Covers MCSE Exam 70-73: Implement
Microsoft Windows NT Work:

G000037257

Organization of chapters, objectives, subobjectives, and review m

Objectives/Subobjectives	Chapter	Exercises
Planning: Plan strategies for sharing and securing resources. Choose the appropriate file system to use in a given situation.	Chapter 1: Planning for Windows NT Workstation 4.0	*pgs. 21-23*
Planning: Create unattended installation files.	Chapter 2: Planning for Unattended Installations	*pgs. 45-50*
Installation and Configuration: Install Windows NT Workstation on an Intel platform. Set up a dual-boot system. Upgrade to Windows NT Workstation 4.0. Configure server-based installation for wide-scale deployment.	Chapter 3: Installing, Upgrading, and Removing Windows NT Workstation	*pgs. 65-70*
Installation and Configuration: Install, configure, and remove hardware components. Use Control Panel applications to configure a Windows NT Workstation computer.	Chapter 4: Configuring Hardware Components	*pgs. 88-92*
Managing Resources: Set up shared folders and permissions. Set permissions on NFTS partitions, folders, and files. Install and configure printers in a given environment.	Chapter 5: Customizing and Configuring Windows NT Workstation	*pgs. 121-125*

continues on page 2

You'll notice that the subobjectives are not listed in the order they are listed in the Microsoft exam objectives. To make the concepts better flow together and to make the learning process easier, we grouped similar subobjectives together so the topic could be covered all at one time. A complete list of current objectives and subobjectives for the exam can be found online at `http://www.microsoft.com/train_cert`.

Objectives/Subobjectives	Chapter	Study Questions and Exercises
Managing Resources: Create and manage local user and group accounts to meet given requirements. Set up and modify user profiles.	Chapter 6: Editing User and System Profiles	*pgs. 143-148*
Connectivity: Add and configure the network components of Windows NT Workstation. Use various methods to access network resources. Use various configurations to install Windows NT Workstation as a TCP/IP client.	Chapter 7: Introduction to Networking Concepts	*pgs. 167-169*
Connectivity: Use various configurations to install Windows NT Workstation as a TCP/IP client.	Chapter 8: Networking with Microsoft Networks	*pgs. 191-197*
Connectivity: Implement Windows NT Workstation as a client in a NetWare environment.	Chapter 9: Networking with NetWare Networks	*pgs. 209-213*
Connectivity: Configure and install dial-up networking.	Chapter 10: Dial-Up Networking and RAS	*pgs. 225-230*
Connectivity: Configure Microsoft Peer Web Services.	Chapter 11: Peer Web Services	*pgs. 239-242*

continues on page 3

Objectives/Subobjectives	Chapter	Study Questions and Exercises
Running Applications: Start applications on Intel and RISC platforms in various operating system environments. Start applications at various priorities.	Chapter 12: Running Applications	*pgs. 260-266*
Monitoring and Optimization: Monitor system performance by using various tools. Identify and resolve a given performance problem. Optimize system performance in various areas.	Chapter 13: Monitoring and Optimizing Windows NT Workstation	*pgs. 295-301*
Troubleshooting: Choose the appropriate action to take when the boot process or a print job fails. Choose the appropriate action to take when the installation process or an application fails. Choose the appropriate action to take when an application fails. Choose the appropriate action to take when a user cannot access a resource. Modify the Registry using the appropriate tool in a given situation. Implement advanced techniques to resolve various problems.	Chapter 14: Troubleshooting Windows NT Workstation	*pgs. 366-383*

Robert Bogue

Emmett Dulaney

Sams
Teach
Yourself
MCSE
Windows NT®
Workstation 4
IN 14 DAYS

SAMS
PUBLISHING

President   *Richard K. Swadley*

Publisher   *Don Fowley*

Associate Publisher   *David Dwyer*

Executive Editor   *John Kane*

Managing Editor   *Sarah Kearns*

Indexing Manager   *Ginny Bess*

Acquisitions Editor
Steve Weiss

Development Editor
Steve Weiss

Project Editor
Kate Shoup Welsh

Copy Editor
Audra McFarland

Indexer
Chris Wilcox

Technical Reviewer
Vincent Averello

Editorial Coordinator
Mandie Rowell

Resource Coordinator
Deborah Frisby

Editorial Assistants
Stacey Beheler
Jen Chisholm
Lori Morgan

Cover Designer
Karen Ruggles

Book Designer
Gary Adair

Copy Writer
David Reichwein

Production Team Supervisor
Andrew Stone

Production
Cyndi Davis-Hubler
Betsy Deeter
Brad Lenser
Chris Livengood
Shawn Ring
Becky Stutzman

Overview

Contents

Dedication

Robert Bogue

For Shelley, my dearest wife, with all my love.

Emmett Dulaney

For Karen, Kristin, Evan, and Spencer. Without their support, so little of what gets accomplished ever would.

Acknowledgments

Robert Bogue

I would like to thank Emmett Dulaney for inviting me to work with him on this project, and Steve Weiss for allowing us both to do the project for Macmillan. I would also like to thank Vince Averello for keeping me straight.

Emmett Dulaney

I would like to thank Steve Weiss of Macmillan for envisioning this project and doing such an excellent job of shepherding it through the process. I would also like to thank Rob Bogue for being the best coauthor one could ask for, and Vince Averello for keeping everyone on their toes. Most of all, though, I acknowledge God, from whom all possibilities flow.

About the Authors

Robert Bogue

Robert L. Bogue owns Thor Projects, a consulting company located in Indianapolis, Indiana. He's also a Microsoft Certified Systems Engineer, a Novell Certified NetWare Administrator, and a certified A+ service technician. In his work at Thor Projects, he specializes in solving the networking and integration needs of small- to medium-sized organizations. Rob's been involved in over 50 book projects on topics ranging from Visual Basic to Windows NT to NetWare to Microsoft Office. He can be reached at Rob.Bogue@ThorProjects.com or at (317) 844-5310.

Emmett Dulaney

Emmett Dulaney writes the monthly "Certification Corner" column for *NT Systems* magazine. An MCSE, CNE, and LAN Server Engineer, Emmett is also a consultant for D S Technical Solutions, and an instructor for a national training company.

Tell Us What You Think!

As a reader, you are the most important critic and commentator of our books. We value your opinion and want to know what we're doing right, what we could do better, what areas you'd like to see us publish in, and any other words of wisdom you're willing to pass our way. You can help us make strong books that meet your needs and give you the computer guidance you require.

Do you have access to the World Wide Web? Then check out our site at
http://www.mcp.com.

 If you have a technical question about this book, call the technical support line at 317-581-3833 or e-mail support@mcp.com.

As the executive editor of the group that created this book, I welcome your comments. You can fax, e-mail, or write me directly to let me know what you did or didn't like about this book—as well as what we can do to make our books stronger. Here's the information:

Fax: 317-581-4663

E-mail: jkane@mcp.com

Mail: John Kane
            Sams Publishing
            201 W. 103rd Street
            Indianapolis, IN 46290

Introduction

Whether you're new to Windows NT Workstation or an old pro at it, taking the Microsoft certification exam can be a stressful event. Passing depends not only on what you know, but how well you take the test. In this book you'll find everything you need to pass the Implementing and Supporting Microsoft NT Workstation 4.0 test (70–73). Not only does this book cover how Windows NT Workstation works, it also offers tips on taking the test.

The Windows NT Workstation test is a valuable exam in that passing it gives you Microsoft Certified Professional (MCP) status; this test counts as one of six exams toward MCSE certification.

Why Take Microsoft Certification Tests?

If you've looked in your local newspaper lately, you've seen ads looking for Microsoft Certified Professionals (MCPs), and especially Microsoft Certified Systems Engineers (MCSEs). No matter where you go, MCPs and MCSEs are in demand. Getting your Microsoft certification is a powerful way of demonstrating your mastery of Microsoft products; this is exactly the kind of expertise the job market is hungry for.

If you're not looking for a new job, Microsoft certification can help you by giving your current company a reason to increase your pay. After your company discovers that you're more valuable, it is more motivated to keep you.

Why Is the NT Workstation Test an Important Part of the MCSE Tests?

Whether your reason for taking the MCSE tests is personal enrichment, desire for promotion, or just more money, it's important to realize where the Windows NT Workstation exam fits into the picture. Windows NT Workstation is one of the three client operating system electives that can be chosen in the Windows NT 4.0 MCSE certification track. The other certification options are Windows 95 and Windows 3.1.

Although Windows 95 is the most widely deployed operating system on the market today and is an excellent choice as a network client, we feel that the Windows NT Workstation test is a more useful part of the MCSE certification. By taking your NT Workstation test, you not only get exposed to the testing format, but you get tested on some of the topics covered on the NT Server and NT Server in the Enterprise exams. This will reduce your study time for the two core tests.

How the Test Works

Microsoft has developed each of the MCP/MCSE tests with the help of instructors, network administrators, and respected members of the networking community. Each test question represents a mastery level of the operating system; questions are not designed to be tricky. This doesn't mean, however, that the test questions are easy. In fact, the test questions generally require a lot of thought. Often, you are asked to evaluate which of the listed criteria are important, and which solutions will work.

To some test takers, the questions that ask for the best answer are tricky. For these questions Microsoft wants only what it considers to be the "best" solution to a problem. Look for these questions in this book, and make sure you read all the answers. Microsoft has made a point of providing possible, but not optimum, solutions to these questions, so it's important to evaluate each answer to see how it weighs against the other answers.

The other curve that most people find is that every test is unique. Just because your friend doesn't get any questions on troubleshooting or connectivity doesn't mean that you don't need to study these topics. It could be that most of your questions come from the troubleshooting or connectivity objectives.

Speaking with other people who have passed the test is an important part of preparing for the test, but you shouldn't focus on only those topics with which others had trouble. Study every topic. A single area of weakness can bring down your score enough to make you fail the test. Another important thing to remember is that the test covers the base product; it doesn't cover service packs or any other add-ins.

> **Note**
> Microsoft has committed to *not* releasing additional product functionality with service packs. Any additional features will be provided via add-ins, or other option package arrangements. This will help prevent the problems caused by service packs in the future.

About Exam 70–73

The NT Workstation exam, as it is referred to, is officially known as "Implementing and Supporting Microsoft Windows NT Workstation 4.0." It is computer-administered, and is intended to measure your ability to implement and administer the product in an enterprise environment. It builds on basic knowledge, and assumes that you, the test candidate, have a great deal of experience with the product. There are 51 questions asked, and you have 90 minutes to answer them. The minimum passing score for Microsoft exams is usually in the

750 range, but may vary by as much as 40 points; your best strategy is always to strive for the highest possible score. The following chart shows the score associated with the number of correct answers:

# of Correct Answers	Score
1	20
2	39
3	59
4	78
5	98
6	118
7	137
8	157
9	176
10	196
11	216
12	235
13	255
14	275
15	294
16	314
17	333
18	353
19	373
20	392
21	412
22	431
23	451
24	471
25	490
26	510
27	529
28	549
29	569

# of Correct Answers	Score
30	588
31	608
32	627
33	647
34	667
35	686
36	706
37	725
38	745
39	765
40	784
41	804
42	824
43	843
44	863
45	882
46	902
47	922
48	941
49	961
50	980
51	1000

There are two types of multiple-choice questions on the exam: single answer (always readily identified by a radio button) and multiple answer (with the correct number of answers given). There are a limited number of "click-on" questions, where you are given a property sheet and told to click the item that you would choose to meet the specifications given. The questions, overall, are verbose, include a large number of exhibits, and provide choices A–D.

The exam is divided into seven objective categories:

■ Planning
■ Installation and Configuration

- Managing Resources
- Connectivity
- Running Applications
- Monitoring and Optimization
- Troubleshooting

 Note Although the exam is multiple choice, and you need only click on radio buttons and boxes to answer questions; the act of taking the exam is called "writing."

Organization of the Book

To help make your study time more productive, and to allow you to review after taking assessment tests, this book is broken into 14 chapters. Each chapter should take less than one hour to complete. If you study just a few hours each day for two weeks, you should be ready to take your Microsoft Windows NT Workstation certification test. Table I.1 lists the major and minor objectives of the Windows NT Workstation test, and where you can find the information you need to pass:

Table I.1. Organization of chapters, objectives, and subobjectives.

Chapter	Objective	Subobjective
Chapter 1: Planning for Windows NT Workstation 4.0	Planning	Plan strategies for sharing and securing resources. Choose the appropriate file system to use in a given situation.
Chapter 2: Planning for Unattended Installations	Planning	Create unattended installation files.
Chapter 3: Installing, Upgrading, and Removing Windows NT Workstation	Installation and Configuration	Install Windows NT Workstation on an Intel platform. Set up a dual-boot system. Upgrade to Windows NT Workstation. Configure server-based installation for wide-scale deployment.

continues

Table I.1. continued

Chapter	Objective	Subobjective
Chapter 4: Configuring Hardware Components	Installation and Configuration	Install, configure, and remove hardware components. Use Control Panel applications to configure a Windows NT Workstation computer.
Chapter 5: Customizing and Configuring Windows NT Workstation	Managing Resources	Set up shared folders and permissions. Set permissions on NTFS partitions, folders, and files. Install and configure printers in a given environment.
Chapter 6: Editing User and System Profiles	Managing Resources	Create and manage local user accounts and local group accounts to meet given requirements. Set up and modify user profiles.
Chapter 7: Introduction to Networking Concepts	Connectivity	Add and configure the network components of Windows NT Workstation. Use various methods to access network resources. Use various configurations to install Windows NT Workstation as a TCP/IP client.
Chapter 8: Networking with Microsoft Networks	Connectivity	Use various configurations to install Windows NT Workstation as a TCP/IP client.
Chapter 9: Networking with NetWare Networks	Connectivity	Implement Windows NT Workstation as a client in a NetWare environment.
Chapter 10: Dial-Up Networking and RAS	Connectivity	Configure and install dial-up networking.
Chapter 11: Peer Web Services	Connectivity	Configure Microsoft Peer Web Services.

Chapter	Objective	Subobjective
Chapter 12: Running Applications	Running Applications	Start applications on Intel and RISC platforms in various operating system environments. Start applications at various priorities.
Chapter 13: Monitoring and Optimizing Windows NT Workstation	Monitoring and Optimization	Monitor system performance by using various tools. Identify and resolve a given performance problem. Optimize system performance in various areas.
Chapter 14: Troubleshooting Windows NT Workstation	Troubleshooting	Choose the appropriate action to take when the boot process or a print job fails. Choose the appropriate action to take when the installation process or an application fails. Choose the appropriate action to take when a user cannot access a resource. Modify the Registry using the appropriate tool in a given situation. Implement advanced techniques to resolve various problems.

You'll notice that not all of the subobjectives are listed in the order they are listed in the Microsoft exam objectives. To make the concepts flow together, and to make the learning process easier, we grouped similar subobjectives together so the topic could be covered all at one time. A complete list of current objectives and subobjectives for the exam can be found online at http://www.microsoft.com/train_cert.

However, you will note that the major objectives are listed in the same order as in the Microsoft objectives. We've made every effort to help you find the information you need to pass—whether it's your first time, or if you've failed a test and need to concentrate on a specific area.

Read Appendix A of this book a day or two before you take the test; it contains testing tips—time-honored ways of improving your score on any test you take. We have used these tips to help us pass tests in the past.

How to Use This Book

Passing the test requires broad understanding of Windows NT Workstation. The test won't ask specific questions about quirks of Windows NT, or the workarounds that might be necessary in certain environments. To get this broad understanding of Windows NT Workstation, you should read and reread each section until you've clicked with the major topics. Each topic covered in this book may or may not be included on your test. As mentioned previously, each test taker gets a unique test. Wherever possible, you will find examples of how the setup works. Remember, however, that these are *examples*; don't infer that the product must be set up that way.

There are two ways that you should approach this book. The first is to read it linearly, chapter by chapter until the end. This will give you an understanding of all the topics in the test and will give you a firm foundation for taking an evaluation test. The second way is to use this book as a reference for issues that occur after you have passed the exam. In many places, we have included information that is not necessary for the exam, but that is nonetheless useful for the real world.

It's recommended that you take the Microsoft self-assessment test before taking the test at a Sylvan Prometric testing center. The assessment test approximates the exam, and will familiarize you with the testing engine. The testing engine used for the sample tests is the same as the one used at the testing center. In addition, the test will report your correct and incorrect answers in each objective. If you look at the results of the self-assessment test, you will know which parts of this book you need to review prior to taking the test. Thus, the book can be used as a resource to improve your understanding of specific topics.

Frequently Asked Questions

Q. If I have already taken the NT Server exam, how much studying do I need to do for the Workstation exam?

A. A great deal of information is carried over between the Workstation and Server exams because of the similarities among the two products. You will want to study the Running Applications section, and everything you can about unattended installations. The Workstation exam shows no mercy when it comes to unattended installations, and expects you to know everything you can on this topic.

Q. If I fail the exam, what is my next course of action?

A. The results of the exam are broken into the seven major objective categories. Look at your weakest areas and better your skills in those. The tear-out card in this book will show you where coverage for each of those objectives is found. Study that material until you know it thoroughly, and then retake the exam. Microsoft imposes no limitation on the number of times you can take an exam.

Q. Is there a way to prepare for the style of questions that are asked?

A. A number of electronic test engines emulate the Microsoft exam. A quick glance at the back pages of any higher-end computing magazine will show half a dozen companies marketing such products. Some of these products are exceptional, and some are very poor—differences in quality relate to how well the engines test your knowledge and emulate questions on the actual exam.

Furthermore, the questions at the end of each chapter of this book mirror exam questions. These will help you test your knowledge, even though they appear in a medium not found in the exam (that is, they appear in written, not electronic, form).

Q. Is the Workstation exam a good one to choose for a first test if you have never taken a certification test before?

A. The Workstation exam is an excellent first exam. The topics you are tested on are generally confined to one product (which cannot be said for all certification exams). Additionally, passing this exam gets you MCP status, and counts as credit toward the MCSE.

Q. If I have questions about the exam that are not addressed in this book, where should I turn?

A. We have made every attempt to cover all exam-relevant material within this book. Nevertheless, there may be questions that are not addressed in a way that rings true to you. If that is the case, please feel free to contact us by e-mail, and we will make every attempt to respond to you within a timely fashion.

Well, it's time to get started. Good luck!

Robert Bogue, MCSE, CNA, A+

Rob_Bogue@ThorProjects.com

Emmett Dulaney, MCSE, CNE

edulaney@iquest.net

Here are the fast facts about this chapter that you may want to know ahead of time. These facts provide great last-minute study material as well. Each bullet point below can be considered a short answer version of a main point explored elsewhere in the chapter.

- Windows NT Workstation supports membership in a workgroup or a domain.

- Windows NT Workstation controls access to resources at a share level.

- File permissions are enforced through shares, and the most restrictive permissions between the share and file permissions are used.

- Windows NT Workstation supports FAT and NTFS file systems. Windows NT Workstation no longer supports HPFS.

- FAT formatted file systems do not support security at a file level.

- FAT formatted file systems are required when dual booting to Windows 95 or DOS.

- NTFS is a fault-tolerant file system with transaction tracking support.

- NTFS supports file-level security information and file-level compression.

Day 1

Planning for Windows NT Workstation 4.0

Objectives

We start our first day by exploring some of the planning issues related to installing Windows NT Workstation. Specifically, this chapter covers the following two sub-objectives:

■ Planning strategies for sharing and securing resources

■ Choosing the appropriate file system to use in a given situation

1.1. Choosing the Appropriate File System to Use in a Given Situation

You choose the appropriate file system for Windows NT based on the needs of the specific environment in which it will be used. In an environment where dual booting to another operating system is required, Microsoft recommends using a FAT formatted file system, but NTFS is recommended for situations where security is a concern.

This section will help you sort out which file system is appropriate given a situation. First, let's review the characteristics of the two file systems that Windows NT supports.

1.1.1. FAT (File Allocation Table)

FAT is the standard filing system in use today. Not only does Windows NT support it, but so do DOS and Windows 95. That means that most of the PCs in use today use FAT as their only filing system.

> **Note**
>
> Windows 95B (or OSR2) released a new version of FAT called FAT32. The Windows NT Workstation test doesn't consider that FAT32 has been released. However, for the real world, you should know that Windows NT is *not* compatible with FAT32, and there is no way to convert a FAT32 partition to a FAT partition. To be able to use the FAT32 space for Windows NT, you must delete the partition and then re-create it as a FAT file system.

Here are the advantages of using FAT in a Windows NT environment:

- FAT is the required file system for floppy disks
- It is compatible with both DOS and Windows 95

In addition to the advantages, there are a few disadvantages:

- No security support
- Poor support for volumes larger than 512MB
- No support for disks over 4GB

> **Note**
>
> Because FAT is limited to 65,536 clusters (which is 2 to the 16th power), it must make the cluster sizes larger and larger for large volumes. The result is that as the cluster sizes get larger, more disk space is wasted because FAT allocates a full cluster to every file even if the file doesn't need it. For example, if the cluster size is 2KB and you need to store a 40 byte file, FAT allocates 2KB for the file. This wastes all but the first 40 bytes.
>
> Any disk over 400MB or so should be formatted NTFS so the cluster size can be kept small.

The FAT file system is the appropriate choice for Windows NT Workstations that need to boot to other operating systems and for formatting floppy disks.

1.1.2. NTFS (NT Filing System)

By the time Windows NT was released, it had become apparent to Microsoft that a new filing system was needed to handle the growing disk sizes, security concerns, and the need for a more stable filing system. To that end, Microsoft included support for a new file system: the NT file system (NTFS). This new file system has several features that FAT and other disk formats do not have. These attributes are discussed in the following sections.

Transaction Tracking

Although FAT was relatively stable if the systems that were controlling it kept running, it didn't do so well when the power went out or the system crashed unexpectedly.

One of the benefits that was designed into NTFS was a transaction tracking system. This made it possible for Windows NT to back out of any uncompleted disk operations that were in progress when Windows NT crashed or lost power. This feature allows NTFS to be more resilient to problems than its predecessor, FAT.

> **Warning**
>
> Even NTFS is not crash-proof. It's highly recommended that you protect your computer with a UPS (uninterruptible power supply) if possible. Windows NT even includes UPS-monitoring software as a part of the base product.

Built-In Security

Another feature designed into NTFS that FAT lacks is support for security information. When FAT was designed back in the early '80s, personal computers were just that—personal. The concepts of networks and sharing information between personal computers were unheard of. Because there was no sharing of resources, security didn't seem very important.

As the PC industry evolved, it became necessary to secure files from other people who might be using the PC directly or from across the network. To handle this, layers of sharing security, such as the share-level security in Windows for Workgroups, were added. In addition, special file encryption programs were developed to encrypt data while it was stored on the hard disk. (*Encryption* is the process of taking a readable file and making it unreadable by means of a process that can be reversed only with a special key.) Still these security layers were add-ons to FAT, an elderly filing system (in PC terms), and they weren't integrated.

However, NTFS's security is flexible and built-in. Not only does it track security in Access Control Lists (ACLs), which can hold permissions for local users and groups, but each entry in the Access Control List can specify what type of access is given—from Read-Only to Change to Full Control, or anywhere in between.

Note

> Some DOS-based programs out there will read NTFS volumes without the limitations of security that you might have defined on the disk. However, this requires physical access to the computer and enough knowledge to get one of these programs. For testing purposes, assume that NTFS cannot be used with any other operating system.

Large Disk Support

In addition to the transaction tracking and security, NTFS also provides improved support for larger disks. Because FAT was designed so long ago, its support of large partitions (over 512MB), leaves something to be desired in terms of speed and efficient use of space.

NTFS was designed to handle volumes that are larger than 512MB without resorting to larger and larger cluster sizes as FAT does. When FAT allocates a file, it must allocate an entire group of disk sectors, called a *cluster*. For FAT to support large volumes, the cluster size must be made larger so that the file allocation table itself can fit within its allotted 64KB. NTFS doesn't have a 64KB limitation for the way that it

1

tracks files. Although it still uses the concept of clusters, it does so only to balance the size of the allocation map and the amount of wasted space at the end of a file.

Both FAT and NTFS allocate space for files in cluster lengths. If a file is, say, 1KB and the cluster size for the volume is 4KB, the 3KB at the end of the cluster will be wasted because it will be marked in the allocation table as having been used.

File-Level Compression

One way in which NTFS gets around allocating a complete cluster for every file is to use the file-compression attribute that was added for the first time to Windows NT 3.51. This attribute allows NTFS to manage file compression on a per file basis, as opposed to FAT-based file-compression schemes that must compress entire sections of the drive.

Note

File-based compression is infinitely superior to partition-based compression because you can compress files that you don't frequently use and leave uncompressed those files that you use frequently. In that way, you can control how much processor overhead you trade for disk space.

Although, DriveSpace in Windows 95 allows you to recompress files based on their last access dates, it doesn't allow you to control whether the files are compressed to the maximum level or are not compressed at all on a file-by-file basis.

Because today's programs require more and more disk space, there is a need to put more and more on the hard disks that we buy. Compression is the method by which we fit more data in the same amount of space. Unlike the different tape speeds available in your VCR, compressed and uncompressed files are no different once the compressed files are decompressed. The only difference is that you must perform an additional step on compressed files before you can use them.

Not too long ago, DOS programs appeared on the scene that allowed you to compress an entire volume, or *partition*. These utilities, such as Stacker, allowed you to store nearly twice as much data in the same amount of space. As the programs improved, more data—as much as four times as much—could be stored in the given amount of space.

Unfortunately, Windows NT didn't and doesn't support FAT-based compression programs. But due to continuing pressure to provide compression support in Windows

NT, Microsoft released changes to NTFS to allow it to support file-level compression. This was a major leap forward in how file compression was handled. In the DOS world, it was always a trade-off between the additional space that compression would buy you and the speed of using uncompressed files (because compressed files must be decompressed in memory before they can be used). On slower processors, file compression meant a performance penalty. However, with NTFS support of file-level compression, the files that are used most often can be left uncompressed to get the speed of accessing without decompression, and the files that are rarely used can be compressed so they don't take up so much space.

Not all files can be compressed. In particular, some of the Windows NT boot files and the paging file cannot be compressed; they must always remain uncompressed. Windows NT will not allow you to set the compression attribute on these files.

Using compression on files that are accessed by a file server can dramatically increase the processor's utilization of the server. If you are running low on disk space, consider the impact on the processor before you use compression.

Feature Review

To review, NTFS has the following specific features that make it desirable to implement on an NT Workstation:

- Transaction tracking
- File-level security support
- File-level compression support
- Large volume support

Now that you know the key features for each format, you can evaluate which one is better in a given situation.

1.1.3. Picking a File System on the Test

The test centers around three main issues for deciding which filing system to support. The first issue is dual booting.

If you will be dual booting to DOS, Windows 95, or OS/2, you must use the FAT file system. FAT is the only file system supported by both Windows NT and other operating systems. Whenever the question says that the system must dual boot to a different operating system, at least one FAT partition is required.

> **Note**
>
> If you install Windows 95 after Windows NT, you will have to repair the Windows NT installation to make NT accessible again.
>
> During the installation of Windows 95, the setup program overwrites the boot sector on the hard drive. Using the Windows NT boot disks, you can repair the NT installation by investigating and fixing the boot sector.

The second issue that the test addresses is security. Security is supported only on NTFS, so if the test requires that the solution support file-level security, NTFS is required. However, if the question deals with access via a network, some share-level security can be set up. Share-level security works with both FAT and NTFS.

Finally, the test requires you to know that FAT file systems can be automatically converted to NTFS with the CONVERT command, but NTFS file systems can't be converted to FAT. The only possible workaround is to back up the partition, delete it, reformat it as FAT, and then restore the data.

1.2. Planning Strategies for Sharing and Securing Resources

One subobjective that actually overlaps with several other subobjectives is "Planning Strategies for Sharing and Securing Resources." In this section, we discuss the basics of networking and sharing strategies. Some of the details of why these make sense are covered in future chapters. Specifically, you'll find more information on how to set up networking in Chapter 7, "Introduction to Networking Concepts."

When planning any environment, you need to decide on a few basics. The first is the network topology: whether it is going to be Ethernet 10BASE2, Ethernet 10BASE-T, Ethernet 100BASET, token ring, or FDDI. Other options are available, but they're not used in most environments and won't be mentioned on the test.

The next decision is whether to use a peer-to-peer or client/server structure on your network.

Finally, you have to decide how to manage shares.

We cover choosing a network topology first.

1.2.1. Choosing a Network Topology

For most people, choosing a network topology is easy. They have experience with a particular method, so they use it again. However, there are a few details that should be considered first. Using each topology has its advantages and disadvantages. The following sections briefly discuss each topology and what it is and is not good for.

Ethernet 10BASE2

Ethernet 10BASE2 is the old coaxial version of Ethernet that is still used in small offices today. Ethernet 10BASE2 offers a few advantages, as listed here:

- It's the simplest network type (it needs only one cable, two terminators, and two "T" connectors).
- No hub is required (which makes it the cheapest network type).
- It offers 10Mbps throughput, which is much more than a small network will need.

Of course, it also has its disadvantages:

- It uses Carrier Sense Multiple Access/Collision Detection (CSMA/CD) to control access. CSMA/CD performs poorly in highly loaded environments.
- In bus-based network architecture, any problem with the network cable will bring down the entire network.
- It offers only 10Mbps throughput, which is not enough for large environments.

Ethernet 10BASE2 is a good solution for cheaply connecting two or three computers. It's not a good solution for large environments because it doesn't have the bandwidth that a large site requires and because a single failure brings down the entire network.

Ethernet 10BASE2 is typically deployed in small medical and dental offices, travel agencies, and so on, where the number of computers will probably never exceed 10.

1

Ethernet 10BASE-T

Ethernet 10BASE-T is closely related to Ethernet 10BASE2. However, instead of using coaxial cable, it uses twisted-pair lines, which are already run in most buildings today and can be used not only for computer networks, but for telephone service as well. As a result, 10BASE-T has some slightly different advantages:

- Operation can continue if a single cable fails.
- It offers 10Mbps throughput, which is much more than a small network will need.

These are the disadvantages of using Ethernet 10BASE-T:

- It uses Carrier Sense Multiple Access/Collision Detection (CSMA/CD) to control access. CSMA/CD performs poorly in highly loaded environments.
- It offers only 10Mbps throughput, which is not enough for large environments without special equipment.
- A hub is required and is a potential single point of failure.

Ethernet 10BASE-T is good for medium to large environments in which a hub can be used and reliability is a concern. It also helps that 10BASE-T uses twisted-pair cabling, which most buildings already have run to each office.

Ethernet 10BASE-T is the most widely deployed technology. It's often used in offices with more than five computers. Every industry—from travel to insurance to manufacturing and more—uses Ethernet 10BASE-T.

Why Is Twisted Pair So Good?

The biggest problem when transmitting a signal from one end of a line to another is handling the interference from other devices and cables operating near the signal that you're trying to transmit. Known as Electro-Magnetic Interference (EMI), this interference slightly changes the signal that you are sending. Sometimes, however, the interference can change the signal so much that it's not recognizable at the other end.

The first method developed to eliminate interference was shielding for the cables. This consisted of a conductor, either a foil or braided wire, that surrounded the wires on which the signal was sent. The shield was then connected to a ground source on one end of the cable. Interference was drained off via the shield so that it couldn't get to the wires conducting the signal.

This worked okay if the shield was properly grounded; however, if it wasn't, the shield actually became an antenna, magnifying the interference on the signal wires. In addition, there was sometimes confusion regarding which end of the shield should be grounded.

The next evolution in cable design was *twisted-pair* cable, which consisted of twisting the pair of conductors that carried the signal. This didn't seem like a big deal, but it made an impressive reduction in the level of interference.

When interference changes a signal, it usually does so by slightly changing the amount of voltage the signal carries. Depending upon which wire is closest to the source, the signal gets either stronger or weaker.

If interference causes the signal to become stronger, it's possible for a signal of 0 to be interpreted by the receiving end as a 1. Even though the signal source is sending out almost no voltage, the interference increases the voltage to a point that it can be read as a one. Conversely, if the interference weakens the signal, it is possible for the receiver to think that a 1 is really a 0. The result is that the receiving end has trouble receiving the 1s that the source is sending.

The way that twisting the wires handles this is by switching which wire is closest so that the interference raises the voltage on one side and lowers it on the other—netting out to 0, or almost 0, change. Although there is still interference around the cable, it negates itself because each wire is closest to the interference for approximately the same amount of time.

In Figure 1.1, you can see an example of what happens when interference runs along the length of a cable. In the first case, in which the pair is not twisted, the net result is that a +7 voltage is applied. In the second case, in which the cable is twisted, only a +1 is applied. You can see that in this example, twisting the pair of conductor wires negates almost all of the interference.

Figure 1.1.

Twisting the pair of wires can significantly reduce the amount of interference.

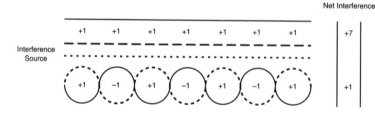

1

Ethernet 100BASE-T

Ethernet 100BASE-T is essentially the same thing as Ethernet 10BASE-T, but it runs at 10 times the speed. It does cost a little more, so it is generally best suited to environments in which cost isn't a big issue. It is also the best choice for environments in which 10Mbps throughput isn't sufficient.

Ethernet 100BASE-T is generally deployed as a backbone for a network primarily running 10BASE-T. The backbone is the central part of a network, near all of the servers.

> Ethernet 100BASE-T requires Category 5 cables. Category 5 cables are twisted very frequently in an attempt to reject interference completely. Category 5 cables are installed in most new buildings today. However, one problem remains: Most of the punch-down blocks used to connect different cables are not Category 5-compliant. This means that even if your cables are Category 5, you still might not be able to run Ethernet 100BASE-T.
>
> Before attempting to move to 100BASE-T from 10BASE-T, you should have your cabling tested. For extensive moves, it might pay to purchase a good cable tester before trying to upgrade to 100BASE-T.

Token Ring

So far we've discussed different variants of the same technology. Token ring is a completely different technology. Instead of using Carrier Sense Multiple Access/Collision Detection (CSMA/CD), it works via a token-passing concept. (There is only one token on the network, and only the computer with the token can transmit.)

There are two varieties of token ring: 4Mbps and 16Mbps. As you might guess, 16Mbps is four times as fast as 4Mbps. In addition, 16Mbps token ring was enhanced to improve performance in other ways.

Here are the advantages of using a token-ring network:

- ■ It provides higher performance than 10Mbps Ethernet.
- ■ A single cable failure between hubs (called Multistation Access Units, or MAUs) won't bring down the ring, whereas a single cable failure in Ethernet will halt operation.
- ■ It offers better performance and the capability to handle higher loads.

As with everything else, there are some disadvantages to using the token-ring topology. They are as follows:

- Token ring is still much more expensive than Ethernet because it hasn't been deployed as widely.

- Only a limited number of networks run token ring, so finding people qualified to support token ring is more difficult.

Token ring has all but disappeared from the mainstream networking marketplace due to its cost. Although it's not recommended for new installations, it does exist in some IBM-centric IS shops.

FDDI (Fiber Distributed Data Interface)

So far, the technologies that we've discussed have been copper-based. By that, I mean that they use copper wires to transmit data between computers. FDDI is the only local communications network that is based on fiber.

 Note Fiber is often used between Ethernet hubs in different buildings and on different floors. However, these are generally proprietary implementations of fiber. They are not often open standards.

FDDI runs at 100Mbps using the same token-passing access as token ring. Even though FDDI runs at only 100Mbps, the actual optical cabling is capable of *much* more throughput.

FDDI is considered overkill for most installations, but the following advantages are persuasive in specialty environments:

- *Security.* FDDI can't be monitored without breaking the cable. Copper can be monitored without breaking the wire—which means the monitoring will go undetected.

- *Elimination of Potential Ground Problems.* Most people don't realize that the "ground" they get for digital signals isn't an absolute. It's a relative thing, and in campus environments, it's possible for two or more ground states to exist. These differing grounds often prevent reliable transmission of data between systems.

- *Speed.* FDDI runs at 100Mbps, which was more than five times as fast as the next-fastest network—token ring—until the advent of 100BASE-T Ethernet.

■ *Distance.* FDDI spans much larger distances than Ethernet can. FDDI is often used as a backbone for a multi-floor network.

■ *Immunity to Interference.* Because fiber transfers information as pulses of light, it is completely immune to EMI.

> Every electrical signal radiates some energy as it travels. That energy could be captured by an enterprising spy to monitor the traffic on the wire without being detected. Most people don't worry about these kinds of attacks because there are normally much easier ways of gaining access to a network—either directly or just to monitor it. However, high-security environments often select FDDI because of this feature.

The obstacle preventing FDDI's acceptance hasn't been its lack of strengths, but rather its list of problems:

■ *Cable breaks.* Fiber is delicate when compared to copper. Whereas copper is fairly resistant to breaks caused by turns in the cable run, fiber is more sensitive to turns.

■ *Installation costs.* Almost anyone can run and terminate copper-based twisted-pair wiring. However, only a trained person with special tools for termination can run fiber. This makes it more expensive to deploy fiber and more difficult to get repairs done quickly.

■ *Hardware costs.* Because there isn't a lot of demand for FDDI, and because the signal is being converted from an electrical signal to an optical signal and back again, FDDI network cards are expensive.

FDDI is generally used only in applications in which security is a big concern. Although its bandwidth was once king, the advent of 100BASE-T has made FDDI almost obsolete.

Topology Summary

As you learned in the past few sections, each topology has its place in different environments. That's why many businesses lament over which topology to choose. In general, make sure you understand the bandwidth of each topology and any special features of the network (such as FDDI's resistance to snooping). The Windows NT Workstation test doesn't focus on topologies, but you might get a few questions on it.

1.2.2. Peer-to-Peer Versus Client/Server

Once you have the ability to connect the computers, it's time to decide how to share services. Will you choose a peer-to-peer relationship in which every computer shares, or serves, resources and uses them as well? Or is a client/server environment with a limited number of servers best for your situation?

Peer-to-peer and client/server are both ways of organizing your network services beyond the connectivity between the computers. Organizing your network is very important and which choice you make can greatly affect the amount of time that will be spent maintaining the network after it's implemented.

We explore the advantages and disadvantages of both peer-to-peer and client/server environments in the following sections.

Peer-to-Peer

Peer-to-peer is the default way of operating when Windows NT Workstation is installed on a network. This is because Windows NT can both provide and use network resources.

Peer-to-peer networks are often used because they are cheap and offer an effective way to get started in networking. However, as is the case with most cheap starts, peer-to-peer is not always the best long-term answer.

Peer-to-peer works well to start out because each workstation can share some of its resources for the other workstations' use. However, as more and more machines are added to the network, more and more resources are being shared across the network, which can make it hard for users to find the resources they need.

Generally, each resource requires a different password for access. As the number of resources increases, so does the number of passwords that users have to remember and administrators have to maintain. And then when someone leaves, the passwords should be changed so that the person can't come back in and look at or destroy files. This means changing the passwords on all the disparate resources and informing all the users of the change. On top of that, most IS auditing firms recommend changing all passwords at least every 180 days—which means that twice a year all the passwords on the network should be changed.

In addition to the security and password issues, system lockups are a problem for peer-to-peer networks. When a particular system locks up, not only is the user sitting in front of that computer unable to get her work done, but so is anyone who uses resources on that computer. No longer is a computer failure's impact limited to a single user; instead, it can have an effect on anyone on the network as well.

Even if the user doesn't totally lock up her computer, she might fill all of the available disk space or run a processor-intensive application, which slows down access for other users. Generally, peer-to-peer networks don't use computers that have an excess of resources to share. They are normally computers with slightly larger hard disks than are needed, and as a result, they can't share a single large database with multiple users.

As you can see, the administration of a peer-to-peer network can become overwhelming if many computers are involved. This is why most networks in use today are client/server networks. They don't have the same administrative problems that peer-to-peer networks do.

Client/Server

Client/server implementations differ from peer-to-peer network implementations in two key ways:

- They require one or more dedicated servers to provide services to all of the clients on the network.
- They are easier to administer because the resources are centralized.

Client/server may seem like overkill for some network implementations, and it is in some cases. However, when a network consists of five or more workstations, it makes sense to start relying on a server whose only job is to take care of network clients.

Client/server networks generally have higher performance than peer-to-peer networks because the server is generally built from higher performing components and can specialize in providing just network services. This higher performance becomes important when a large number of users are waiting on network resources. Just a few seconds a day multiplied by 1,000 users can be a significant number. So not only does the response time from the server go down, but the workstation's performance itself will go up because it isn't also spending its time trying to serve other network users.

Server hardware is also generally designed to handle more users, so in a client/server network, hardware problems on the server are fewer. Server computers also often feature:

- *ECC (Error Checking and Correcting).* A type of memory that automatically corrects single-bit memory failures.

- *Dual-power suppliers.* Even if there is a power supply failure, the computer keeps running and performance isn't affected.
- *RAID hardware controllers.* RAID is a method of protecting data against a drive failure and providing improved performance. If a single drive in a RAID 5 stripe set fails, the server will continue to operate.

By centralizing on a few servers instead of many servers across the organization, special considerations can be made for the server hardware, such as UPS power. A UPS (uninterruptible power supply) protects the server from a power outage for a period of time. UPSs are generally used to give servers the time they need to shut down normally in the event of a power failure.

Backup is also facilitated in a client/server network. Backups are an important means of protecting against hardware failures and user errors. Centralized servers (in a client/server situation) can be backed up via a connected tape drive. In a peer-to-peer network, on the other hand, backups are complicated because each computer providing services must be backed up across the network, which is slower and more prone to errors. It also requires that all of the systems be left on all night.

Next, we review Microsoft's implementation of peer-to-peer and client/server networks.

The Workgroup Model

The workgroup model is Microsoft's implementation of peer-to-peer networking. Each computer has its own security database that determines which directories and files can be shared, to whom they can be shared, and what passwords are required. Windows NT Workstation, Windows 95, OS/2, and Windows 3.1 all support the workgroup model.

The key things to remember about the workgroup model are

- There is no specific server requirement to run a workgroup. Any combination of Windows 95, Windows NT, OS/2, and Windows 3.11 can be used.
- It is an implementation of a peer-to-peer network and, therefore, has the same administrative problems and resource-availability problems that all peer-to-peer networks have.
- Each computer manages security individually.

All Windows 95, Windows NT, OS/2, and Windows 3.11 computers will join a domain if they are not specifically connected to a domain and resources are shared.

Most members of a workgroup operate with share-level security, in which the share itself is assigned a password. This is the method that Windows 3.11 and Windows 95 use by default. Windows 95, however, can also use user-level security when a Windows NT computer or a Novell NetWare server is present. With user-level security, each user is assigned a user name and password. Resource permissions are then granted to the user ID.

This is more secure than share-based security because each user has his or her own password. When someone leaves, all the administrator has to do is delete the person's user ID. With share-level security, every share password that the former employee knew should be changed.

 Note　It's a good idea to put one Windows NT Workstation on a workgroup network to provide a central user database.

The Domain Model

Microsoft's answer to client/server networking is the domain model. The domain model requires that a Windows NT Server be installed as a Primary Domain Controller (PDC) to maintain the security of the domain. For this reason, a Windows NT Server is always present in a domain. Windows NT Workstation is the only operating system that can become a full member of a domain. However, both Windows 95 and Windows 3.1 can use domain security to control their logins.

A domain works by having each of the client computers subscribe to the domain for its security. When every member uses the same security database, the administrator does not have to go around to each computer and change passwords when someone leaves. The changes are made to one central database that controls security for all of the systems in the domain.

A domain is formed with Windows NT Server, an operating system designed to service network clients. Thus, the domain model fits both criteria of being a client/server network.

Microsoft has domain strategies that allow domains to be used in the largest companies. However, a single domain scales to about 15,000 users, which is more than enough for all but the largest companies.

Which Model Fits Best?

The workstation test focuses on your understanding of how sharing and securing resources in a domain is different from sharing and securing resources in a workgroup.

The key differences are these:

- In a workgroup, each workstation that shares resources must have a user account for the user trying to use the resource (or the guest account must be enabled).
- In a domain, access to resources is assigned to individual users or local groups. The local groups are added to global groups in the domain.

The workstation test, unlike the server and enterprise tests, has a very limited number of questions about domains. All you need to know are the basic concepts about domains and know how to share and secure resources. You'll learn about specifically sharing resources and assigning permissions in Chapter 5.

Lab

The Lab section reviews what you have learned thus far and gives you an opportunity to think about various real-world situations and which solution is best for each one. Answers to the review questions are at the end of the section.

Review Questions

1. You're installing Windows NT Workstation for a client. The client tells you that he wants to keep his existing Windows 95 installation. Which file system should you use?

   A. FAT

   B. NTFS

   C. HPFS

   D. CDFS

2. You're installing a new Windows NT Workstation in an unsecure environment. Which file system should you use?

   A. FAT

   B. NTFS

   C. HPFS

   D. CDFS

3. You have a FAT-based Windows NT Workstation that doesn't dual boot into another operating system. You're running out of space and want to use disk compression. What do you do? (Choose all that apply.)

   A. Run Doublespace.

   B. Set the compression attribute on the files and folders you want to compress.

   C. Convert the volume to NTFS.

   D. Go to the Control Panel's System applet and turn on file compression.

4. You have a small office environment and need to install a network. What kind of Microsoft network are you going to install?

   A. Peer-to-peer

   B. Client/server

   C. Workgroup

   D. Domain

5. You have a large company in which you want to install a network. What do you need in order to have a domain?

   A. Windows NT Workstation

   B. Windows 95

   C. Microsoft Domain Controller for Networks

   D. Windows NT Server

6. You need to share a large database containing several gigabytes of data to several users. Which type of network do you need to use?

   A. Peer-to-peer

   B. Client/server

   C. Workgroup

   D. Domain

7. Billy has a Windows NT computer. He wants to be able to dual boot to Windows 95. His computer currently has a single drive partitioned as one large NTFS volume. How can Billy get Windows 95 installed?

   A. Install Windows 95 and select the Dual-Boot option.

   B. Back up the NTFS volume, delete the partition, create and format a FAT partition, install Windows 95, and then install Windows NT.

   C. Convert the NTFS volume to FAT using the CONVERT utility, and then install Windows 95.

   D. Install Windows 95, and then install Windows NT again.

8. You're discussing network options with a small company that is struggling with cash flow. Which networking type should you propose?

   A. Peer-to-peer

   B. Client/server

   C. Workgroup

   D. Domain

Answers to Review Questions

1. A When there is a requirement to dual boot between any two operating systems other than Windows NT, FAT is required.

2. B Whenever security is a concern, NTFS should be used because it is the only file system that supports security.

3. B, C Only Windows NT supports file-level compression and only on NTFS volumes. Doublespace is not supported because it's a file system-based compression utility. To enable compression in this scenario, you must convert the volume to NTFS and then set the compression attribute. Turning on file compression in the System applet is not a possible option.

4. C Although peer-to-peer is the correct solution for a small office, it's not the correct Microsoft solution, which the question specifically asks for.

5. D A Windows NT domain requires Windows NT Server.

6. B Because the resources needed to share the database on the network will be large, a peer-to-peer network organization may not be able to handle the load; thus, a client/server network type is recommended. A domain is not a valid answer here because the question asks for the networking type, not the Microsoft networking type.

7. B NTFS file systems can't be converted to FAT. You must delete, re-create, and reformat the partition to change it to FAT.

8. A Because they are struggling with cash flow, they don't have the money to install the dedicated resources that a client/server network would require. A workgroup is the correct Microsoft solution, but the question didn't ask for the Microsoft solution.

1

Day 2

Planning for Unattended Installations

Welcome to Day 2. This chapter is one of the more important chapters in the entire book. Today we cover the one objective that most people will never have any direct experience with.

Most people will run across the other objectives in this book if they work with the product enough. However, unattended installations are used in only the biggest environments, so you're not likely to be involved with deploying Windows NT using unattended installations.

Test Tip

The emphasis on unattended installations on the test is unmistakable. Microsoft definitely wants the MCP to know how to roll out Windows NT in large environments.

Objective

This chapter deals with only one subobjective of the Planning objective:

■ Creating unattended installation files

This subobjective gets significant attention on the MCSE test.

Both of the authors of this book find the unattended installation subobjective to be one of the more difficult to grasp because it is so far outside of the average person's normal experience with Windows NT.

If after reading this chapter, you still want more information on this subject, you can get a Microsoft white paper called "MS Windows NT Workstation Deployment Guide – Automating Windows NT Setup (Windows NT 4.0 Workstation and Server)" from Microsoft's Web site. It's only about 95 printed pages, but it details every option for every tool.

2.1. Understanding Unattended Installations

Configuring computers can be one of the most time-consuming tasks an IS department faces. Consider for a minute that installing Windows NT Workstation can take 30-45 minutes. Installing Office will take another 30-45 minutes. Add in a few dozen utilities and corporate applications, and you can easily exceed two hours of time for each PC you deploy.

> Although this chapter focuses on using the unattended installation method with Windows NT Workstation, most of the same procedures apply for Windows NT Server. If you need to deploy a large number of NT servers, you can use the same techniques.

If your company is small, deploying only one workstation a month, for example, investing 2–3 hours to deploy a workstation might not seem that bad. However, if you're in a company that deploys—or redeploys—workstations at a rate of two or more a week, you begin to see computer configuration as a drain on critical resources.

Microsoft, being one of those large corporations that has to deploy hundreds of computers a week, has integrated features into Windows NT to facilitate automated setups. These features and utilities can take the need for user intervention out of installing workstations. Instead, they enable an administrator to just drop a CD in the drive of a machine that needs to be built or rebuilt and then run a single command.

However, running unattended installations isn't for the faint of heart. Even with Windows NT facilitating some of the setup, an administrator must jump many hurdles in order to get an unattended installation to work on every computer.

> Microsoft's Systems Management Server is an excellent addition to the scripting of an unattended installation. SMS allows applications to be installed and updated on any SMS client. SMS can manage a few clients or several thousand. If you decide to implement unattended installations, look to SMS to push additional applications.

Despite the functionality that the tools provide, there are some problems with using the included tools.

- *Installation of services using SYSDIFF.* Services must be installed via applications or commands after setup is complete.

- *Installation of multiple hardware profiles.* You can set up only the hardware profile for the current configuration of the system when the Setup program has been run.

- *Installation of sound cards.* Sound cards must be set up after the Windows NT setup is complete.

- *Installation of printers.* Printers must be set up after the Windows NT setup is complete.

- *Installation of multilanguage versions of Windows NT.* The automated tools are not supported.

- *Configuration of Windows NT auditing.* There are no "hooks" for automating Windows NT auditing setup.

- *Configuration of Windows NT replication.* There are no "hooks" for automating Windows NT replication setup.

- *Installation of ISA Plug and Play drivers.* There is no support for automating the installation of Plug and Play drivers.

You will need to know these limitations for the test. Try to commit them to memory.

Another consideration for the test is why these unattended installation files are so important. In other operating systems, such as DOS and Windows 95, a single computer can be set up exactly as every computer should be set up, and the hard drive can then be placed in a disk duplicator and duplicated as many times as necessary. This system has always worked great. Once a particular system is configured correctly, it's a piece of cake to create exact copies of that system.

This, however, presents a problem with Windows NT because each Windows NT workstation and server has a (presumably) unique system ID. This system ID is used in domain memberships and is supposed to uniquely identify a system. If the system ID isn't unique, you might encounter weird problems that Microsoft Technical Support won't be able to help you resolve.

> **Warning**
>
> Do not try to get around the complexities of creating an unattended installation script by duplicating hard drives. In the end, Microsoft Technical Support will be unable to provide support for your configuration.

> **Note**
>
> Some of these limitations can be overcome by the use of the Rational Visual Test tool. The Visual Test tool was first developed by Microsoft to automate testing of its applications, and it subsequently became a product. In 1997, Microsoft decided that it no longer wanted to develop the product and sold it to Rational.
>
> The tool automates user actions by tracking the objects with which the user interacts, and then it attempts to interact with those objects again. Although Visual Test is another language to learn, it can be used to automate installations where other tools can't.
>
> Short of writing Visual C++ programs, you can't beat Visual Test for creating bulletproof application installations.

2.2. Unattended Installation File (UNATTEND.TXT)

The starting point with any unattended installation is the UNATTEND.TXT file. The UNATTEND.TXT file, along with the uniqueness database file (discussed in section 2.3, "Creating a Uniqueness Database"), control how Windows NT Workstation is set up. Although UNATTEND.TXT can be used to configure almost every aspect of the Windows NT Workstation setup process, it can't be used directly to configure other applications.

2.2.1. Specifying an Unattended File During Setup

The first step in using an unattended setup file is knowing how to tell the Setup program to use it. To instruct Windows NT to use an unattended installation file, you enter the option /U: on the command line, followed by the full path and filename of the unattended installation file.

The two Windows NT Setup programs are designed to be run from different operating systems. The first program, WINNT, is designed to be run from all operating systems except Windows NT. The second program, WINNT32, is designed to be run from previous or damaged versions of Windows NT. We discuss both versions of Setup in more detail in Chapter 3. At this point, it doesn't matter whether the Setup program is WINNT or WINNT32; both programs support the unattended installation option.

The unattended installation file should fit within the 8.3 character limitation of DOS. In fact, all the files that you use in your unattended installation should comply with the DOS 8.3 naming convention. The Setup tools include built-in functions for renaming files to use long filenames after the installation is complete. This is discussed in more detail in the section "Creating a $$RENAME.TXT File."

Here is a sample command line for the Setup program:

```
WINNT32 /U:B:\THORPROJ.TXT /B
```

This command line calls for the use of the unattended installation file in drive B called THORPROJ.TXT and will copy the boot files to the drive so no floppy disk swapping will be necessary.

> **Note** Although the unattended installation file can have any name, you'll find that Microsoft refers to it as UNATTEND.TXT in most documents.

2.2.2. Some Sample Unattended Installation File Entries

Now that you know how to tell the Setup program to use an unattended installation file, you need to know how to create one. The first thing to do is to get a copy of the UNATTEND.TXT file from the platform directory on the Windows NT CD-ROM. The sample file included with Windows NT 4.0 is shown in Listing 2.1.

> **Test Tip** Although we go into detail here about the unattended installation file, you need not memorize specific entries. The test doesn't cover entries directly; it references only the [Unattended] section specifically. However, it's good for you to have an understanding of the file and what the major settings are.

Listing 2.1. UNATTEND.TXT **file from the** \I386 **directory of the Windows NT CD-ROM.**

```
; Microsoft Windows NT Workstation Version 4.0 and
; Windows NT Server Version 4.0
; (c) 1994 - 1996 Microsoft Corporation. All rights reserved.
;
; Sample Unattended Setup Answer File
;
; This file contains information about how to automate the installation
; or upgrade of Windows NT Workstation and Windows NT Server so the
; Setup program runs without requiring user input.
;
; For information on how to use this file, read the appropriate sections
; of the Windows NT 4.0 Resource Kit.

[Unattended]
OemPreinstall = no
ConfirmHardware = no
NtUpgrade = no
Win31Upgrade = no
TargetPath = WINNT
OverwriteOemFilesOnUpgrade = no

[UserData]
FullName = "Your User Name"
OrgName = "Your Organization Name"
ComputerName = COMPUTER_NAME

[GuiUnattended]
TimeZone = "(GMT-08:00) Pacific Time (US & Canada); Tijuana"

[Display]
ConfigureAtLogon = 0
BitsPerPel = 16
XResolution = 640
YResolution = 480
VRefresh = 70
AutoConfirm = 1

[Network]
Attend = yes
DetectAdapters = ""
InstallProtocols = ProtocolsSection
JoinDomain = Domain_To_Join

[ProtocolsSection]
TC = TCParameters

[TCParameters]
DHCP = yes
```

After you get this file, you will want to change a few options. Some of these options will be machine specific; if so, they should not be specified in the unattended installation file, but in the uniqueness database (explained in the section "Creating a Uniqueness Database (UDB)"). Essentially, the uniqueness database file contains exceptions, or additions to the base unattended installation file, that make it unique to the machine so you don't have to create an entire unattended installation file for each computer.

The first thing you will notice when viewing the UNATTEND.TXT file (see Listing 2.1) is that it has the same format as an INI file. It contains section headings enclosed in brackets and one or more entries in each section.

There are several key sections within the file. We'll explore options from the sections listed below:

- [Unattended]
- [UserData]
- [Network]

We explore these options to give you a better understanding of the unattended installation file and the things that it can do. The test will not ask you about specific entries in the file.

[Unattended]

The [Unattended] section of the unattended installation file must be present or the file will be ignored. This section is a sort of master control section. It determines which sections, if any, of the rest of the file will be processed during setup. Here are some of the key entries:

- The OEMPreinstall option can be set to Yes or No. The default value of No indicates that the OEM directory (described in the section "Building an OEM Directory") will not be copied or used. If your goal is simply to install Windows NT without any applications, the default value of No is fine. However, most people will set this to Yes so that the OEM directory and all its features can be used. The sections [MassStorageDrivers], [KeyboardDrivers], [PointingDeviceDrivers], [OEMBootFiles], and [OEM_Ads] must all be included if the OEMPreInstall is set to Yes.

- The NoWaitAfterTextMode is used to prevent Windows NT from prompting for a key before rebooting after the Text mode portion of setup. A value of 1 tells Windows NT not to wait for a keypress after Text mode. This option is valid only if OEMPreinstall is set to Yes. It's recommended that this value be set to 1 for unattended installation scripts. If this value isn't set, the installation will not be truly unattended.

- The `NoWaitAfterGuiMode` is similar to `NoWaitAfterTextMode`, but it is used to prevent Windows NT from prompting for a keypress at the end of the GUI mode portion of setup. As with `NoWaitAfterTextMode`, it's recommended that this value be set to 1 for unattended installation scripts.

- The `ConfirmHardware` option specifies whether the user should confirm hardware. The setting of No (the default setting) is recommended for unattended installation scripts. The `ConfirmHardware` option isn't available when `OEMPreinstall` is set to No.

- The `NTUpgrade` option indicates how the Setup program should handle existing installations of Windows NT. Generally this option should be set to No. This prevents the unattended installation script from accidentally overwriting an existing version of NT. However, if you're planning to use the script to regenerate machines that have become damaged, the best option might be Single.

  If the value is set to Yes, Setup upgrades the first installation it finds. If it is set to No, Setup halts if it finds a previous version of NT. When it's set to manual, Setup prompts the user to specify which Windows NT installation to upgrade.

  It's important to note that this can be specified only in the answer file—not the uniqueness database—so you won't be able to use a single script to repair or build new systems. You will need a unique file for each type of installation.

- The `TargetPath` option specifies where Windows NT will be installed. If the option is *, the Setup program generates a unique directory name. It's recommended that you set this to a specific directory so future scripts will know exactly where to find system files on all of your computers. Normally this directory is `C:\WINNT`.

Note

If you don't want to create multiple script files to handle the options that Microsoft won't let you change in the uniqueness database file, you do have another option. You can use an INI file-changing utility to change the entry in the unattended installation file before starting Setup. One such utility can be found on the Thor Projects Web site at `http://www.ThorProjects.com/Programs.htm`. (The utility is shareware and has a minimal licensing charge.) You can use `ChangeINI` in batch files that run Setup in order to eliminate the need to maintain multiple `UNATTEND.TXT` files.

[UserData]

The [UserData] section contains the user name, company name, and computer name. Normally, the only options specified in this section in the unattended installation file are the FullName and OrgName. The other parameters are generally specified in the UDB file. Here are the four key parameters:

- The FullName option is used to specify the user's full name. If you use the full name of the user who will be running this computer, this entry is normally placed in the UDB file. However, many companies are placing a standard value in this field, such as A company employee, in which case the entry can be made in the unattended installation file.

- The OrgName option is used to set the company name. This is generally set in the unattended installation file because it is normally the same for every computer installed.

- The ComputerName option is used to set the computer's NetBIOS name. This option is almost exclusively set in the UDB file because every NetBIOS name must be unique.

- The ProductID option enters the product ID number into the Windows NT product. This information might be consistent, as it is when the Multiple Office License Program (MOLP) is purchased, or it might be different, if each machine has its own license, for example.

Even though most of this information is included in the UDB file, it's an important section in the unattended installation file.

> **Note**
> If you're pursuing unattended installations for your organizations and haven't investigated Microsoft's Multiple Office License Program (MOLP), you should. It offers licensing discounts for organizations that can meet minimum requirements.

[Network]

The networking section tells the Setup program how to set up networking on the Windows NT Workstation. This is important because most Windows NT Workstations, especially those that would need an unattended installation file, are installed on a network. This section is important for getting a fully functional unattended installation file. The following are the key options:

- The `Attended` option specifies whether Windows NT should prompt the installer for information on the network. The suggested setting for automated installation scripts is No. When you choose No, Setup uses the settings in the unattended installation file and the UDB file to set up the network.

- The `JoinWorkgroup` option, which is mutually exclusive of `JoinDomain` option, specifies the workgroup that the workstation should join. No special settings must be created for a workstation to be added to a workgroup.

- The `JoinDomain` option specifies the domain in which the workstation should be installed. Note that either the `CreateComputerAccount` option must be used, or there must be an existing computer account in the domain.

- The `CreateComputerAccount` option allows the unattended installation to automatically create a computer account in the domain for the computer being installed. However, because the user name and password used to do this are listed in clear text, Microsoft doesn't recommend using this option. It represents a potential security problem.

Many other sections and entries can and should be placed in the unattended installation file to make it complete. However, even the sections that we've covered here offer more detail than the test gets into.

2.3. Creating a Uniqueness Database (UDB)

No matter how careful or detailed you are, maintaining multiple installation scripts for each computer and changing the appropriate entries will eventually lead to havoc. With each version that you attempt to maintain, the likelihood that you'll confuse versions or fail to make all of the necessary changes increases.

In anticipation of this, Microsoft allows *most* entries that exist in an unattended installation file to be overwritten by entries in a uniqueness database. The uniqueness database is a standard file, just like the unattended installation file, and it uses the same INI file-type sections and entries. By making changes in the uniqueness database file for a particular computer, you can essentially modify the base unattended installation file, making it unique to that particular computer. This keeps you from having to create a new unattended installation file for each computer.

2.3.1. How to Tell Setup to Use a UDB File

Just as it is pointless to create an unattended installation file if Setup doesn't know how to use it, it is also pointless to make a uniqueness database if Setup doesn't use it.

The command line switch that tells Setup to use a UDB file is /UDF:ID,*Filename*. The ID can be alphanumeric and must match an ID in the uniqueness database. If the filename is missing, Setup assumes it is to use the file $UNIQUE$.UDB on a floppy that the user will be prompted for.

> **Note**
> The command switch is /UDF: instead of /UDB: because in the beginning, the files were called "uniqueness data files." However, Microsoft decided to change the name to "uniqueness database files" because each file contains more than one unique ID, thus implying a database. Although some people may object to Microsoft calling a flat ASCII file a database, it provides an effective way of keeping a single master configuration file for all of your computers.

If a problem prevents Setup from locating the file or ID, Setup offers the user the opportunity to retry or cancel. If the user cancels, Setup continues, using the defaults from the unattended script.

2.3.2. Specifying Unique IDs

The first section of a UDB file is the [UniqueIDs] section. This section tells the Setup program which IDs are in the file and which sections each of those IDs uses. Listing 2.2 shows a sample [UniqueIDs] section of a UDB file. The machine names are from my network. And note that they are machine names, not user names, although I could have just as easily used user names or even numbers.

Listing 2.2. Sample uniqueness database file.

```
[UniqueIds]
BEAST=UserData, GuiUnattended, Network
HYDRA=UserData, GuiUnattended, Network
MAMMOTH=UserData, GuiUnattended, Network
```

2.3.3. How Setup Uses the Sections in the Uniqueness Database File

After you establish the [UniqueIDs] section of a UDB file, you need to set up the sections within it. These sections are identical to those in the unattended installation file. You create the same headings and entries, understanding that some entries can't be in the UDB file.

Listing 2.3 shows a sample [UserData] section. As you can see, it's identical to the [UserData] section in the unattended installation file.

Listing 2.3. [UserData] section of a UDB file.

```
[UserData]
FullName = "Robert L. Bogue, MCSE, CNA, A+"
OrgName = "Thor Projects, Inc. (www.thorprojects.com)"
ComputerName = MAMMOTH
```

The entries in Listing 2.3 will override the entries in the unattended installation file if they are present. If the entries are not present in the installation file, the values from the UDB will be used as if they were in the unattended installation file.

Although there's no reason to do it here, you can also clear values that are set in the unattended script by creating the necessary entry and placing no value after the equal sign. As a result, the default value will be used.

2.3.4. Associating Sections with the Appropriate IDs

If you looked closely at Listings 2.2 and 2.3, you probably noticed that all of the computers use the same [UserData] section. However, this will cause problems if the [UserData] section is handled as it is above because every computer will have the same name.

In the UDB file, you can also express section headings as *ID:Section*, where *ID* is the ID name and *Section* is the section's standard name. Listing 2.4 shows an example of this for the [UserData] section.

Listing 2.4. Sample [UserData] sections from a UDB file.

```
[BEAST:UserData]
FullName = "Single 100Mhz Pentium"
OrgName = "64MB/3GB"
ComputerName = BEAST
```

```
[HYDRA:UserData]
FullName = "Dual 166Mhz MMX Pentium"
OrgName = "64MB/4GB"
ComputerName = HYDRA

[MAMMOTH:UserData]
FullName = "Single 200Mhz Pentium Pro"
OrgName = "128MB/12GB"
ComputerName = MAMMOTH
```

As you can see, each ID gets its own section, and the section contains all the necessary values. In Listing 2.4, I used the full name to describe the processor(s) and the company name to describe the memory and hard disk space. You can use names, a standard value, or whatever you feel is appropriate.

2.3.5. Handling Settings That Can't Be in a UDB File

Despite the wide array of options that can be set in the UDB file, there are some that Microsoft won't let you set. There are two approaches to handling this:

- Create separate unattended installation files, or use a tool to change the unattended installation file, so that a batch file can be created to make the specific changes that are necessary. This creates the setup exactly as you need it.

- Post-process the installation using the OEM directory to correct installation differences that couldn't be handled in the UDB file.

Which method you choose is up to you; I recommend that you manage the unattended installation files because it will take less time and will allow you to start the setup and then walk away.

2.4. Building an OEM Directory

One of the best things about the unattended installation is its capability to install more than just the base Windows NT installation. Most of the functionality to add additional applications is handled by the OEM directory stored under the distribution directory. This directory can be located almost anywhere.

To understand where the directory must be created, suppose you've created a share called AUTONT on the server DISTRIBUTION. The distribution directory would be referred to as \\DISTRIBUTION\AUTONT. The OEM directory would be \\DISTRIBUTION\AUTONT\OEM.

The OEM directory enables Setup to use custom HALs, drivers, and other files. It also makes it possible for system files to be replaced, entire directory structures to be created, and programs to be run.

In the root of the OEM directory is a file called CMDLINES.TXT. This file contains all the commands that you want executed after the GUI portion of the setup is complete.

Often the OEM directory structure is used to run the SYSDIFF program discussed in the following section, "Using SYSDIFF.EXE." Using that utility is much easier than manually developing the files and directory structures of the OEM directory that we discuss here. The SYSDIFF tool is actually the recommended way of building an unattended installation. However, there are some things that the SYSDIFF utility can't do that can be scripted into the OEM directory structure. For instance, SYSD-IFF can't install services, but installation of services can be scripted into the OEM directory structure.

The following sections discuss some of the options that are available in the OEM directory structure.

2.4.1. Installing Custom HALs and Drivers

The standard installation of Windows NT is good for a standard PC on which you don't want to install any updated HALs, SCSI drivers, or pointing device drivers. However, if you need to install updated files on your Windows NT system, the best time to do so is during the Text mode phase of the setup. In that phase, none of the files are in use so they can be replaced—or more likely, the correct drivers can be installed.

All the files that are selected in the Text mode portion of Setup (including the HAL, SCSI driver, pointing driver, and so on) are placed in a directory called \TEXTMODE under the OEM directory. Also placed in this directory is a TXTSETUP.OEM file that tells Setup which files are used for what. The TXTSETUP.OEM file interacts with the unattended installation file. You will have to make some changes to the unattended installation file in order to use this directory.

2.4.2. Creating a $$RENAME.TXT File

One of the design limitations that results from having Setup copy files from the Text mode portion of the setup routine is that long filenames are not necessarily supported. Because of this, all the files in the OEM directory must have short filenames that fit the 8.3 DOS naming standard.

This doesn't, however, preclude the use of programs that use or need long filenames. Each directory under the OEM directory can contain a file called $$RENAME.TXT. The $$RENAME.TXT file controls how Setup will rename files from their 8.3 names to long filenames.

The file is very simple and follows the INI file format. The file can contain multiple sections that indicate the directories the files are in. By default, the $$RENAME.TXT file works on files in the current directory. Listing 2.5 shows a sample $$RENAME.TXT file.

Listing 2.5. Sample $$RENAME.TXT that renames short filenames to long filenames.

```
[]
MYCRPPRG.LNK="My Corporate Program.lnk"
TIMSYNUT.LNK="Time Synchronization Utility.lnk"
CRPRPTMN.LNK="Corporate Reporting Menu.lnk"
```

As you can see, the short filename is listed first, followed by an equal sign, followed by the long filename in quotation marks. The file format is simple, but it's very important that you key in the filenames correctly. A single error can prevent the installation from occurring as it was intended.

2.4.3. Replacing System Files and Installing Applications

Sometimes the first release of drivers or those included on the Windows NT CD aren't exactly bug free. As time goes on, Microsoft and other vendors release service packs, patches, bug fixes, or whatever they want to call their fixes.

In Microsoft's case, they release most of their fixes as hot fixes and then bundle them into service packs. The service packs have nice installations and will automatically install if you want, but often the hot fixes have only instructions on how to install them instead of an actual install program. The result is that you have to place some files in specific locations, replacing the older files. This can be a tedious process. But now the OEM directory structure can automate this process for new installations.

A special $$ directory under the OEM directory contains files that are designed to replace files located in the %WINDIR%. For instance, $$\SYSTEM32\REPL\IMPORT\ SCRIPTS matches the NETLOGON share, which is generally C:\WINNT\SYSTEM32\REPL\ IMPORT\SCRIPTS on most NT installations.

Another use for the $$ directory is placing files in the %WINDIR% directories. For instance, you may want to include the company logo as a bitmap so that it can be used as a background (or mandated through the use of profiles).

2.4.4. Copying Files to the Hard Disk After Setup

The $$ directory structure shouldn't generally be used to install applications. If you want to install Windows NT application or data files, you create directories under the OEM subdirectory using the drive letters for names. During the installation, these will be copied to the appropriate drives.

Suppose you have a corporate pricing database that you want each workstation to have a copy of. The standard place for this directory is C:\PRICEDATA. To have the Setup program copy this data for you, you can create the directory \OEM\C\ PRICEDATA and place any files needed for the database in that directory.

2.5. Using SYSDIFF.EXE

To this point in the chapter, we've been discussing things that you can manually script, but each one required your time. The manual scripting methods require that you do a fair amount of research to get all the settings in the correct place in the correct file.

The SYSDIFF tool is different. SYSDIFF is an automated tool that enables you to quickly and easily replicate most environments. Like any automated tool, SYSDIFF has its limitations. However, most of those limitations are problems that occur only in very specific environments and can be handled via other means.

One of SYSDIFF's limitations is that the installation directory must be located in the same place on both the system creating the differences file and the machine to which the differences file is applied. This means that if you generate a differences file from a machine on which Windows NT is installed in the C:\WINNT directory, every other machine on which you use the differences file must also have Windows NT installed in C:\WINNT.

One disadvantage is that this prevents you from creating and testing a differences file on the same machine. You must use another machine to test the differences files after they are created.

The SYSDIFF tool has five modes:

- /snap, which creates a snapshot
- /diff, which creates a differences file
- /apply, which applies a differences file
- /dump, which displays the contents of a differences file
- /inf, which creates the OEM structure

The SYSDIFF tool works by creating a snapshot of the system before any applications are installed or configuration settings are changed. This is done with the /snap mode.

After the snapshot has been created, updates are made to the system, and then the /diff mode is used to create a differences file. The differences file can be moved from machine to machine and is designed to allow programs to be added to the system in an automated fashion.

Once the differences file has been copied to another system, it can be applied by using the /apply mode. This causes the same changes to be made to the new computer that were recorded between the snapshot and when the differences file was created on the original system. Finally, the /dump and /inf modes are used to debug and tweak the differences file.

All these modes will be explored in the following sections.

2.5.1. /snap

The first step in monitoring changes is to get a baseline. This is true when you are trying to determine what changes a program makes, just as it is true with performance monitoring.

It's important to realize that SYSDIFF measures changes in the system configuration. To measure a change you have to first take a measurement, and then take another measurement and compare the differences. The /snap mode enables you to take this initial picture off the system.

To take a snapshot of the current system, you use the command SYSDIFF /snap snap_file where snap_file is the fully qualified name of the file in which you want the snapshot contained.

> **Warning**
>
> Don't try to use the SYSDIFF tool on anything other than a new or clean configuration. Even if you don't know it yet, each application you install, each setting you change, and so on may actually have to be changed on every machine.
>
> Because the differences file records changes, you don't want to have any newer files or anything else in the environment that might cause the Setup program to skip copying a file. Likewise, you want to make any required configuration changes after you take the snapshot file.
>
> If you fail to heed this warning, your differences files will not completely replicate the system.

2.5.2. /diff

Once you have your frame of reference for determining what changes have occurred, you need to actually make the changes. Add files, change configuration options, and make any changes that you will want to replicate to multiple machines.

When you finish making changes, use the SYSDIFF command with /diff mode to create another snapshot of the system, compare it with the first, and create a differences file. All of these steps are done at once as part of the /diff mode. To create a differences file, you use the command SYSDIFF /diff *snap_file diff_file*, where *snap_file* is the snapshot file that was created with the /snap mode and *diff_file* is the differences file that you will use to apply the changes to other systems.

2.5.3. /apply

The final step in replicating the changes to multiple systems is to apply those changes to each workstation. This can be done with the /apply mode of the SYSDIFF tool.

As we mentioned in an earlier warning box, the differences file can be applied only to installations of Windows NT that use the same installation directory. You cannot install to Windows NT machines that were installed to directories with other names.

There is one other issue regarding the use of the /apply command: By default, the SYSDIFF program records changes very literally, which is what you want in most cases. However, in the case of user IDs, it's not necessarily what you want. For instance, say you log into your workstation as "Joe," and you build the differences file. Well Joe has a unique system identifier that won't be present on other systems.

Suppose you install programs that modify Joe's profile. Those changes will not carry over to the other machines because the users on the other workstations do not use Joe's profile.

The way you get around this is to use the /m option to indicate that changes made to your user profile should be made to the default user profile instead. This means that every new user will get a copy of these profile changes, and this eliminates the problem of user changes not being available to every user.

To apply the differences file created with the /diff mode and restore the user changes to the default user, use the command SYSDIFF /apply /m *diff_file*, where *diff_file* is the name of the differences file.

2.5.4. /dump

One of the problems with a tool such as SYSDIFF is that you don't always know what the tool is actually doing. If you're planning to deploy a large number of workstations, it's recommended that you use the /dump mode to get a readable form of what the SYSDIFF tool will do when the /apply mode is used. This helps you determine if there are any visible problems, such as files that aren't being copied because they are already on the system or changes you may have accidentally made between the times you created the snapshot and created the differences file that you don't want to be replicated.

To get a dump of a differences file, use the command SYSDIFF /dump *diff_file* *dmp_file*, where *diff_file* is the differences file and *dmp_file* is the file in which you want the human-readable output.

2.5.5. /inf

As we mentioned previously, there are certain things that the SYSDIFF tool just can't do. Instead of not using the SYSDIFF tool because of these limitations, you can use SYSDIFF to create the differences file and then convert that differences file into the OEM directory structure. This is probably the quickest, easiest, and best way to start developing an OEM directory structure to automate installations.

The command line to create the OEM directory structure from a differences file is SYSDIFF /inf /m *diff_file* *dist_dir*, where *diff_file* is the differences file created with /diff and *dist_dir* is the distribution directory on the network under which you want the OEM directory to be created.

As it did with the /apply mode, the /m switch indicates that the user settings should be made a part of the default user profile, not the user profile where the changes actually were made. If you make changes to the user configuration but fail to use the /m switch, the OEM directory will be useless.

After creating the OEM directory, you can modify it to add additional information and changes, including changes that SYSDIFF can't handle. You can also correct or eliminate any problems that you may have induced by changing settings that you shouldn't have after creating the snapshot or by adding settings that you accidentally made before creating the snapshot file.

Lab

Today's lab tests and exercises your understanding of the unattended installation facilities built into Windows NT. Answers to the review questions are at the end of the section.

Review Questions

1. Which of the following is the command line option that specifies a uniqueness database file?

    A. /UDB:

    B. /UDF:

    C. /U:

    D. /UF:

2. Which of these sections is a required part of the unattended installation file?

    A. [UserData]

    B. [GuiUnattended]

    C. [Network]

    D. [Unattended]

3. What is the purpose(s) of an unattended installation file?

    A. To provide answers for setup prompts.

    B. To install applications after Windows NT setup is complete.

    C. To allow the control of Windows NT without a user being present.

    D. To automatically create user accounts on Windows NT.

4. Which of the following are valid uniqueness database IDs?

    A. 1

    B. 2,000

    C. MACHINE_NAME

    D. USER_NAME

2

5. Which section is present in the uniqueness database file but isn't present in the unattended installation file?

   A. [Unattended]

   B. [UniqueIDs]

   C. [UserData]

   D. [Network]

6. A user enters a command specifying the use of a uniqueness database file with an ID of 123. However, no uniqueness database file has the ID 123. What will happen when the user cancels the dialog box requesting the uniqueness database file?

   A. Setup will abort.

   B. Setup will continue but will use only the settings in the unattended installation file.

   C. Setup will continue but will ignore the uniqueness database file and the unattended installation file.

   D. Setup will continue. It will use the first entry in the uniqueness database file.

7. In which file is the [UserData] section normally found?

   A. The unattended installation file

   B. The uniqueness database file

   C. SYSDIFF

   D. CMDLINES.TXT

8. You've created a custom installation directory, and you want to run some applications after setup is complete. Which file should you use?

   A. The unattended installation file

   B. A uniqueness database file

   C. CMDLINES.TXT

   D. SYSDIFF

9. Which of the following files would not be valid under the OEM directory?

   A. OEM.LST

   B. MYFILES.LST

   C. LISTING_OF_FILES.TXT

   D. $$RENAME.TXT

10. Which mode of SYSDIFF must be used first?

    A. /apply

    B. /diff

    C. /snap

    D. /inf

11. Which mode of SYSDIFF creates human-readable output?

    A. /inf

    B. /dump

    C. /diff

    D. /apply

12. Which mode of SYSDIFF is used to create a differences file?

    A. /snap

    B. /apply

    C. /create

    D. /diff

13. You have a complex installation that requires features SYSDIFF doesn't support. What is the *best* way to develop the installation?

    A. Copy the hard drives from one machine to another.

    B. Manually create an unattended installation and OEM directory.

    C. Create an unattended installation file, use SYSDIFF to process the changes that it can and convert the differences file into the OEM structure, and then modify files as required to tailor the installation.

    D. Use a tape drive to back up a master machine and restore that backup to each machine.

2

14. What happens when an entry exists in both the uniqueness database file and the unattended installation file?

    A. Setup uses the one in the unattended installation file.

    B. Setup uses the one in the uniqueness database file.

    C. Setup prompts the user to select which value to use.

    D. The installation is aborted.

15. If the SYSDIFF utility is run on a system with a Windows NT installation directory of C:\WINNT, the differences file can be applied to:

    A. All machines.

    B. All machines that have Windows NT installed on the C: drive.

    C. All machines that have Windows NT installed in the C:\WINNT directory.

    D. All machines that have Windows NT installed in a \WINNT directory on any drive.

Answers to Review Questions

1. B   Although the files are called uniqueness database files, the option is /UDF:.

2. D   If the unattended installation file doesn't contain an [Unattended] section, the file will be ignored.

3. A   The primary purpose of the unattended installation file is to answer the setup prompts. Answer B is not correct because the unattended installation file cannot directly cause other programs to be set up; the OEM directory must be used to do this.

4. A, B, C, D   The uniqueness database file IDs can be either alpha or numeric.

5. B   The [UniqueIDs] section isn't present in the unattended installation file because that section is used only to determine which parts of the uniqueness database file apply to the specific ID that was referenced.

6. B   If a uniqueness database file is corrupted, is unreadable, or doesn't have the specified ID, the Setup program ignores it.

7. B   Because the [UserData] section contains machine-specific data (the machine name), it is located in the uniqueness database file.

8. C   The CMDLINES.TXT file in the OEM directory is used to control which commands are run after setup is complete.

9. C   All the files in the OEM directory must have valid 8.3 DOS filenames. The $$RENAME.TXT file renames them from their short names to long file-names.

10. C   The first step in using the SYSDIFF tool is to create a snapshot.

11. B   The /dump mode dumps the differences file into a human-readable output file.

12. D   The /diff mode uses a snapshot file to produce a differences file.

13. C   The *best* option is to use the SYSDIFF tool to generate as much of the OEM directory structure as possible.

14. B   The uniqueness database file overrides any settings in the unattended installation file.

15. C   SYSDIFF images can be used to install files only when the Windows NT installation directory is the same.

Exercises

The exercises here are meant to allow you to practice what you've learned today.

Exercise 2.1: Creating a Differences File

For this exercise, you'll need one new installation of Windows NT Workstation, the Windows NT CD-ROM, and at least one application that you can install.

You are going to create a differences file that can be applied to other systems to auto-mate the installation of the application or applications. Follow these steps:

1. Log in to the Windows NT server as administrator.

2. Copy the SYSDIFF.EXE and SYSDIFF.INF files from the \SUPPORT\DEPTOOLS\ I386 directory on the Windows NT CD-ROM to the Windows NT directory. (This assumes that you're using an Intel-based NT system; if you're not, sub-stitute the correct platform directory.)

3. Run SYSDIFF /snap C:\snap.img. This creates the snapshot that you'll need later to create the differences file.

4. Install any applications that you want to distribute, and then change any set-tings that you want to be changed on all the systems.

5. Run SYSDIFF /diff C:\snap.img C:\diff.img. This creates a differences file that can be applied to other systems.

Exercise 2.2: Applying a Differences File

In this exercise, you'll need a system on which Windows NT was installed into the same directory as it was in Exercise 2.1. This system should not be the same system on which the differences file was created unless that system has been reformatted.

This exercise shows you how to apply an image file.

1. Copy the SYSDIFF.EXE and SYSDIFF.INF files from the \SUPPORT\ DEPTOOLS\I386 directory on the Windows NT CD-ROM to the Windows NT directory. (This assumes that you're using an Intel-based NT system; if you're not, substitute the correct platform directory.)

2. Copy the differences file you created in Exercise 2.1 to the root of the C: drive.

3. Run SYSDIFF /apply /m C:\diff.img.

4. Delete the SYSDIFF.EXE and SYSDIFF.INF files from the Windows NT directory, and then delete the DIFF.IMG file from the root of C:.

5. Reboot Windows NT.

6. Log in as administrator.

7. Run User Manager (choose Start, Programs, Administrative Tools).

8. Select User and then New User to open the New User dialog box.

9. Enter **TestUser** in the Username field and click Add.

10. Click the Close button to close the New User dialog box.

11. Close User Manager.

12. Select Start, Shutdown.

13. Select Close All Programs and Log In as a Different User.

14. Log in as TestUser.

15. Verify that the settings and applications you used to create the differences file are working. The /apply mode applied the differences to the system on which the command was run.

2

Day 3

Installing, Upgrading, and Removing Windows NT Workstation

Welcome to Day 3. Today we cover the basics of installing Windows NT Workstation, removing it, and setting up dual-boot configurations.

Objectives

Today we cover the first part of the Installation and Configuration objective. Specifically, this chapter covers the following subobjectives:

- ■ Installing Windows NT Workstation on an Intel platform given a specific situation

- ■ Setting up a dual-boot system in a given situation

- ■ Upgrading to Windows NT Workstation 4.0 in a given situation

- ■ Configuring server-based installations for wide-scale deployment in a given situation

3.1. Install Windows NT Workstation on an Intel Platform in a Given Situation

The Windows NT Workstation exam emphasizes a few key points of installing Windows NT on an Intel-based computer. They are

- Hardware compatibility
- Installation method options
- The phase of installation in which particular options appear

We'll explore these key points of installation in the following sections.

3.1.1. Hardware Compatibility

One of the biggest complaints with Windows NT has been its rather restrictive hardware requirements. Compared to DOS, Windows, or even NetWare, Windows NT is very picky about the hardware it will run on.

It's not really NT's fault, though. When Windows NT was designed, the goal was to extract the best performance from each component. So the designers adhered strictly to the hardware specifications. The problem is that some hardware vendors cut corners and *don't* strictly adhere to those same requirements, which sometimes causes problems when running NT.

If there were no way to determine what hardware NT would run with, it would be chaos trying to deploy Windows NT in your organization. You would never know which computers Windows NT would properly install on and which ones would have problems. Luckily, Microsoft had the foresight to develop a hardware compatibility list (HCL). The HCL lists all of the hardware that has been tested and can be run successfully with Windows NT. It is strongly recommended that you choose a computer that is on the HCL for new installations of Windows NT. If you install Windows NT on a platform that's not supported, you might not receive any assistance from Microsoft Technical Support.

Microsoft makes the HCL easy to get to. An HCL is included on the Windows NT CD as a help file in the \SUPPORT directory. It is also available on TechNet, Microsoft's subscription information and patch release program, and on Microsoft's Web page at http://www.microsoft.com/hwtest/hcl.

3.1.2. Using the Hardware Qualifier

Although the HCL lists many devices that have been tested with Windows NT, thousands of others haven't been tested with Windows NT. Windows NT provides a way to quickly determine if you will have problems with any particular hardware.

In the \SUPPORT\HQTOOL directory on the Windows NT CD, you will find a batch file called MAKEDISK.BAT. This batch file allows you to create a hardware qualification disk that will create an NTHQ.TXT file you can use to determine what Windows NT is detecting the hardware as.

This tool can't fix hardware problems, nor can it specifically tell you what might be a problem. What you need to know for the test is that this tool exists and can be used to troubleshoot problems with the setup.

3.1.3. Choosing an Installation Method

3

If you've determined that your hardware will support Windows NT, it's time to install the program. In this respect, Windows NT is very flexible. It can be installed via:

- Floppy disks and CD
- CD only (if bootable CDs are supported)
- CD from a previous version of Windows or DOS
- A network share from a previous version of Windows or DOS

These installation methods really break down into two similar installation paths: installation from bootable media (both floppy and CD) and installation from a previous operating system by using either WINNT or WINNT32. The following sections cover these options in detail.

Floppy Boot/CD Boot

The most common way to install Windows NT is via the setup floppies or bootable CD-ROM. This is because these are the only two methods available when no existing operating system is installed on the computer, and because this is the only way that all of the partitions can be changed during setup.

> **Note**
>
> Even though you can change partitions when using other installation methods, you cannot change the partition used for the temporary files. Floppy- or CD-booted setups are the only ones that support changing every partition because they don't have any files on any partition that are needed to complete the setup.

If your system supports it, the fastest way to install Windows NT is to use the bootable CD. To test whether your system supports bootable CDs, just put it in your CD drive and turn the computer on. One of three things will happen:

- Windows NT Setup will start, indicating that you have a bootable CD-ROM drive.

- You'll get a message that there is no bootable or system disk, or your previous operating system will start. Either case indicates that your CD-ROM drive isn't bootable.

- Your computer will lock up and will have to be reset before you can do anything else. This indicates that your CD-ROM is bootable, but the Windows NT CD and your CD-ROM drive are not boot-compatible. You can try to update the firmware on the CD-ROM controller to try to get it to work.

> **Note**
>
> Every RISC-based computer can boot from CD-ROM. This is the only way of installing to RISC computers because they don't boot from a floppy. Either they boot to a firmware menu that will allow you to run a program, or they boot to a special menu that gives you the option of installing Windows NT. Refer to the hardware manual for a RISC computer for exact installation steps for Windows NT. Because the installation steps are slightly different for each RISC computer, you will not be tested on how to install Windows NT on any RISC computer.

Even if you can't boot from CD-ROM, you'll need the CD for the floppy disk installation. As soon as the floppy disk installation has loaded the appropriate drivers and SCSI drivers, it will prompt you for the CD-ROM.

> If you lose the setup floppies, you can replace them. Simply use three blank high-density 3.5" floppies and run the WINNT or WINNT32 command with the /ox command line option. This creates the floppy disks but does not attempt to set up Windows NT on the computer.

Installing over a Previous Version of DOS or Windows

Even if Windows NT can't upgrade a previous version of Windows, the setup program can use the previous version of Windows to support some of the initial file copying, making the installation process quicker.

If you're running a previous version of Windows NT, if you have an installation you want to repair, or if you just want to install another copy of Windows NT on a computer that already has it, you can use the WINNT32.EXE program located in the \I386 directory to start the installation process. You use the WINNT32.EXE program whenever you're already running Windows NT and want to start the installation process.

If you're not already running Windows NT, you can still start the installation process without using the boot floppies. To do so, run the WINNT.EXE program in the \I386 directory of the CD-ROM. This starts a DOS-based installation program.

With either program, you'll want to use the /b command line option, which tells the Setup program to copy the boot files to the hard drive so that floppy disks are not needed.

> You can't change the C partition when installing over a previous version of Windows. The C partition is used to hold the installation and setup files.

3.1.4. The Installation Process

No matter which installation method you choose to use, you have two basic phases of setup: the text phase and the GUI phase. The test asks you what happens in each phase. Use Table 3.1 to memorize which parts of the installation occur in each phase.

Table 3.1. The two phases of setup.

Text Phase	
Storage controller detection	Detects all SCSI and IDE controllers installed in your system.
License agreement	The license agreement for Windows NT Workstation, to which you must agree before continuing the installation.
Verification of detected equipment	Verification that the computer, display, keyboard, and pointing device that were detected match what you have installed. The display will be detected for the specific chipset and model during the GUI portion of the setup.
Partition selection	You must create or select a partition on which to install Windows NT.
Format selection	You must decide which type of file system you want—FAT or NTFS—and if you want to reformat an existing partition or leave the existing format in place.
Directory selection	After the formatting is complete, you'll have to choose which directory to install Windows NT in. The default directory is \WINNT.
Secondary disk examination	Windows NT checks the drive for any directory problems or file allocation table problems that might prevent a successful installation.
Copying of files required for GUI setup	Finally, the program copies the files necessary for the GUI portion of setup.
GUI Phase	
Select installation type	Select the type of installation you want: Typical, Portable, Compact, or Custom.
Enter name and company name	Your name and your organization's name are used by default as registration information for applications installed in the future.
Enter the CD key	You must enter a valid CD key. The CD key generates a product number that

	Microsoft uses to uniquely identify your installation of Windows NT Workstation.
Enter the computer name	This is the NetBIOS computer name. This name must be unique on the network, or users will have problems accessing other machines.
Set the administrator password	Windows NT creates the Administrator account as part of setup. NT allows you to set the administrator's password here.
Determine whether you want an emergency repair disk	Windows NT asks whether you want an emergency repair disk to be created during setup. Even if you choose no, you can still create one with the RDISK.EXE utility.
Select the components to install (Custom installations only)	Select the specific components that you want installed. You can select entire groups or individual programs.
Select network participation	You must specify how your workstation will participate in the network, and whether you will connect to the network via a network card or modem. The next four steps will not appear if you do not indicate that you are wired to a network.
Select installed network adapters	You can select your adapter manually or use the Start Search button to have NT find your network card.
Select network protocols	You're prompted to select network protocols; TCP/IP is selected by default.
Select services	You must specify what services to install. By default, the services needed for the NT Workstation to be both a workstation and a server are installed.
Select workgroup/domain membership	You must elect whether to join a workgroup or an existing domain.

3

continues

Table 3.1. continued

Set time zone	You must set the time zone for the server. This setting is important for replication and other services.
Change video display settings	Next you must select and test video display settings.
Create an emergency repair disk	If you chose to create an emergency repair disk earlier in the installation process, it will be created now.

3.2. Set Up a Dual-Boot System in a Given Situation

Having more than one operating system installed at one time was popularized by OS/2 and its boot partition manager. That little program allowed you to install multiple operating systems and select which one booted the computer.

Windows NT has the same functionality. Every time that you boot up your computer, it displays a list of operating systems that can be started. This list, called the *boot menu*, exists whether or not there is another operating system installed, so you can specify options on how NT should boot. Its real power, however, lies in its capability to allow you to have more than one operating system installed at one time.

In the following sections we discuss how to set up a dual-boot situation.

Warning Don't format partitions with NTFS or convert FAT partitions to NTFS if you dual boot your machine. Operating systems other than Windows NT don't understand and can't use NTFS.

Note The boot menu is controlled by the BOOT.INI file in the root of the C: drive. You can edit it to add additional operating system options or to change the description of an option. This file is flagged as read-only and hidden; you will have to remove the hidden and read-only attributes to make changes to it.

> You must be careful when editing the BOOT.INI file. If you make an error when editing the file, you can potentially prevent Windows NT from booting altogether. You can make some changes easily, such as changing how long it takes for the default operating system to boot or changing the default operating system.

3.2.1. Installing NT to Dual Boot an Existing Operating System

When Windows NT is installed on a computer that has another operating system installed on it, and Windows NT isn't installed in the same directory as the previous operating system, Windows NT creates a dual-boot situation between NT and the previous operating system. Windows NT places an entry for the previous operating system on the boot menu so you can boot up that operating system. Windows NT also creates two entries on the boot menu for itself.

Warning

> Windows 95 OSR2 Release (sometimes known as Windows 95B) supports a new partition type called FAT32. Windows NT 4.0 does not support FAT32. If your drive is formatted with FAT32, you will need to delete the partition with all the files, create a FAT partition, and restore the files.

3.2.2. Installing a New Operating System After Windows NT

Installing another operating system on top of Windows NT is a little more difficult than installing NT on top of another operating system. When the new operating system is installed, it takes control away from Windows NT's boot manager, rendering it useless.

You can fix this by performing the following sequence when installing the new operating system:

1. Create a Windows NT emergency repair disk using the RDISK utility.

2. Shut down Windows NT and install the new operating system.

3

3. Boot with the setup floppy #1.

4. Insert setup floppy #2 when prompted.

5. When you reach the initial welcome screen, select Repair.

6. When asked which things you want Setup to do, deselect everything except Inspect Boot Sector.

7. Specify any hard disk controllers or allow Windows NT to detect them.

8. Insert your emergency repair disk, and then press Enter when prompted.

9. Remove the emergency repair disk and reboot the computer.

You'll see that Windows NT has been restored, and that there is an option on the boot menu for the new operating system you installed.

3.3. Upgrading to Windows NT in a Given Situation

Windows NT can upgrade earlier versions of Windows NT and only two other operating systems. They are

- Windows 3.1
- Windows for Workgroups 3.11

Windows NT will perform an upgrade only if Windows NT is installed into the same directory the previous operating system was installed in. Windows NT cannot upgrade Windows 95, OS/2, UNIX, or any other operating system.

When Windows NT upgrades a previous version of NT, virtually all the settings are maintained, including the security database, common and personal groups, file associations, and so on. However, Windows NT might not be able to migrate certain settings. For example, it cannot migrate video card settings because the video driver structure has changed.

When upgrading Windows 3.1 or Windows for Workgroups 3.11, Windows NT keeps groups, file associations, and the Registry.

> **Note**
>
> Windows 3.1 did have a Registry, but it was much simpler than that of Windows NT or Windows 95. It basically contained file associations and information relating to DDE and OLE. Most of this information exists under the HKEY_CLASSES_ROOT key in the Windows NT Registry.

3.4. Removing Windows NT

Windows NT is an impressive operating system that is stable, scalable, and reliable. However, it's not a fit for every user or every computer. Because it is not the panacea of operating systems, there may be situations in which you need to remove Windows NT.

Windows NT does not have an uninstall program. Instead, follow these steps to remove Windows NT from a computer.

1. Load Windows NT and use Disk Administrator to delete any NTFS partitions (except the system partition if it's NTFS).

2. Load DOS 6.*x*'s FDISK.

3. If the system partition is NTFS, delete it.

   If the system partition isn't NTFS, delete the \WINNT directory and the following files from the root directory:

BOOT.INI	PAGEFILE.SYS
NTLDR	NTDETECT.COM

4. Install the new operating system, or reinstall the operating system to activate its bootup loader.

Often, instead of deleting the files from the system partition, it's easier to delete all the partitions and install the new operating system as you would on a brand new system.

3.5. Configure Server-Based Installation for Wide-Scale Deployment in a Given Situation

We spent all of Day 2 talking about how to use the Windows NT installation files to develop unattended scripts. Today, we cover how to use these files to deploy a number of machines via the network.

3

Test Tip Server-based installations work only for Intel-based systems. RISC-based systems must be installed via a local CD.

3.5.1. Copying Files to the Server

The first step in configuring a server-based installation is to copy the \I386 directory from the Windows NT CD-ROM to a shared directory on a Windows NT or Windows 95 server, or to copy it to a location on a NetWare volume.

For instance, let's say you have a server called SERVERA with a share called INSTNT and a CD-ROM drive to which the letter D has been assigned. To get the files on the share, you would use the command XCOPY D:\I386*.* \\SERVERA\INSTNT /s.

3.5.2. Copying Unattended Files

After the Windows NT files are copied to the share, you need to copy the unattended files. You should copy at least the unattended installation file and any files and directories in the OEM directory structure. You may want to copy the uniqueness database file to this directory as well.

For instance, suppose you have the same system described in the previous example, and you have used the net use command to assign the letter S to the share \\SERVERA\INSTNT. From the directory that contains the OEM directory, unattended file, and uniqueness database files, you would issue the command XCOPY *.* S:*.* /s.

3.5.3. Running the Installation

When the installation is complete, you issue the WINNT or WINNT32 command against the shared directory, with the /b option to eliminate the need for the floppy disks and possibly the /U: and /UDF: options to specify the unattended file and uniqueness database files (respectively).

For example, you could use the command WINNT /b /U:UNATTEND.TXT /UDF:WKSNTA, UNIQUE.UDB to install Windows NT using the unattended installation file and the uniqueness database file named UNIQUE.UDB.

Lab

Today you learned how the Windows NT installation process works, how it can be used to upgrade systems, and how to set up a server for wide-scale distribution. The labs here will exercise your understanding of today's material. Answers to the review questions are at the end of the section.

Review Questions

1. Which directory is copied to the server to support server-based installations?

    A. `\%platform%`

    B. `\RISC`

    C. `\MIPS`

    D. `\I386`

2. You're installing Windows NT over Windows 95, and you want to upgrade Windows 95. How do you do this?

    A. Install Windows NT into the same directory as Windows 95.

    B. Install Windows NT into a different directory from Windows 95.

    C. This can't be done.

    D. Install Windows NT in any directory, and the upgrade will happen automatically.

3. You're installing Windows NT over Windows 95, and you want to dual boot to Windows 95. How do you do this?

    A. Install Windows NT into the same directory as Windows 95.

    B. Install Windows NT into a different directory from Windows 95.

    C. This can't be done.

    D. Install Windows NT in any directory, and the upgrade will happen automatically.

4. Which of the following are part of the Text phase of setup?

    A. Setting the time zone

    B. Agreeing to the license

    C. Selecting a partition

    D. Selecting the components to be installed

3

5. Which of the following are part of the GUI phase of setup?

   A. Entering the administrator password

   B. Creating an emergency repair disk

   C. Storage controller detection

   D. Secondary disk examination

6. You're installing Windows NT over Windows 3.1, and you want to upgrade Windows 3.1. How do you do this?

   A. Install Windows NT into the same directory as Windows 3.1.

   B. Install Windows NT into a different directory from Windows 3.1.

   C. This can't be done.

   D. Install Windows NT in any directory, and the upgrade will happen automatically.

7. Which of the following are part of the Text phase of setup?

   A. Setting up the network card

   B. Establishing or choosing the partition on which Windows NT is to be installed

   C. Joining a workgroup or domain

   D. Selecting the services to be installed

8. Which of the following are part of the GUI phase of setup?

   A. Entering the CD key

   B. Agreeing to the license agreement

   C. Entering the user and organization names

   D. Entering the computer name

9. You've installed Windows NT already, and you want to install Windows 95 so that you can dual boot to it. What is the best way to do this?

   A. This is not possible.

   B. Backup Windows NT, install Windows 95, and then restore Windows NT.

   C. Create an emergency repair disk, install Windows 95, boot with the emergency repair disk, and then repair Windows NT.

   D. Create an emergency repair disk, install Windows 95, boot with the setup disks, and then repair Windows NT's boot sector using the emergency repair disk.

10. Dual booting is controlled by which file?

    A. `DUALBOOT.INI`

    B. `BOOT.INI`

    C. `MULTIBT.INI`

    D. `MSDOS.SYS`

Answers to Review Questions

1. D Windows NT Workstation can be installed only via the network on Intel systems, and the directory for Intel-based systems is `\I386`. The `%platform%` directory isn't right because it's always the `\I386` directory. The `\RISC` directory doesn't exist, and `\MIPS` doesn't work because server-based installation is supported only for Intel systems.

2. C Windows NT can't upgrade Windows 95 under any circumstances.

3. B The Setup program automatically creates a dual-boot situation when Windows NT isn't installed into the same directory as the previous operating system.

4. B, C Both agreeing to the license and selecting the partition are part of the Text mode of setup.

5. A, B Both entering the administrator password and creating the emergency repair disk are part of the GUI mode of setup.

6. A When Windows NT is installed into the same directory as Windows 3.1 or Windows for Workgroups 3.11, the installation is upgraded.

7. B Choosing the partition is the only listed action that occurs during the Text mode of setup.

8. A, C, D Only accepting the license agreement happens in the Text phase of Windows NT setup.

9. D Answer B won't work because Windows 95 won't be able to boot. Answer C is wrong because the emergency repair disk isn't bootable.

10. B Dual booting is a function of the Boot menu, which is controlled via the `BOOT.INI` file in the root of the C: drive.

Exercises

The exercises in this chapter walk you through installing Windows NT workstation and performing a quick test to see if your CD-ROM supports bootable CDs.

Exercise 3.1: Installing Windows NT from a Previous Version of Windows

Time Estimate: 30 minutes

Windows NT can be installed over previous versions of Windows or DOS. In this exercise, we'll walk through the process of installing Windows NT over an existing version of DOS.

1. Insert the Windows NT CD-ROM.

2. From the D:\I386 directory of the CD-ROM, run WINNT.EXE with the /b option. All the files necessary files for Windows NT are copied to your hard drive, including boot files.

3. Reboot the computer, and the Windows NT setup screen appears.

4. Press Enter to set up Windows NT.

5. Allow Windows NT to detect mass storage devices. When it's finished, press Enter to accept the mass storage devices NT detected.

6. When the license agreement appears, press Page Down until the end of the agreement is visible, and then press F8 to accept it.

7. Windows NT detects the basic hardware. It displays the system type, keyboard, mouse, and video display for you to verify. Press Enter to continue.

8. Select the partition on which you want to install Windows NT. You can also create or delete partitions here.

9. Select the directory in which you want to install Windows NT. (The default is \WINNT.)

10. Allow NT to perform a secondary examination of the hard disks. This time it checks the drive for any problems.

11. Restart the computer by pressing Enter.

12. When the GUI appears, click the Next button.

13. Select the kind of installation you want, in this case, Typical. Then choose the Next button.

14. Enter your name and your organization's name. Click the Next button when you finish.

15. Provide the CD key if prompted. Choose the Next button to continue.

16. Provide a computer name, and then choose the Next button to go on.

17. Enter and confirm the administrator password. Click the Next button to proceed.

18. Select Yes to create an emergency repair disk, and then choose the Next button.

19. Specify that you want to install the most common components. Choose the Next button.

20. Click next to install NT Networking.

21. Select Do Not Connect This Computer to a Network at This Time, and then choose the Next button.

22. Select Finish.

23. Select a time zone and click Close.

24. Click OK to accept Windows NT's detection of a video display.

25. Press the Test button to test the settings Windows NT selected as defaults.

26. Answer Yes to the dialog box that asks if you saw the bitmap properly.

27. Click OK to clear the message about having successfully tested the display settings.

28. Click OK to clear the Display Properties dialog box.

29. Insert the floppy disk that you want to use for the emergency repair disk.

30. Click the Restart Computer button.

You've just installed Windows NT Workstation on your computer!

Exercise 3.2: Determining If Your CD Is Bootable

Time Estimate: 10 minutes

Determining whether your CD-ROM controller and drive support bootable CDs is an easy task. Follow these steps:

1. If the computer is already on, shut it down and turn it off.

2. Turn on the computer.

3. Go into the BIOS of the SCSI controller and look for any option that is for bootable CDs. Make sure that it is on. (Generally this is labeled Bootable CD support or something similar, but it might be listed under removable media.)

4. Insert the Windows NT Workstation CD and reboot the computer via the Reset switch or by turning the computer off and back on.

If the computer doesn't load Windows NT and actually locks up, the machine has bootable CD-ROM support, but it is not compatible with Windows NT. If the computer starts the previous operating system, bootable CDs are not supported.

If the computer starts the Windows NT Setup program, the computer supports bootable CDs and is compatible with Windows NT.

Day 4

Configuring Hardware Components

Welcome to Day 4! After what might have seemed to be a grueling few days, we're going to take it easy today. We're going to talk about how to configure Windows NT Workstation with various hardware.

Objectives

Today we cover the second set of subobjectives for the Installation and Configuration objective. Specifically, we're going to cover these tasks:

- Installing, configuring, and removing hardware components for a given situation
- Using Control Panel applications to configure a Windows NT Workstation computer in a given situation

We'll spend all our time today working with the Windows NT Control Panel. You add, configure, and remove hardware and configure Windows NT via the Control Panel.

4.1. Install, Configure, and Remove Hardware Components for a Given Situation

Windows 95 made configuring hardware devices easy. Full support of Plug and Play meant that many devices automatically configured themselves. Installing a new sound card could be as easy as installing the card in the system and starting Windows 95. Windows 95 would then take over and prompt you for the correct drivers to make the sound card work. What's better is that from the Add New Hardware applet, you could add any type of hardware—even if it wasn't Plug and Play.

Unlike Windows 95, Windows NT doesn't have an Add New Hardware applet/wizard in the Control Panel. Each hardware device must be configured in its own Control Panel applet.

Windows NT 4.0 doesn't yet have full support for Plug and Play, so we have to manually configure most devices and run from applet to applet in the Control Panel trying to get all the right settings to make the hardware work.

PCI-based devices almost always automatically configure themselves, even in Windows NT.

Getting the hardware settings right might seem to be a daunting task, especially if you're used to Windows 95's nearly automatic hardware installation routines. However, it's not as difficult as it might seem.

Windows NT does have minimal support for Plug and Play devices. It allows you to use Plug and Play devices that have been configured via another Plug and Play–aware operating system or via vendor-provided utilities. This is why Windows 95 is often installed on Windows NT Workstation computers. Windows 95 can automatically configure Plug and Play devices, eliminating the need to track down the vendor-specific Plug and Play setup utilities for cards.

Windows NT also has a Plug and Play add-in located in the \DRVLIB\PNPISA directory on the Windows NT CD-ROM. Although it's not fully tested or widely supported, it will work in a pinch. The Windows NT Workstation exam doesn't test you on the NT Plug and Play device drivers.

> **Warning**
>
> If you use Windows 95 on a machine on which you have also installed Windows NT, you'll need to be very careful when adding or removing hardware—particularly Plug and Play hardware. Windows 95 will change IRQ, DMA, and IO address settings, which can prevent Windows NT from communicating with the device or, in the worst cases, from even booting.
>
> Once you've configured the devices in both Windows 95 and Windows NT, go back into Windows 95 and disable automatic resource selection for all the devices you use in Windows NT.

The Windows NT exam focuses on determining which applet is used to add or configure hardware. The next several sections cover the hardware that is specifically mentioned in the exam guidelines.

4.1.1. Network Adapter Drivers

One of the most common additions to a Windows NT Workstation is a network card. As more and more systems, at home or at work, are being networked, a network card is becoming an essential part of every computer, not just those used in large business.

You add network adapters by way of the same Network Control Panel applet that all network services are installed in. You then use the Adapters tab in the Network applet to configure adapters. Figure 4.1 shows the Network applet with the Adapters tab selected.

> **Note**
>
> You can also get to the Network applet by selecting the Network Neighborhood, right-clicking its icon, and selecting Properties.

Figure 4.1 shows that the current system has both a 3Com Etherlink III card and a Comtrol RocketPort. The 3Com Etherlink III is used to connect to the local Ethernet.

Figure 4.1.

The Adapters tab of the Control Panel's Network applet.

 Note

The Comtrol RocketPort is a multiport serial board. While it doesn't technically belong in the Network applet, this is where most multiport serial boards are installed because there isn't a multiport serial board applet for them. You might also see ISDN devices installed in the Network applet.

If you install a device and then you can't find it under any other applet, check the Adapters tab of the Network applet. It is often the catch-all for miscellaneous communications devices.

Each device listed may or may not have a properties sheet that can be modified. Most devices do have a properties sheet like the one shown in Figure 4.2. On the properties sheet, you can configure the hardware resources that the card will use and any network card-specific properties, such as which interface to use.

Figure 4.2.

3Com Etherlink III properties.

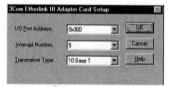

To get to the properties of a network adapter, you can either double-click the adapter in the list or click the adapter once and select Properties.

The properties of a network card are also shown when the card is installed. If you click the Add button on the Adapters tab, you will see a list of all the network adapters for which Windows NT initially had drivers. If you don't find your adapter on this list, you can choose the Have Disk button, shown in Figure 4.3, to enter the path to the drivers for your adapter.

Figure 4.3.

Choose the known network adapter you want to add, or click the Have Disk button to add an unknown network adapter.

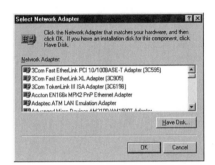

After you select the adapter, you will probably be prompted for the Windows NT CD-ROM so NT can copy the drivers to the system. When the files have been copied, you'll see the properties screen, as shown in Figure 4.2. Click OK in the Properties dialog box to return to the Adapters tab of the Network applet.

When you finish working in the Network applet, click the Close button. You'll be prompted to reboot your computer so that the network adapter driver can be loaded. Chapters 7–9 cover this process in more detail.

4.1.2. SCSI Device Drivers

Even if you don't have a SCSI controller in your system, Windows NT behaves as if you do. As far as Windows NT is concerned, any disk controller not supported by BIOS is a SCSI controller and, as such, is configured via the SCSI Adapters applet in the Control Panel.

Windows NT uses SCSI controllers to boot and is very sensitive about their configuration. It is strongly recommended that you back up your system before you make modifications to the SCSI controllers in your system.

4

The SCSI Adapters applet, shown in Figure 4.4, shows two SCSI controllers. The first one is an Adaptec AHA-1510, and the second is an AHA-2940UW. The AHA-1510 has a CD-ROM (OPTICS_S 8622 SCSI), a CD recorder (YAMAHA CDR100), and a 4MM tape drive (WangDAT Model 3200) attached to it. The AHA-2940 has three hard drives attached, of which only the first two are visible.

Figure 4.4.

The SCSI Adapters applet shows all connected disk controllers.

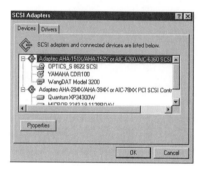

Both the controller and the attached devices have properties sheets that you can access via the Properties button. Simply select the device or controller for which you want to view settings and click the Properties button. A properties dialog box like the one shown in Figure 4.5 appears. Even though you will be able to see the resources via the properties dialog boxes, you will not be able to change them.

Figure 4.5.

YAMAHA CDR100 properties.

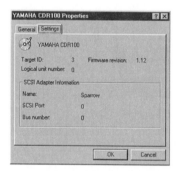

To actually change the SCSI device drivers installed in Windows NT, you must select the Drivers tab of the SCSI Adapters dialog box. As you can see in Figure 4.6, this tab has buttons for adding and removing SCSI adapters.

Figure 4.6.

The Drivers tab of the SCSI Adapters dialog box.

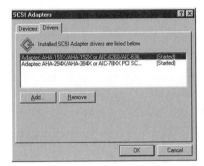

If you want to add a new SCSI controller to your system, click the Add button. This displays a dialog box that prompts you to identify the model of SCSI controller you're installing. Identify the model and click OK, and a properties sheet for your SCSI controller appears, displaying any properties that need to be configured.

4.1.3. Tape Device Drivers

After you install SCSI controllers, you need to back up the disks. This is generally done via a tape drive. Tape drives are essential to Windows NT because they are used to back up the system. The backup utility included with Windows NT backs up to tape only; it will not back up to floppy disks or removable media such as Zip or Jazz disks.

All tape devices are controlled through the Tape Devices applet. As shown in Figure 4.7, the Tape Devices applet has two tabs: Devices and Drivers.

Figure 4.7.

The Tape Devices applet.

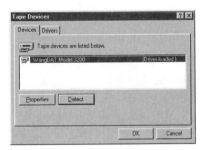

This Devices tab is very similar to the Devices tab in the SCSI Adapters applet. However, it is only a single level because tape devices don't have devices connected to them, and it contains a Detect button that the other does not.

The properties of the tape drive are the same as the ones that were visible in the SCSI Adapters applet. The properties sheet contains basic information, as well as the SCSI ID and firmware revision of the device.

You can add a new device by clicking the Detect button. Windows NT then scans through its database of drivers and attempts to load the appropriate ones. Normally this detection is successful. If the detection isn't successful, you can click the Drivers tab and choose the Add button. This displays a list of tape drives supported by Windows NT. Select the correct tape drive and click OK. You'll be prompted for the Windows NT media so NT can copy files.

You do not have to reboot Windows NT in order for the tape driver to be installed.

4.1.4. UPSes

Next to a tape drive, UPSes are probably the second most important "safety" device for computers. A UPS, or Uninterruptible Power Supply, enables a computer to continue operating even if there is a short interruption in power from the utility company.

UPSes come in various capacities and sizes. The smallest UPSes for PCs are about 250VA. Large data center UPSes can be well in excess of 100KVA. VA is short for Voltage-Amp. It refers to the amount of power that a UPS can output. At normal 110 volt output, a 250VA UPS can output about 2 Amps of current. This is enough to drive a small PC and a 14-inch monitor, but it wouldn't power a high-end PC with a 17-inch monitor.

The other characteristic of UPSes—which isn't normally listed prominently on their specification sheets—is the length of time the device can keep your computer running. UPSes use a battery to supply power, and batteries can supply only a finite amount of power before giving out.

Because Windows NT likes to be shut down properly even in the event of a power loss, it provides a very simple UPS monitoring utility. This utility signals Windows NT when it is time to shut down because the UPS has been activated and its battery is about to fail. Although the UPS is about to fail, Windows NT has enough time to shut down successfully.

As you can see in Figure 4.8, the UPS is connected via a COM port, and it has several options you can configure. They are

- *Power Failure Signal.* A signal from the UPS to indicate that utility power has failed.

If this option is selected, you'll be given the chance to specify when Windows NT informs the user that the power has failed.

■ *Low Battery Signal at Least 2 Minutes Before Shutdown.* This specifies that the UPS should provide a low-battery signal to indicate that it's time to shut down Windows NT, at least 2 minutes before the UPS fails.

If this option is *not* selected, you'll be given the opportunity to set the estimated UPS battery life.

■ *Remote UPS Shutdown.* This indicates that the computer can shut down the UPS remotely. This feature turns off the UPS to prevent the battery from being completely depleted.

Figure 4.8.

The UPS applet.

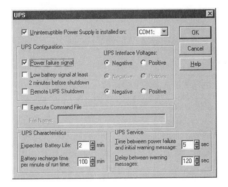

4

Lead-acid batteries, like those used in most UPSes, aren't the same as the NiCad, NiMH, and Lithium Ion batteries used in most notebook computers. You've probably heard that it is good to fully discharge a battery before recharging it. This is true of NiCad, NiMH, and Lithium Ion batteries but not the lead-acid batteries that are used in UPSes. Fully discharging a lead-acid battery can cause long-term damage. It's always best to leave at least some charge in a lead-acid battery.

Most UPS vendors have their own enhanced UPS software that you can purchase with their UPSes or download for free. Their software is generally much more flexible; it's recommended that you use any such software that's available to control the UPSes.

4.1.5. Multimedia Devices

Multimedia devices, such as sound cards, video capture cards, and joysticks, are all controlled from the Multimedia applet. When you open the Multimedia applet, the Multimedia Properties dialog box, shown in Figure 4.9, appears.

Figure 4.9.

The Multimedia applet controls all audio, video, MIDI, and CD audio devices.

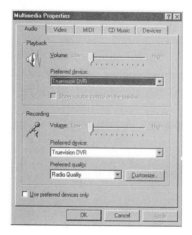

To add or configure a device, you must select the Devices tab to see the options shown in Figure 4.10.

Figure 4.10.

The Devices tab shows the installed multimedia devices.

Configuring a device is as simple as selecting the device and then clicking the Properties button. Some property sheets also have a Settings button that you must click to change the settings of the device.

Adding a device is equally simple. Either click the Add button and select your device from the list that appears, or insert a disk and select Unlisted or Updated Driver. Depending on which device you choose, you might have to complete certain settings dialog boxes in order for it to operate correctly.

4.1.6. Display Drivers

Every Windows NT system has a video card. Windows NT requires at least a VGA-compatible video card to work. Windows NT controls this video card through the Display applet.

The Display applet, shown in Figure 4.11, controls not only the specifics of the video card and monitor used with Windows NT, but also the background, screen saver, color schemes, desktop, and Web appearance (if IE 4.0 is installed).

Figure 4.11.

The Display applet controls the video and monitor settings as well as the background, screen saver, color scheme, and desktop.

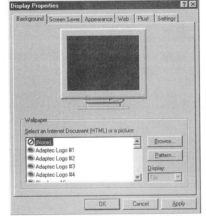

4

To change the video card drivers or the monitor refresh rate, click the Settings tab. You'll see the options shown in Figure 4.12. The settings on this tab are based on what the video card is capable of doing. Unlike Windows 95, this dialog box doesn't take into account the limitations of the monitor.

You can change the color depth without worrying about whether the monitor will be able to handle it. However, both the resolution and the refresh rate need to be tested before applying the changes. Windows NT will inform you that you need to test the settings if you don't test them before selecting the Apply button. Figure 4.13 shows the warning message you get from Windows NT.

Figure 4.12.

The Settings tab controls how the video card and monitor are set up.

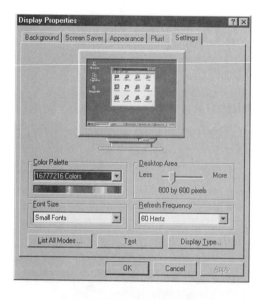

Figure 4.13.

Windows NT warns you that you should test options before changing them.

Note

The Refresh Frequency setting controls how fast the screen is refreshed. The higher the number, the less flicker your eyes will notice as you're working at the computer, and the more relaxed your eyes will be. A high refresh frequency reduces eye fatigue.

The Desktop Area setting indicates how many pixels are represented on your screen. As the number of pixels increases, the size of each pixel decreases. When pixel size is decreased, fonts are smaller and harder to read. However, you should select the highest resolution that you can tolerate because your characters and pictures will appear sharper, and most programs today allow you to zoom in or out of a document anyway.

If your driver isn't correct and it's limiting your options, or if you need to install an updated driver, click the Display Type button to access the Display Type dialog box shown in Figure 4.14.

Figure 4.14.

The Display Type dialog box shows which chipset has been detected and where the driver came from, in addition to the driver name.

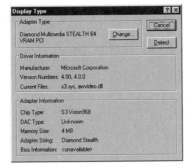

If you select the Change button on the Display Type dialog box, you'll see a list of possible adapters to install. This is a quick way of specifying the new driver. However, sometimes you don't know the exact driver that you need. In that case, you can use the Detect button on the Display Type dialog box to put Windows NT into a special detection mode that will require two reboots.

4.1.7. Keyboard Drivers

The input device with which we computer users are most familiar is the keyboard. Each of us uses the keyboard every day to enter information.

Most of us sit down to a Standard 101/102-key keyboard or one of the new "Windows Keyboards" with the additional Windows keys (which makes it about a 104-key keyboard). Although most of us use the 101/102-key keyboard layout, there are other keyboard types, some of which are created specifically to address handicapped persons' special needs, alternate layouts, and so on. Regardless of which keyboard you use, you must select it in the Keyboard Control Panel applet.

For the test, you simply need to know that you can change the keyboard driver via the Keyboard applet in the Control Panel.

4.1.8. Mouse Drivers

With the advent of Windows, the mouse became our second most important input device. It became the method by which we start programs, move files, and maneuver around documents.

As we became more familiar and dependent upon our mice, they started adding new features: a third button or, in the case of the Microsoft IntelliPoint mouse, a new wheel with which the user can scroll through documents.

Should you need to change your mouse for any reason, you need to go to the Mouse applet in the Control Panel.

4

4.2. Use Control Panel Applications to Configure a Windows NT Workstation Computer in a Given Situation

Most of today's lesson has covered the functions of icons in the Control Panel. This subobjective is no different. Table 4.1 includes the information that you should know about each Control Panel applet to pass the workstation test.

Table 4.1. Control Panel applets and functions.

Applet	Function
Accessibility Options	Controls options for changing the way that Windows operates to make it easier for those with physical impairments. This is where you would change settings to control whether keys need to be held down, to ignore some repeated keystrokes, or to have NT notify you with a sound when toggle keys (such as Caps Lock) are pressed. You can also choose to have Windows give a visible sign each time a sound is made, or allow you to use the keyboard as if it were a mouse.
Add/Remove Programs	Allows you to install or remove compatible 32-bit applications and change which Windows NT options have been installed.
Console	Controls how DOS sessions appear within Windows NT.
Date/Time	Allows you to change the time, date, and time zone.
Dial-Up Monitor	Displays connection information and allows you to terminate current dial-up connections.
Fonts	Displays the Fonts directory, allowing you to add, delete, and view fonts.
Mail and Fax	Used to change the services installed in MAPI profiles and to manage MAPI profiles, which are used in mail-enabled applications such as Microsoft Exchange and Microsoft Outlook.

Applet	Function
Modems	Maintains information on each modem installed and on the geographic location of the system so Windows NT can make adjustments to telephone numbers dialed to accommodate changing locations.
ODBC	Installs and removes drivers for remote databases and other data sources used by applications such as Access.
Regional Settings	Controls the way that Windows NT displays numbers, currency, dates, and times.
Services	Lists all of the installed services and allows you to start, stop, or pause them. Also allows you to change how the services start up.
System	Controls system-level settings, such as hardware and user profiles, environment variables, virtual memory, and startup options.

4

Lab

The following questions will help you review the material we've covered today and to prepare yourself for the Microsoft test. Answers to the review questions are at the end of the section.

Review Questions

1. Which Control Panel applet is used to configure a hard disk controller?

    A. SCSI Adapters

    B. Hard Disk Controllers

    C. System

    D. Device Manager

2. You've purchased a new sound card. Which Control Panel applet do you use to configure it?

    A. Sound Cards

    B. Network

    C. Multimedia

    D. Modems

3. You've moved to England and need to make changes to the way your computer shows dates and times. Which Control Panel applet do you use?

    A. Date/Time

    B. System

    C. Services

    D. Regional Settings

4. You just purchased a new tape drive. Which Control Panel applet do you use to install it in Windows NT?

    A. Add New Hardware

    B. SCSI Adapters

    C. Tape Devices

    D. System

5. You need to change the Microsoft Exchange settings for your user profile. Which Control Panel applet do you need to use?

   A. Mail

   B. Modems

   C. Network

   D. Mail

6. You've purchased a new modem and installed it in your system. However, Windows NT does not recognize it. Which Control Panel applet do you need to use to configure the modem?

   A. Devices

   B. Add New Hardware

   C. Modems

   D. System

7. You just bought a new monitor, and you want to change your video adapter settings to take advantage of it. In which Control Panel applet can you change the video adapter settings?

   A. Video

   B. Adapter

   C. Display

   D. Monitor

8. You have an IBM AS/400, and you need to be able to use its data in Access. Which applet do you use to configure this?

   A. Accessibility Options

   B. Network

   C. ODBC

   D. Databases

4

9. Joe gives you two cool new fonts, and you want to print them out. Which Control Panel applet would you use?

    A. Printers

    B. Fonts

    C. Display

    D. Add/Remove Programs

Answers to Review Questions

1. A All hard disk controllers are considered to be SCSI controllers. Hard Disk Controllers and Device Manager are not actual Control Panel applets.

2. C Sound cards are multimedia devices and are installed through the Multimedia Control Panel applet.

3. D Date and time formatting as well as currency settings are handled through Regional Settings.

4. C Tape devices are installed via the Tape Devices applet. There is no such thing as an Add New Hardware applet in Windows NT. SCSI Adapters can be used to display installed tape drives attached to SCSI controllers, but it cannot be used to install the tape drive.

5. D The Mail Control Panel applet is used to control MAPI profiles.

6. C The Modems Control Panel applet is used to configure and troubleshoot modems. The Devices applet doesn't contain modem configuration information; Add New Hardware isn't a valid Windows NT applet; the System applet doesn't contain modem configuration information.

7. C The correct Control Panel applet is the Display applet. It controls all settings related to how Windows NT is displayed, including video adapter, background, screen saver, color scheme, and desktop settings.

8. C ODBC is used to configure database access. Accessibility Options allows you to make Windows NT easier to use for people who have physical impairments; Network can configure the connectivity but not the database access; Databases isn't a valid Windows NT Control Panel applet.

9. B The Fonts applet controls the addition or removal of fonts.

Exercises

Today's exercises are designed to get you comfortable with using Windows NT's Control Panel to add and remove hardware.

Exercise 4.1: Installing the Drivers for a Sound Card

Time Estimate: 15 minutes

Adding a sound card in Windows NT can be simple and painless. Before beginning this exercise, you should have purchased and physically installed a sound card in your system. You should make note of the configuration parameters, such as IO address, IRQ settings, and DMA channels to provide to the driver.

To install the sound card drivers, follow these steps:

1. Start the Control Panel by selecting Start, Settings, Control Panel.
2. Start the Multimedia applet by double-clicking it.
3. Click the Devices tab to select it.
4. Choose the Add button to display the Add dialog box.
5. Select the audio card from the list, or select Unlisted or Updated Driver to be prompted for the location of the driver files for the card.
6. When prompted, enter any resource information needed by the audio card driver. Generally an IO address, IRQ, and DMA are needed for an audio card.
7. Click OK to close the Multimedia Properties dialog box.
8. Select Yes when prompted to reboot your computer.

Some sound cards also come with additional utilities that you can install through their installation and setup programs. However, Windows NT provides the basic utilities needed to test your new sound card.

Exercise 4.2: Changing Video Cards

Time Estimate: 15 minutes

Changing a display driver can be a little more tricky than installing another kind of driver because you can't have two displays installed at the same time. The following steps will help you to install a new video card:

1. Start the Control Panel by selecting Start, Settings, Control Panel.
2. Start the Display applet by double-clicking it.
3. Click the Settings tab to select it.

4. Choose the Display Type button to open the Display Type dialog box.

5. Click the Change button to display a list of compatible video drivers.

6. Select the (Standard Display Types) option from the Manufacturers list, and select VGA Compatible Display Adapter from the Display list.

7. Click OK to enter the changes you made in the Change Display dialog box.

8. Select the Cancel button to close the Display Type dialog box.

9. Click OK in the Installing Driver dialog box that appears.

10. Click the Close button to close the Display Type dialog box.

11. Click Close to close the Display Properties dialog box.

12. Select Yes when prompted to restart your computer.

13. When the boot menu appears, turn off your computer.

14. Remove the old video card.

15. Install the new video card.

16. Turn the computer back on.

17. Log in to Windows NT.

18. Run the Control Panel by selecting Start, Settings, Control Panel.

19. Run the Display applet by double-clicking it.

20. Click the Settings tab to select it.

21. Choose the Display Type button to access the Display Type dialog box.

22. Click the Change button to display a list of compatible video drivers.

23. Select the appropriate driver for the new video card. If the driver isn't listed or if the manufacturer provided an updated driver, choose the Have Disk button.

24. Click Cancel to close the Display Type dialog box.

25. Click OK in the Installing Driver dialog box that appears.

26. Click the Close button to close the Display Type dialog box.

27. Click Close to close the Display Properties dialog box.

28. Select Yes when prompted to restart your computer.

You've successfully installed the new video card, and display driver. You can change the resolution of the video card the next time you log into your Windows NT Workstation.

Day 5

Customizing and Configuring Windows NT Workstation

Welcome to the fifth day and a new set of objectives! The Managing Resources section is one of the most important in the real world and is tested upon fairly evenly on the exam. There are five subobjectives for Managing Resources; we will look at three today and two tomorrow.

Objectives

This chapter deals with the first three subobjectives of the Managing Resources objective. Today, you will learn about:

- ■ Setting up shared folders and permissions
- ■ Setting permissions on NTFS partitions, folders, and files
- ■ Installing and configuring printers in a given environment

5.1. Setting Up Shares

Sharing, as the name implies, is the method by which resources are made available on a network for others to use. This can take place with a workgroup, a few users, or an enterprise. When you decide to share a resource, you make it available to users on other machines to access via the network. In Windows NT, the two objects most commonly shared are directories and printers.

Only the power user or administrator has permission to create shares in Windows NT Workstation. In addition to the creation of shares, the Server service must be running and the network card properly functioning for the share to be valid.

There are three ways to create shared directories:

- From My Computer
- From Explorer
- From the command prompt

These methods are examined in the following sections.

5.1.1. Sharing with My Computer or Explorer

Sharing directories in Windows NT Workstation is a simple thing to do and can be accomplished in a number of ways. The two easiest ways are to use Explorer or My Computer.

Follow these steps to create a shared directory from within Explorer:

1. Right-click on the directory you want to share and choose Sharing from the shortcut menu.
2. Open the Sharing tab of the Properties dialog box (see Figure 5.1).
3. Configure the directory appropriately.

An alternative to reaching the Sharing tab in Explorer is to choose File, Properties.

To enable sharing from My Computer, select the directory, open the File menu, and choose Sharing.

Figure 5.1.

The Sharing tab for a directory.

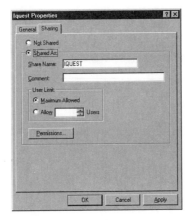

In both cases, the name of the directory becomes the default share name. Although this is the default, you are not stuck with it. The share name is free text, which means you can enter a completely different value if you want. In all cases, the name should be something that network users can easily identify, as they are the ones who will see and select the value. It should also be 15 characters or fewer in length (eight characters or less if MS-DOS computers will access it). The comment field is optional. Anything you might enter there becomes a tag of free text that appears next to the share name to users who are browsing in Explorer or Network Neighborhood.

 Note You can choose View, Details to see the comments.

The User Limit section enables you to limit the number of concurrent users who can access the directory. This is useful for licensing issues and helps you prevent too many users from accessing applications for which you have a small number of accounts.

Clicking the Permissions button opens the Access Through Share Permissions dialog box, shown in Figure 5.2. From there you can build an access control list for the share to prevent unauthorized network access.

The ATS permissions exist whether you are using FAT or NTFS and are completely independent from any local NTFS permissions. The one thing to note for the exam is that ATS permissions apply to the entire share; you cannot assign file-level permissions through sharing (although you can if the partition on which the share resides is NTFS).

Figure 5.2.

The Access Through Share Permissions dialog box.

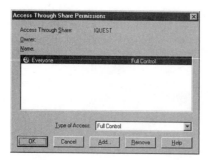

ATS permissions are

- *Change.* Assigns Read (R), Execute (X), Write (W), and Delete (D) permissions to the share.

- *Full Control.* Assigns R, X, W, and D permissions to the share; if the share is NTFS, Change Permissions (P) and Take Ownership (O) permissions are added. When you create a share, the default is for everyone to have full control.

- *No Access.* Overrides all other permissions. It still allows users to connect to the share, but nothing shows up in File Manager except the message You do not have permission to access this directory.

- *Read.* Assigns only R and X permissions to the share.

As with all Windows NT permissions, user and group permissions accumulate, with the exception of No Access, which overrides all other permissions.

5.1.2. Sharing from the Command Prompt

The NET command, coupled with the SHARE parameter, enables you to create shares from the command prompt using this syntax:

```
NET SHARE <share_name>=<drive_letter>:<path>
```

For example, to share the C:\IQUEST directory as download, you would use the following command:

```
NET SHARE download=C:\IQUEST
```

Figure 5.3 shows the result.

Figure 5.3.

Sharing can be established from a command prompt.

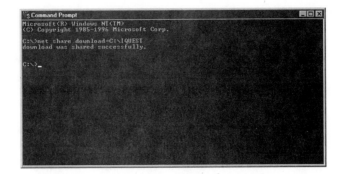

Certain parameters can be used with NET SHARE to set other options. The following list summarizes the most common parameters:

/DELETE	Stops a share.
/REMARK	Adds a comment for browsers.
/UNLIMITED	Sets the user limit to maximum allowed.
/USERS	Sets a specific user limit.

After a share is created, the icon associated with it appears in My Computer and Explorer with a hand beneath it, as shown in Figure 5.4.

Figure 5.4.

Shared directories can be identified by the hand under the folder.

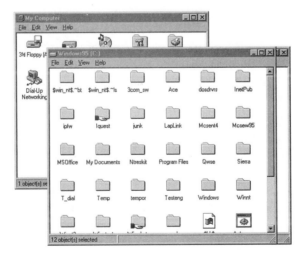

5

5.1.3. Hiding Shares

Whether a share is created from My Computer, Explorer, or the command prompt, it can be "hidden" so that it doesn't appear in most places where shares are listed. To hide a share, you end the share name with a dollar sign ($) like this:

```
NET SHARE download$=C:\IQUEST
```

This does not prevent users from connecting to the share. However, in order to do so, the user must supply the entire filename and path (including the $) because the share is hidden in Network Neighborhood and every browse list.

On every Windows NT-based computer, two hidden shares are created automatically:

- **C$.** The root of the computer's drive. If there are other hard drive partitions, a similar share will be created for them as well.
- **ADMIN$.** The %systemroot% of the partition on which Windows NT is installed.

Both of these shares offer full control to administrators and no access to regular users. They provide a means by which administrators can easily access key directories across the network.

5.1.4. Accessing the Share

Users can access the shared directory and its contents through Network Neighborhood or the Find command. In Network Neighborhood, you see a list of all available resources from which you can select the one to which you want to connect. With the Find command, you can look for a specific resource. This topic is covered in more detail in the networking chapters.

5.2. NTFS Permissions

The benefit of sharing is letting users share their resources with other users. What sharing lacks, however, is a good system of security going down to the file level. (Sharing, you will recall, stops at the directory level.) If you have installed the NTFS file system (as opposed to FAT), you can apply another level of complex security arrangements to your system.

NTFS uses the concept of *ownership* in which the creator of the resource is the owner of the resource and determines what can be done with it. The owner of a directory can grant a user access by way of directory and file permissions. This is discussed in greater detail in section 5.3.2.

The following are the defined permissions that can be assigned to users:

- *Add.* The user cannot read or view the contents of the directory but can write files to the directory. If he attempts to write a file to the directory, he receives the message `You do not have permissions to access this directory.` However, he can save or copy files to the directory.

- *Add & Read.* The user can view and read from the directory and save new files to the directory, but he cannot modify existing files in any way.

- *Change.* The user can view and read from the directory and save new files to the directory, modify and even delete existing files, and change attributes on the directory and even delete the entire directory. This is the most extensive permission you would ever want to assign to anyone.

- *Full Control.* The user can view, read, save, modify, or delete the directory and its contents. In addition, the user can change permissions on the directory and its contents, even if he does not own the resource. The user also has permission to take ownership at any time.

- *List.* This restricts the user from accessing the directory, although the user can view the contents list for the directory.

- *No Access.* This restricts the user from accessing the directory by any means. The directory appears in the directory tree, but instead of a file list of the directory contents, the user sees the message `You do not have permissions to access this directory.` Whereas most permissions are cumulative, this permission overrides all others.

- *Read.* The user can read data files and execute program files from the directory, but he can make no changes of any sort.

5

To summarize, each level of permissions enables a user to perform from one action to a combination of six actions against a resource. These are the six actions:

Read (R)
Write (W)
Execute (X)
Delete (D)
Change Permissions (P)
Take Ownership (O)

Table 5.1 breaks down the actions by permission level.

Table 5.1. User permissions by level.

Level	Directory Permissions	File Permissions
No Access	None	None
List	RX	Unspecified
Read	RX	RX
Add	WX	Unspecified
Add & Read	RXWD	Unspecified
Change	RXWD	RXWD
Full Control	RXWDPO	RXWDPO

The two custom levels of permissions are Special Directory Access and Special File Access, both of which enable the owner (or any user granted the P permission) to custom-build an access control entry by using any combination of the six basic actions.

5.2.1. Setting Permissions

Setting NTFS permissions on a file or directory is almost as easy as creating a share, and it also can be done from either Explorer or My Computer. Follow these steps to set NTFS permissions:

1. Select the resource for which you want to set permissions.

2. Choose File, Properties.

3. Select the Security tab.

4. Click the Permissions button. This opens the File Permissions dialog box shown in Figure 5.5.

Figure 5.5.

The File Permissions dialog box enables you to add user permissions.

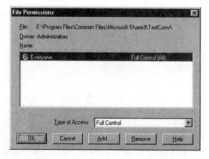

5. To add a user or group to the ACL, click the Add button. (To remove a user, select the user and click the Remove button.)

6. When you click the Add button, the Add Users and Groups dialog box appears, which includes a list of all groups in your account database (see Figure 5.6). If you want to grant access to a user, click the Show Users button. By default, only group names are displayed.

Figure 5.6.

The Add Users and Groups dialog box.

7. Choose the users or groups you want to add and click the Add button to enter their names in the Add Names list box at the bottom of the dialog box.

8. Modify the permission level for each account using the Type of Access drop-down list. When you finish setting permissions, click OK.

9. Click OK again to close the File Permissions dialog box.

5

You use the previous steps to set permissions on individual files. You perform similar steps to set permissions for a directory, but the Directory Permissions dialog box (shown in Figure 5.7) appears instead of the File Permissions dialog box.

The biggest difference is that the Directory Permissions dialog box contains two check boxes: Replace Permissions of Subdirectories and Replace Permissions on Existing Files. If you choose the Replace Permissions on Existing Files box, the permissions that apply to the directory also apply to the files within that directory, but not to subdirectories or files within subdirectories. If you choose Replace Permissions on Subdirectories, the permissions that apply to the directory apply to all directories in the directory tree but do not apply to any files within those directories. If you choose both boxes, the permissions you set apply to the entire directory tree and its contents. Conversely, if you do not choose either box, permissions you apply affect only the top-level directory.

Figure 5.7.

The Directory Permissions dialog box.

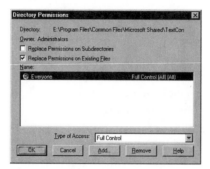

5.2.2. Ownership

You learned earlier that one way in which NTFS differs significantly from FAT is that for every NTFS file and directory, one account is designated as its owner. The owner is, by default, the only account that has the right to access a resource, modify its properties, and secure it from outside access.

Traditionally, the owner of a resource is the user who created it, and only one user can own a resource at any time (although a member of the administrators group cannot be the sole owner of any resource.) To find out who owns a file or directory, perform the following steps:

1. In My Computer, select a directory and then a file.
2. Choose File, Properties.
3. Click the Security tab (see Figure 5.8).

Figure 5.8.

The Security tab of the Properties dialog box.

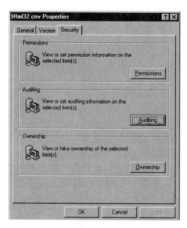

4. Click the Ownership button, and the Owner dialog box appears, as shown in Figure 5.9.

Figure 5.9.

The owner of the file is identified.

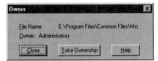

If the current owner has granted you permission to take ownership, you can transfer ownership away from the current owner. To do so, click the Take Ownership button in the Owner dialog box. For purposes of the exam, the important concept is that ownership is taken, never given.

5.2.3. Auditing

In addition to assigning rights and permissions, an administrator can *audit* the access to objects. Windows NT can be configured to track all successful and unsuccessful attempts to access NTFS resources for various purposes. When this feature is enabled, the record of all access attempts appears in the Security log and can be viewed with Event Viewer.

To enable auditing for an NTFS file, follow these steps:

1. Right-click the file in My Computer and choose Properties.
2. Click the Security tab of the File Properties dialog box.
3. Click the Auditing button. The File Auditing dialog box shown in Figure 5.10 appears.

Figure 5.10.

The File Auditing dialog box.

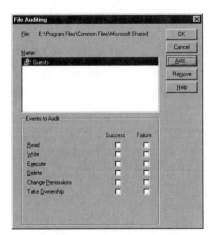

5

4. Click the Add button to add a group or user to the audit list. If you want to delete a group or user from the audit list, select the user in the Name list and click the Remove button.

As you can see in the figure, you can audit successful or failed attempts on any of the actions listed. You can also specify which groups or users you want to audit.

If you *copy* a file to a directory configured for auditing, the copied file inherits the directory's auditing configuration. However, if you *move* a file, the file retains its original auditing configuration.

5.3. Installing and Configuring Printers

Printing architecture has come a long way since the days of DOS-based applications. For the exam, you should understand the steps involved in the Windows NT printing process and how to configure all aspects of a printer in Windows NT.

5.3.1. Architectural Overview

The best way to understand the printing architecture of Windows NT is to look at the steps involved in printing a document. These are the basic steps involved in the printing process:

1. A Windows NT application sends a print job, and Windows NT checks to see if the version of the printer driver on the client is up-to-date with the version on the print server. If it's not, Windows NT downloads a new version of the printer driver from the print server to the client.

    The following steps apply for EMF spooled jobs; the processing of RAW jobs is done on the client machine at this point in the process.

2. The printer driver sends the data to the client spooler. A remote procedure call is made to the server spooler, in essence sending the data to the server spooler on the print server.

3. The server spooler sends the data to the Local Print Provider.

4. The Local Print Provider passes the data to a print processor that renders it into a format legible to the printing device. If a separator page is used, it is added and sent at the beginning. The Local Print Provider passes the rendered data to the print monitor.

5. The print monitor points the rendered data to the printer port and the printing device.

The following sections examine the important components of these steps in detail.

All About Printer Drivers

The printer driver is responsible for generating the data stream that forms a print job. It amounts to two DLLs (Dynamic Link Libraries) and a printer-specific minidriver (akin to a configuration file):

- *The Printer Graphics Driver DLL.* This is the rendering or managing portion of the driver; it's always called by the Graphics Device Interface.

- *The Printer Interface Driver.* This is the user-interface or configuration-management portion of the printer driver; it's used by an administrator to configure a printer.

- *The Characterization File.* This file contains all the printer-specific information, such as memory, page protection, soft fonts, graphics resolution, and paper orientation and size. The two DLLs need this file to gather printer-specific information.

Because the printer driver is specific to the operating system and the hardware platform, you cannot use a Windows 95 printer driver with Windows NT or use an Intel printer driver on an Alpha machine.

The automatic updating of the printer driver on the client is a key component of Windows NT printing. As shown in Figure 5.11, when you first configure a Windows NT printer, the Setup wizard asks for the operating systems and hardware platforms of all client machines that will be accessing the printer. It is the wizard's responsibility to place the appropriate drivers on the server so they are available for downloading to clients.

Figure 5.11.

When you first configure a Windows NT printer, the Setup wizard asks for the operating systems and hardware platforms of all client machines that will access the printer.

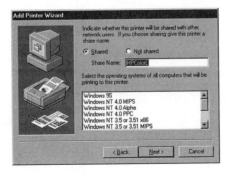

5

All About the Spooler

The spooler consists of a series of DLLs that accept, process, and distribute print jobs. It operates in the background to manage the whole printing process. All told, the spooler service performs these functions:

- Keeps track of job destinations
- Keeps track of ports
- Routes print jobs to ports
- Manages printer pools
- Prioritizes print jobs

To function, the Spooler service has to run on both the client and the print server machines. A key point to know for the exam is that the spool file folder, by default, is the `%systemroot%\system32\spool\PRINTERS` directory. This can be changed using the Advanced tab of the Print Server Properties dialog box, as shown in Figure 5.12. (You can also use Registry Editor to set the spool directory.)

Figure 5.12.

The Advanced tab of the Print Server Properties dialog box allows you to change the spool location.

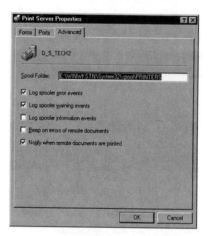

The next stop in the process is the print router. There is little to say about the print router except that it receives the print job from the spooler and routes it to the appropriate print processor.

All About the Print Processor

Rendering is the process of translating print data into a form that a printing device can read. The printer driver starts the process of rendering, and the print processor completes it. However, the tasks performed by the print processor differ depending on data type.

The primary Windows NT print processor is called WINPRINT.DLL. It works with the following data types:

- *RAW data.* Data that's already rendered and ready for the printer.
- *TEXT.* RAW text with very minimal formatting (intended for printing devices that don't directly accept ASCII text).
- *EMF (Enhanced Metafile).* A standard file format in Windows NT and Windows 95 wherein the Graphical Device Interface generates information before spooling. Because the processor, memory, and other resources on the machine are typically beefier than the resources on the printer, the end result is that the control is returned to the user in less time than if she had to wait for the printer directly.

Again, I must stress the importance of understanding that RAW data renders on the client, and EMF renders on the server.

All About Print Monitors

Print monitors control access to specific devices, monitor the status of devices, and communicate with the spooler. The print monitor controls the data stream to printer ports and is responsible for writing a print job to the output destination and taking care of port access.

To install a print monitor, select the Ports tab of the Print Server Properties dialog box (see Figure 5.13). Click Add Port, and the Printer Ports dialog box shown in Figure 5.14 appears. Click the New Monitor button.

Figure 5.13.

The Ports tab of the Print Server Properties dialog box.

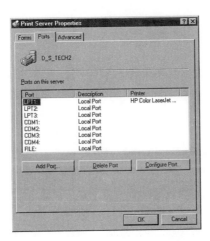

5

Figure 5.14.

The Printer Ports dialog box.

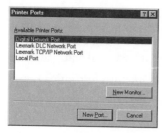

The print monitor can do all of the following:

- Detect unsolicited errors (such as Out of Paper, Toner Low, and so on).
- Handle end-of-job notification.
- Monitor printer status for printing errors.

5.3.2. The Printers Folder

The primary interface between the user and Windows NT Workstation printing is the Printers folder. This is available through Control Panel, My Computer, or the Settings item in the Start menu.

> **Note**
> The Printers folder replaces Print Manager, the printing interface in previous versions of Windows and Windows NT.

From the Printers folder, you can install, configure, administer, and remove printers; watch print queues; pause, purge and restart print jobs; share printers; and set printer defaults.

Printers can be installed on the workstation or through a connection to a remote printer. Installing your own printer is somewhat involved and requires administrator or power user rights; the remote connection installation, on the other hand, is quite easy.

To start either installation, double-click the Add Printer icon in the Printers folder to open the Add Printer wizard. Figure 5.15 shows the first screen of the Add Printer wizard. The next two sections walk you through the two methods of installing a printer.

Figure 5.15.

The Add Printer wizard.

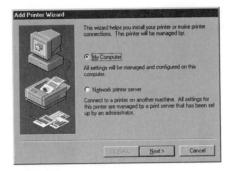

5.3.3. Adding a Printer on Your Own Machine

As I mentioned earlier, to add a printer on your own machine, you must be an administrator or power user. When you start the Add Printer wizard, it asks you what port you want to use (see Figure 5.16). You cannot proceed until you have checked one of the available ports or added a new port. Throughout the wizard, you click the Next button in each screen when you have fulfilled the requirements of the screen.

Figure 5.16.

The Add Printer wizard first requires that you select a port.

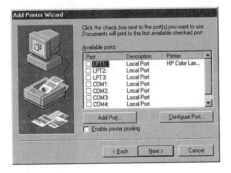

5

Notice the option for printer pooling in Figure 5.16. This option is discussed in detail in the section "Setting Up a Printer Pool," later in this chapter.

Next you must specify the manufacturer and model of the new printer from the list shown in Figure 5.17. If you have an unlisted printer, click the Have Disk button and install the driver from a disk.

Figure 5.17.

Select your printer from the lists of manufacturers and models.

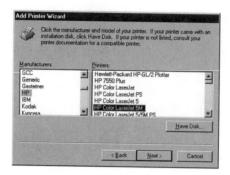

Next you must supply a printer name, as shown in Figure 5.18. The only other choice you make here is to indicate whether you want the printer to become the default printer for Windows-based programs.

Figure 5.18.

You must specify a printer name.

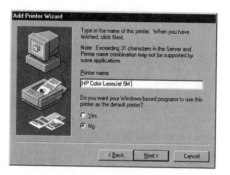

The printer name can be as long as 32 characters and doesn't have to reflect the name of the driver in use. As with other resources and shares, placing a dollar sign ($) at the end of the name hides it from all other users even though you choose to share it.

Note

The $ has to go after the share name, and it does not matter if it is in the printer name. As a side note, Microsoft's KnowledgeBase article number Q110062 mentions that Print Manager does show hidden printer shares.

Coincidentally, the next wizard screen asks if you want to share the printer with other computers on the network (see Figure 5.19). You must specify a share name if you are going to share it (the default is the name you entered in the previous screen).

Figure 5.19.

Choose whether to share the printer and make it available to other network users.

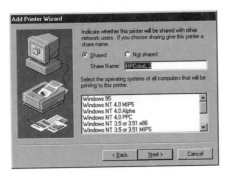

If you are sharing the printer, you must also identify the operating systems of the computers that will be sharing the printer so the appropriate printer drivers can be installed.

Upon completion, the Add Printer wizard displays the Properties dialog box for the new printer.

5.3.4. Adding a Network Print Server

This is a much simpler operation than installing a printer locally. In the first screen of the Add Printer wizard, you choose the network printer server option. The wizard opens the Connect to Printer dialog box and asks for the name of the shared printer to which you want to connect.

Click the computer the printer is attached to and select the printer. To verify settings, the wizard asks if you want the printer to serve as a default printer. The wizard then completes the installation by placing an icon for the printer in your Printers folder.

Note

If the printer to which you are attaching is on a Windows 95 machine, you have to extract the printer INF files into a directory and point Windows NT to that directory.

5.3.5. Configuring Printers

All standard configuration settings for a Windows NT Workstation 4 printer are available through these three options on the Printers folder's File menu:

- Document Defaults
- Server Properties
- Properties

Document Defaults

To use this method, select the printer and choose File, Document Defaults. The Default Document Properties dialog box shown in Figure 5.20 appears.

Figure 5.20.

The Default Document Properties dialog box.

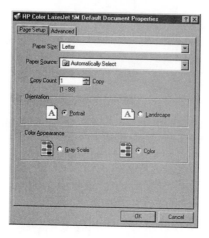

The Page Setup tab of the dialog box contains document settings for the documents that are to print on the selected printer. Those settings are fairly self-explanatory. From the Advanced tab, you can change the graphics resolution, color adjustment, print quality, size, source, and orientation settings.

Server Properties

To use this method, select the printer and choose File, Server Properties. The Print Server Properties dialog box, shown in Figure 5.21, contains information specific to the computer's print server activities.

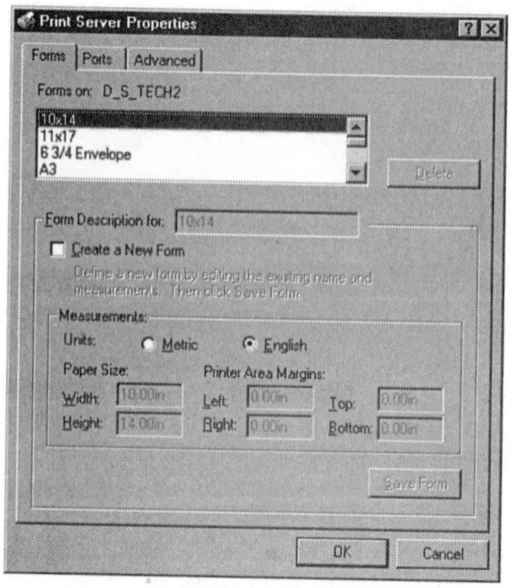

Figure 5.21.

The Print Server Properties dialog box.

This dialog box contains the following three tabs:

- *Forms.* Defines the print forms available on the computer.
- *Ports.* Maintains a list of available ports. You can add, delete, or configure a port.

> **Note**
>
> This Ports tab is the same as the Add Printer wizard's Ports tab except that you don't have to select a port here because you are viewing the available ports and are not associating a port with a particular printer.

- *Advanced.* Provides the location of the spooler and an assortment of logging and notification options.

Properties

Most configuration settings for a printer are located in the printer Properties dialog box. To open the printer Properties dialog box, select a printer in the Printers folder. Then right-click the printer and choose Properties.

The following subsections discuss the six tabs of the printer Properties dialog box.

The Printer Properties General Tab

The General tab, shown in Figure 5.22, lets you install a new driver for the printer. Pay particular attention to the three buttons on the tab.

Figure 5.22.

The printer Properties General tab.

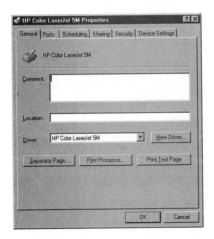

The first button, Separator File, enables you to choose one of three predefined separator pages or to create one of your own. For the exam, it is important to know that Windows NT, by default, does not separate print jobs or use a separator page. However, three separator pages are included with Windows NT:

- PCL.SEP. Switches Hewlett-Packard printers to PCL mode.
- PSCRIPT.SEP. Switches Hewlett-Packard printers to PostScript mode.
- SYSPRINT.SEP. A separator page for PostScript printers.

The second button is the Print Processor button. The default print processor is WINPRINT.DLL, but it can be updated or replaced. As I mentioned earlier in the chapter, WINPRINT.DLL supports five data choices (as shown in Figure 5.23):

- RAW
- RAW (FF appended)
- RAW (FF auto)
- NT EMF 1.003
- TEXT

Figure 5.23.

The data choices supported by WINPRINT.DLL.

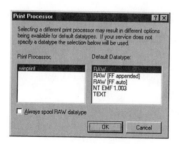

The third button, Print Test Page, enables you to test a printer connection.

The Printer Properties Ports Tab

This tab, shown in Figure 5.24, lets you choose a port for the printer, add a port, or delete a port. By clicking the Configure Port button, you can specify the Transmission Retry time for all printers that use the same driver.

The Printer Properties Scheduling Tab

This tab, shown in Figure 5.25, lets you determine when the printer will be available or unavailable and set the printer priority.

Figure 5.24.

*The printer
Properties Ports tab.*

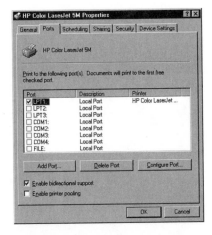

Figure 5.25.

*The printer
Properties
Scheduling tab.*

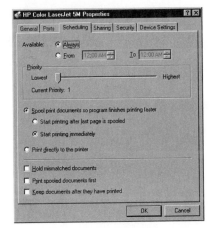

Note

The Printer Priority setting is in no way related to the print job's priority. The priority for a printer defaults to 1 but can be any number between 1 and 99. When more than one printer is printing to the same printing device, it is useful to change the priority because the printing device allows the one with the highest priority to print first.

The Printer Properties Sharing Tab

This tab, shown in Figure 5.26, lets you share the printer with other computers on the network. It is useful if you did not originally install the printer as a shared printer but decide later that you want to share it.

Figure 5.26.

The printer Properties Sharing tab.

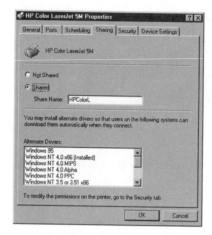

The Printer Properties Security Tab

This tab, shown in Figure 5.27, lets you configure permissions, auditing, and ownership for the printer. Like all Windows NT objects, printers are protected by the Windows NT security model.

Figure 5.27.

The printer Properties Security tab.

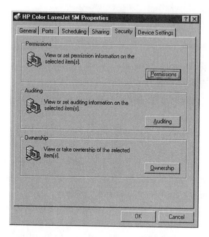

To view or set permissions for the printer, click the Permissions button. The four possible permission levels for printer access are

- *No Access.* Completely restricts access to the printer.
- *Print.* Allows a user or group to submit a print job and to control the settings and print status for that job.

■ *Manage Documents.* Allows a user or group to submit a print job and to control the settings and print status for all print jobs.

■ *Full Control.* Allows a user to submit a print job and to control the settings and print status for all documents as well as for the printer itself. In addition, the user or group may share, stop sharing, change permissions for, and even delete the printer.

It's important to know and remember that these permissions affect both local and remote users. The following table outlines the default permissions on newly created printers.

Administrators	Full control
Creator/Owner	Manage documents
Everyone	Print
Power Users	Full control on workstations and servers

To change the permission level for a group, select the group in the Name list and choose the new permission level from the Type of Access drop-down list. You can add a group or user to the permissions list by clicking the Add button and using the Add Users and Groups dialog box that appears.

> Note
>
> The printer Properties Security tab also enables you to set up auditing for the printer and to take ownership of the printer.

5

The Printer Properties Device Settings Tab

This tab, shown in Figure 5.28, keeps settings for the printing device. The information on this tab differs depending on what your printing device is.

5.3.6. Setting Up a Printer Pool

Printer pools offer an efficient means of streamlining the printing process in many environments. By the simplest definition, a *printer pool* is a single logical printer that prints to more than one printing device. It prints jobs sent to it to the first available printing device, thereby providing the throughput of multiple printing devices with the simplicity of a single printer definition. Windows NT ensures that no single device is ever sent more than one document at a time if other devices currently are available. This ensures efficient utilization of the printing devices.

Figure 5.28.

The printer Properties Device Settings tab.

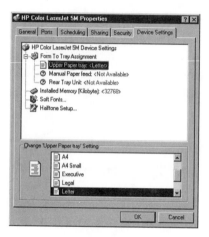

A network must meet these criteria in order to use a printer pool:

- There must be a minimum of two printing devices capable of using the same printer driver. Because the pool is viewed and treated as a single logical device, it must be managed by a single printer driver.

- While nearness is not required, the printing devices should be located close to one another. This is because users have no means of specifying a device within the pool and are given no notification of which device will actually print the job. For efficiency to work, users should not be walking from floor to floor looking for a job but should be able to check all the printing devices quickly.

To create a printer pool, you configure the printer to print to more than one port. Naturally, you must also attach a printing device to each of the specified ports.

5.3.7. Using MS-DOS–Based Applications

MS-DOS–based applications differ from Windows-based applications in that they provide their own printer drivers. They typically also render data to the RAW data type or to straight ASCII text. Because of this, an application that prints graphics and formatted text must have its own printer driver for the printing device, whereas the application can print ASCII text without a vendor-supplied printer driver.

Note

Most MS-DOS–based applications cannot handle UNC names. Therefore, when printing to a remote printer, you must often map a physical port to the remote printer. This can be done with the following command:

```
NET USE LPTX: \\PSERVER\PRINTER_NAME
```

Lab

This lab exercises your understanding of today's material. Answers to the review questions are at the end of the section.

Review Questions

1. To create a share in Windows NT Workstation, a person must be a member of which two groups?

    A. Everyone

    B. Power user

    C. Administrator

    D. Supervisor

2. In which of the following ways can shared directories be created? (Select all correct answers.)

    A. From the desktop Properties menu

    B. From Explorer

    C. From My Computer

    D. From the command prompt

3. Under what file systems do Access Through Share (ATS) permissions exist?

    A. FAT

    B. NTFS

    C. CDFS

    D. NFS

4. Which of the following are not ATS permissions?

    A. Modify

    B. Read

    C. Full control

    D. No access

5

5. Which command is used to create shares from the command prompt?

   A. NET

   B. SHARE

   C. MAP

   D. REPL

6. A share can be hidden by using which character?

   A. #

   B. _

   C. $

   D. !

7. The special character used to hide a share must be placed where?

   A. At the beginning of the name

   B. At the end of the name

   C. Anywhere within the name

   D. One space before the name

8. Which of the following file systems utilize the concept of ownership?

   A. NTFS

   B. FAT

   C. CDFS

   D. NTFS and FAT

9. Which of the following is not an NTFS permission?

   A. Add

   B. Read

   C. Scan

   D. Change

   E. Full control

10. Auditing can be performed in Windows NT when using which file systems?

   A. FAT

   B. CDFS

   C. NTFS

   D. Any file system

11. You can audit the successes and failures of which of the following events?

   A. Read

   B. Write

   C. Execute

   D. Change

   E. Delete

12. By default, what does Windows NT use as a separator page?

   A. A blank page

   B. The name of the job

   C. The name of the user

   D. Nothing; Windows NT does not use a separator page

13. Which of the following is a means of streamlining the printing process in many environments by using more than one physical printer to print jobs?

   A. Print pooling

   B. Print sharing

   C. Print spooling

   D. Print rendering

14. MS-DOS–based applications can print what jobs without a vendor-supplied printer driver? (Select the best answer.)

   A. Graphics

   B. Text

   C. Text and Graphics

   D. None of the above; a vendor-driver is always required

5

Answers to Review Questions

1. B, C Only a power user or administrator has permission to create shares in Windows NT Workstation.

2. B, C, D Shared directories can be created from Explorer, My Computer, or the command prompt.

3. D Access Through Share (ATS) permissions exist in both FAT and NTFS.

4. A ATS permissions include change, read, full control, and no access.

5. A The NET command is used to create shares from the command prompt.

6. C A share can be hidden by using a dollar sign ($).

7. B The $ goes at the end of the share name.

8. A NTFS uses the concept of ownership; FAT and CDFS do not.

9. C NTFS permissions include add, read, change, list, full control, and no access.

10. C Windows NT, when using NTFS, can be configured to audit all successful and failed attempts to access an object.

11. A, B, C, E Auditing can be done on Read, Write, Execute, Delete, Change Permission, and Take Ownership.

12. D By default, Windows NT does not separate print jobs or use a separator page.

13. A Printer pools are efficient means of streamlining the printing process in many environments.

14. B MS-DOS–based applications can print ASCII text without a vendor-supplied printer driver, but they need such a driver for printing graphics.

Exercises

The exercises here are meant to allow you to practice what you've learned today.

Exercise 5.1: Creating Print Forms

You can create your own print forms from within the Forms tab. To create your own form, follow these steps:

1. Click on an existing form in the Forms On list.

2. Select the Create a New Form check box.

3. Change the name of the form and change the form measurements to the new settings.

4. Click the Save Form button.

Exercise 5.2: Sharing a Printer

To share a printer, follow these steps:

1. Open the printer Properties dialog box and select the Sharing tab.

2. Specify a share name (or accept the default, which is the first eight characters of the printer name).

3. Specify what operating systems are used by the other workstations that will be accessing the printer (so Windows NT can automatically download the necessary print drivers to the connecting computers).

4. Click OK.

Exercise 5.3: Find the Owner of a File

To find out who owns a file or directory, do the following:

1. From My Computer, select the `%systemroot%` directory.

2. Highlight the `BOOT.INI` file.

3. Choose File, Properties.

4. Click the Security tab.

5. Click the Ownership button.

Exercise 5.4: Turn on Auditing for a File

To enable auditing for an NTFS file, follow these steps:

1. Double-click the root drive in My Computer.

2. Find the `BOOT.INI` file and right-click it.

3. Choose Properties.

4. Click the Security tab of the file Properties dialog box.

5. Click the Auditing button.

6. Click the Add button and add the everyone group.

7. Choose Success and Failure for Read.

8. After collecting logon information for a few days, open the Event Viewer and check the information in the Security log.

5

Day 6

Editing User and System Profiles

Welcome to the sixth day and the last of the Managing Resources objectives. Like Day 5, this section is one of the most important in the real world, and is tested upon fairly evenly on the exam.

Objectives

This chapter deals with the last two subobjectives of the Managing Resources objective. Today, we will look at:

- Creating and managing local user accounts and local group accounts to meet given requirements
- Setting up and modifying user profiles

6.1. Creating Local User and Group Accounts

On Day 5, you learned about ownership and that every object created beneath NTFS has an owner. If the file system is NTFS, that information is kept, whereas if it is FAT, the information is not kept. Critical to this entire discussion is the understanding that every user and group created in Windows NT is unique. What makes it unique is a value associated with it called a Windows NT Security Identifier, or SID.

SIDs are issued to accounts when they are created and are never used again. If you delete a user and then add her back in immediately—using the exact same information—the files that were associated with that user before are not associated afterward because the SID is different. For that reason, user and group accounts should *never* be deleted from Windows NT; instead they should be disabled.

There are two types of accounts in Windows NT: user and group accounts. *User accounts* belong to one person only (rights and permissions assigned affect only that one person); *group accounts* belong to collections of users who hold common rights and permissions. A group account can consist of only one user or any number of users (unlimited) who share the same permissions.

The Microsoft security model stresses placing user accounts into group accounts and managing the permissions at the group level. Because there are fewer groups than users, it is easier to manage, and easier to keep track of. Users can belong to as many groups as they need to, and there are a number of built-in groups already created for common tasks.

In this section, you will learn about users and groups individually in logical order and by bouncing between the two.

6.1.1. Default User Accounts

Two user accounts are created when you install Windows NT Workstation: administrator and guest. The administrator account is the first account created during installation. This account is also a member of the administrators group.

Note

Do not underestimate the value of this correlation. The administrator user account is permanent—you cannot disable or delete it. You can, however, remove it from the administrators group and place it in the guests group. This leaves a virtually powerless administrator account.

The guest account is also permanent and is, by default, a member of the guests group. By itself, the account has no real power. It differs from administrator in one important way: You can disable it.

6.1.2. Default Group Accounts

Windows NT Workstations have six built-in groups:

- *Administrators.* Members can gain access to all files and resources on the system.
- *Backup operators.* Members have the rights to back up and restore files using the NTBackup program.
- *Guests.* This is a pretty powerless group with minimal access to the system.
- *Power users.* These users have 90% of the power administrators do, but they cannot fully administer the workstation. The big difference is that they can create accounts, but not administrator-level accounts.
- *Replicator.* This is a special service group used by Windows NT to perform replication.
- *Users.* These users are beefed up guests who can do daily tasks on a workstation. By default, all newly created accounts join the users group.

It is important to know that Windows NT categorizes groups into two types: global groups and local groups. A *global group* is a collection of user accounts within the domain that has *no* power by itself. Local groups, on the other hand, exist for the purpose of assigning rights and permissions to resources on the machine. All the default groups that are created during installation are local groups.

 Note | Global groups must be assigned to local groups to gain access to local resources. If you think its confusing, you're right—it is. Know the basics, but don't sweat it too much. This is a big topic on the Windows NT Enterprise exam, but it's not stressed until then.

6

6.1.3. Creating User Accounts

Windows NT Workstation includes a tool called User Manager that is used to create and administer user and group accounts. To access User Manager, open the Start menu, choose Programs, Administrative Tools (Common), and User Manager. A screen similar to the one in Figure 6.1 appears.

For the exam, be ready for a trick topic that can appear. Windows NT Workstation includes this utility called User Manager. Windows NT Server includes a utility called User Manager for Domains. The utilities are the same, except that User Manager for Domains can manage global groups. Be sure you know which utility comes with which version of Windows NT.

Figure 6.1.

The main screen of User Manager.

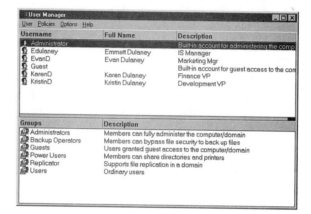

To add a user account, go to the User menu and select New User. The New User dialog box, shown in Figure 6.2, appears.

Figure 6.2.

The New User dialog box.

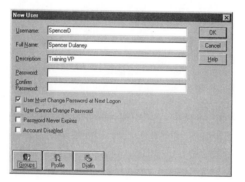

The name in the Username field must be unique. No other user or group can have the same user name. The user name can be as long as twenty characters and is not case sensitive.

This is the only field for which an entry is required when creating a new user account. Technically, the Password field must also be completed to make the account valid, but you can leave the entry blank for now and let the user supply a value the next time he logs in. This is against good practice, however; you really should enter a value (and type it again on the next line for confirmation) to keep anyone intent on no good from stumbling upon the recently created user account that lacks a password.

The password entered in the Password field is case sensitive and can be as long as 14 characters. As you type it, the program shows only asterisks onscreen to prevent others from looking over your shoulder and seeing the password you type.

The other parameters in the dialog box are optional, and most take free text:

- *Full Name.* Can include spaces and initials.
- *Description.* Can be used to track departments, projects, locations, teams, and so on.
- *User Must Change Password at Next Logon.* Forces the user to change the password immediately after logging on the first time.
- *User Cannot Change Password.* Keeps users from making any change to their passwords at any time. This is only practically useful for the guest account, though it can also be used for shared user accounts.
- *Password Never Expires.* Overrides any blanket password expiration date defined in the Account policy. This option is often useful for service accounts.
- *Account Disabled.* Turns off the account but does not remove it from the database. As I mentioned earlier, you should always disable user accounts instead of removing them. To understand why, consider this example. If Rob is fired on Monday and is rehired on Friday, you can reactivate the account. If Rob never returns and his position is filled by Vince, you can rename the account and reactivate it. All rights and permissions for the original user are then transferred to the new user.

Three buttons appear at the bottom of the New User dialog box:

- *Groups.* Displays the Group Memberships dialog box (see Figure 6.3) in which you can add and remove group memberships for the user. Adding the user to a group that already has the rights she needs is the easiest way to assign rights. (Notice that the user was automatically made a member of the users group as are all new user accounts.)

6

Figure 6.3.

The Group Memberships dialog box.

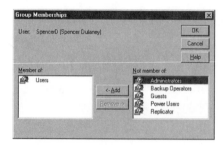

Note

Notice that all the icons in Figure 6.3 associated with groups show a computer in the background. This indicates that they are local groups. When the icon shows the world, it indicates that the group is a global group.

■ *Profile.* Displays a dialog box in which you can add a user profile path, a logon script name, and a home directory path to the user's environment profile (see Figure 6.4). You'll learn about profiles in more detail in section 6.2.

Figure 6.4.

The User Environment Profile dialog box.

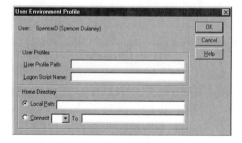

■ *Dialin.* Displays the Dialin Information dialog box in which you can specify whether the user can access the account through a dial-up connection. You also can configure call-back properties (see Figure 6.5).

Figure 6.5.

The Dialin Information dialog box. The dial-up connection must be made via the RAS service on this particular Windows NT workstation.

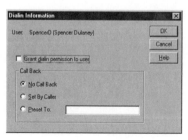

6.1.4. Creating Group Accounts

You can create new groups by using the New Local Group option on the User Manager User menu. Figure 6.6 shows the New Local Group dialog box that appears.

Figure 6.6.

The New Local Group dialog box.

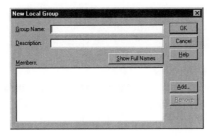

To add members to the new local group, click the Add button. Both users and global groups can join a local group.

Note

If you select users in User Manager's main screen before choosing New Local Group, those users automatically appear in the membership list for the new local group.

6.1.5. Other User Menu Options

The User menu in User Manager contains a number of other choices, as shown in Figure 6.7. It is worthwhile to look at each of them in passing.

Figure 6.7.

The User menu options of User Manager.

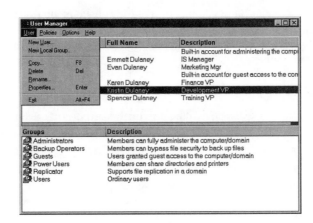

6

The Copy command allows you to take one account and copy it to another, essentially using it as a template with which to create a new account. Instead of configuring the same parameters over and over for 100 users, you can use one user's profile as a template with which to create the other 99—changing only the one or two parameters that differ.

The Delete option removes a selected user or group account. It should never be used, though, for reasons stated earlier in the chapter. But, for purposes of hammering it home for the exam, I'll say it one more time. Never delete an account; always disable it.

The Rename option enables you to rename one account with another name. This is useful in a situation like that suggested earlier, in which Vince took over for the never-returning Rob. After it was renamed, Rob's disabled account (now Vince's) could be reenabled.

The Properties option takes you to the same dialog box that pressing Enter does. This dialog box contains the information you filled out for the account when it was created. If necessary, you can make changes here to reflect changing conditions.

6.1.6. The Policies Menu

The Policies menu has three important components:

> Account
> User Rights
> Audit

The Account Policy

Selecting the Account command from the Policies menu displays the Account Policy dialog box, shown in Figure 6.8. The options here apply to the whole system and center around the concept of passwords.

This dialog box contains the following parameters:

- *Maximum Password Age.* Specifies how long a password can be used before the user must change it. Where security is a concern, the longer the password is in use, the greater the chance someone will discover it. The default is 42 days, but that value can range from 1–999. Users get a warning 14 days before the password is set to expire; they can change it anytime between then and the time the maximum password age is reached.

Figure 6.8.

The Account Policy dialog box.

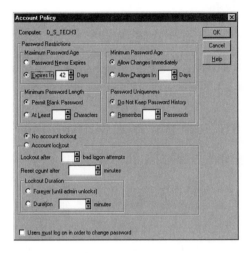

- *Minimum Password Age.* Indicates the minimum amount of time a password has to be used after it has been set. Users stumbled upon a certain trick years ago when they found a password that they liked and wanted to keep beyond the maximum password age: When it came time to change their passwords, they simply entered the original value again. Administrators stopped this by requiring unique values. But users got around that by changing the password to something odd and then changing back to the old one again. Minimum Password Age prevents this by not allowing users to make another password change for the number of days you specify. This value can range from 1–999.

- *Minimum Password Length.* Specifies a minimum length for a password. Setting a minimum forces most users to choose a longer password than they normally would. You can require up to 14 characters.

- *Password Uniqueness.* Prevents users from setting the same password more than once. When this feature is enabled, Windows NT remembers the specified number of passwords (up to 24) that a user has set. As long as a password is in a user's password history cache, the user cannot reuse it.

- *Account Lockout.* Forces Windows NT to lock out an account after a certain number of bad logon attempts (when an incorrect password is given for a valid user name). If you choose this option, you have to complete the other parameters in the frame. If you do not choose this option, you do not complete the other parameters in the frame. By default, the account lockout feature is turned off.

6

■ *User Must Log On in Order to Change Password.* Limits a user's options for changing his password. As a user's password nears expiration, he is prompted at each logon to change it. If he does not do so and the maximum password age is reached, he can no longer log on until the password is changed. If this selection is cleared (the default), the user is presented with the Change Password dialog box one last time and is not allowed to proceed until he changes the obsolete password. If this selection is checked, users are allowed to change the password only after logging on, and because the user cannot log on after the password is expired, the administrator must change the user's password from within User Manager before the user can log on again.

The User Rights Policy

Selecting the User Rights command from the Policies menu opens the User Rights Policy dialog box shown in Figure 6.9. Here you can see all actions that can be performed on the system, as well as who can perform them.

Figure 6.9.

The User Rights Policy dialog box.

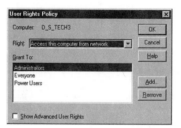

Right, as it is used here, means the ability to perform a particular action on the system. The Right drop-down list contains actions that can be performed, such as those listed here:

■ Shut down the system

■ Restore files and directories

■ Take ownership of files or other objects

The Grant To list contains the names of all users and groups who have the right to perform the action selected in the Right drop-down list. You can add and remove users and groups from the Grant To list by using the Add and Remove buttons.

To add a user to the list of those who can perform the function, click the Add button to bring up the Add Users and Groups dialog box shown in Figure 6.10. Locate the user you want to add, click Add, and then click OK.

To remove a user from the Grant To list, select the user and click the Remove button.

Figure 6.10.

The Add Users and Groups dialog box.

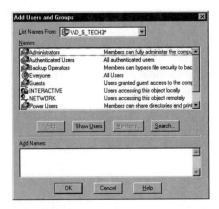

The Audit Policy

Selecting the Audit command from the Policies menu brings up the dialog box shown in Figure 6.11.

Figure 6.11.

The Audit Policy dialog box.

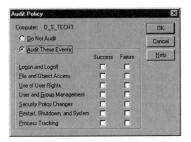

This dialog box enables you to track account-related events based upon successes or failures. The event information is stored in the security log and can be viewed with Event Viewer.

6.2. User Profiles

A *profile* is description—a collection of attributes about something or someone. When police are trying to track down a criminal, they collect all the information they know about the perpetrator and build a profile based upon what they know. The same principle applies in Windows NT.

6

Windows NT uses two types of profiles: user and hardware. A user profile is a collection of all the attributes known about the user: what wallpaper she likes as well as her screensaver, printer connections, recently used documents, and so on. This information is saved when the user exits and restored when she logs on again.

Hardware profiles perform a similar function: They identify the attributes of the system. On most systems, there is only one hardware profile (whereas there is one user profile for every user who uses the system). The exception to this rule is a mobile system, such as a laptop. Such systems can have multiple hardware profiles: one for the system when it is standing alone in a hotel room somewhere, for example, and one for when it is cradled in a docking station back at the office (where it also connects to the network, printers, and other resources).

> Note
>
> System policies are often confused with profiles. Profiles identify, while policies restrict. A profile would say that your wallpaper is giddy whales. A policy would say that you cannot use the Registry Editor. System policies are created in the System Policy Editor, which is included with Windows NT Server. The System Policy Editor is not included with Windows NT Workstation and is not covered on the exam.

6.2.1. Creating User Profiles

As stated, a user profile is a collection of all configuration data applicable to a specific user. A profile is maintained for every user, and every user can change his or her own environment without affecting the environment of other users.

Profiles can hold any or all of the following:

- Settings for the user-specific Control Panel entries
- Persistent network drive connections
- Remote printer connections
- Personal program groups
- User environment variables
- Bookmarks in Help
- Preferences for Win32 applications
- Most recently accessed documents in Win32 applications

All this information is saved in two files within a certain subdirectory that's unique for each user. By default, a user's profile subdirectory is located under the system root directory. For example, the profile for user BOB would be in:

```
winnt_root\Profiles\Bob
```

The pertinent files in the subdirectory are `NTUSER.DAT`, the Registry component, and `NTUSER.DAT.LOG`, a transaction log file.

> **Note** The `NTUSER.DAT.LOG` transaction file provides fault tolerance for `NTUSER.DAT`.

In addition to those two files, the subdirectory also holds a number of other subdirectories that contain items such as shortcuts. Other common subdirectories include:

- `Start Menu`
- `SendTo`
- `Personal`
- `Favorites`
- `Desktop`
- `Application Data`

In addition there are four hidden directories: `NetHood`, `PrintHood`, `Templates`, and `Recent`.

In all cases, the subdirectory names are self-explanatory. Now that you know what user profiles are, it is important to know that Windows NT supports two types: local and roaming. A local profile is stored on a local machine and does not follow a user around if she wanders from machine to machine. A roaming profile is stored in a central location and can follow the user to other computers on the network.

6.2.2. Local Profiles

Unless it's set up otherwise, Windows NT Workstation gets user-specific settings from a local user profile on the workstation at which the user is sitting in the manner described earlier. If the user has never logged on before, a new profile is created for her using settings in the following subdirectory:

```
%systemroot%\Profiles\Default User
```

6

The next time the user logs on at the workstation, Windows NT accesses the local user profile and configures all user-specific settings to match the information in the profile. For most purposes, this is sufficient. It is not sufficient, however, when a user constantly changes machines. If a user configures the desktop the way she wants it, that desktop should be available to her at any machine she might sit at. That is where the concept of roaming profiles comes into play.

6.2.3. Roaming Profiles

Roaming profiles are identical to local profiles except that they are stored on and accessed from a central server. That server can be Windows NT Server or NetWare. In either case, in User Manager, you specify the path to the roaming profile subdirectory, as shown in Figure 6.12. In the User Profile Path text box, include the full UNC path to the profile, including a computer name, a share name, and the directory path.

Figure 6.12.

Configuring a roaming profile.

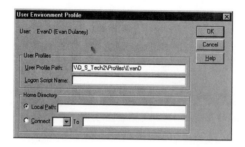

Note

If you are creating a template that you want to apply to all newly created users, use the %USERNAME% variable in the last position to specify that the path will include the user name. If the user name directory does not exist, it will be created.

When a user logs on, Windows NT checks to see if the account database contains a roaming profile path for the account. If the account does contain a path, NT checks to see if the user has her profile type set to Local in the User Profiles tab of the Control Panel's System application (see Figure 6.13).

Figure 6.13.

Configuring local and roaming profiles.

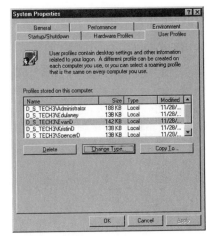

If the profile type is set to Local, Windows NT always uses the locally stored version of the profile. If the profile type is set to Roaming, NT compares the local version of the profile with the roaming profile specified in the account database to see which is more current. If the local version is more recent, NT asks if you would like to use the local version instead of the roaming version. Similarly, if the remote server is not available or if the connection is unnecessarily slow, NT asks if you would like to use the local version instead of the roaming version. If none of those circumstances exist, Windows NT downloads the roaming version.

At any time, you can change the profile type from roaming to local or local to roaming. To do so, click the Change Type button shown in Figure 6.13 to access the dialog box shown in Figure 6.14. Then make your selection.

Figure 6.14.

Changing between local and roaming profiles.

6.2.4. Mandatory Profiles

Any changes made to a profile are saved at logoff and show up in the profile again the next time the user logs on—with one exception. *Mandatory profiles* can be created so that a user accesses the same profile every time she logs on. During the course of the user's session, she is free to make whatever changes she wants. But when she logs off, the changes are not saved, and the next time she logs on, she is presented with the same profile she had at the previous logon.

Creating a mandatory profile is remarkably easy. Simply create a roaming profile subdirectory and specify the path to that directory in User Manager. Then copy a user profile to the specified subdirectory and rename the NTUSER.DAT file NTUSER.MAN. The .MAN extension makes the file a read-only file and prevents changes from being written to it. This might be useful if you wanted to restrict what users could do and prevent them from making profile changes. It is an administrative nightmare, however, if users install software, create shortcuts, and so on because their changes will never be saved from one session to another.

Lab

This lab will exercise your understanding of today's material. Answers to the review questions are at the end of the section.

Review Questions

1. Which of the following are unique identifiers associated with accounts?

    A. Domains

    B. Permissions

    C. Attributes

    D. SIDs

2. Evan storms out of the building after meeting with the boss. Everyone hears him mumble, "this is not fair," and promise to never return to the building as long as he lives. As a conscientious administrator, what should you do with Evan's user account?

    A. Auction it to the highest bidder.

    B. Delete it.

    C. Disable it.

    D. Rename it.

3. What two user accounts are created during Windows NT Workstation installation?

    A. Administrator

    B. Guest

    C. Supervisor

    D. Admin

4. Which of the following are Windows NT Workstation built-in groups?

    A. Administrators

    B. Managers

    C. Backup operators

    D. Power users

6

5. Which of the following is a collection of user accounts that is powerless by itself?

    A. Local group

    B. Guest group

    C. Domain users

    D. Global group

6. Which of the following exists for the purpose of assigning rights and permissions to resources on the machine?

    A. Local group

    B. Guest group

    C. Domain users

    D. Global group

7. The utility used to create and manage user and group accounts is

    A. User Manager for Domains

    B. User Manager

    C. Server Manager

    D. Profile Administrator

8. When creating a number of new user accounts, you must make which of the following values unique? (Select all that are correct.)

    A. Password

    B. Username

    C. Account Policy

    D. Profile

9. The account policy centers around which of the following?

    A. Passwords

    B. Profiles

    C. Audit parameters

    D. Hardware

10. Auditing enables you to track account-related events based upon what?

    A. Success

    B. Failure

    C. Logon

    D. Logoff

11. What variable can be used to create a unique subdirectory for every user?

    A. %USER%

    B. %PASSWORD%

    C. %MAIL%

    D. %USERNAME%

12. Which of the following is defined as a collection of user-specific settings saved on the local machine?

    A. Local profile

    B. Roaming profile

    C. Mandatory profile

    D. System Policy

13. Roaming profiles can be stored on which of the following machines? (Choose all that apply.)

    A. Any Windows NT Server

    B. Any Windows NT Workstation

    C. Any NetWare server

    D. Any Windows-based client

14. Which of the following prevents users from saving setting changes from one logon to the next?

    A. Local profile

    B. Roaming profile

    C. Mandatory profile

    D. System Policy

6

Answers to Review Questions

1. D SIDs are unique Security Identifiers associated with accounts.

2. C User and group accounts should *never* be deleted from Windows NT; instead they should be disabled.

3. A, B Two user accounts are created during Windows NT Workstation installation: administrator and guest.

4. A, C, D Windows NT Workstation has six built-in groups: administrators, backup operators, guests, power users, replicator, and users.

5. D A global group is a collection of user accounts and is powerless by itself.

6. A A local group exists for the purpose of assigning rights and permissions to resources on the machine.

7. B User Manager is the utility used to create and manage user and group accounts. It is available only in Windows NT Workstation. Although its counterpart, User Manager for Domains, performs the same function, it is available only in Windows NT Server.

8. B The user name is the only value for every user that must be unique. All other values can be the same.

9. A The account policy centers around passwords and applies to the whole system.

10. A, B Auditing enables you to track account-related events based upon successes or failures.

11. D The %USERNAME% variable can be used to create a unique subdirectory for every user.

12. A Local profiles are collections of user-specific settings saved on the local machine.

13. A, C Roaming profiles can be stored on any Windows NT or NetWare server. They are used to provide the same desktop to the user regardless of which workstation the user is sitting at.

14. C Mandatory profiles prevent users from saving setting changes from one logon to the next.

Exercises

The exercises here are meant to allow you to practice what you've learned today.

Exercise 6.1: Setting an Account Lockout Policy

The Account Lockout policy enables you to lock an account after a specified number of failed login attempts. To create one, follow these steps:

1. In User Manager, choose Policies, Account.

2. Click the Account Lockout radio button.

3. In the Lockout After Bad Logon Attempts field, enter the number of bad logons required to trigger the lockout.

4. In the Reset Count After field, enter the timeout period for resetting the bad logon count.

5. Choose a lockout duration by clicking the Forever (Until Admin Unlocks) option or by clicking the Duration option and entering a specific time limit (in minutes).

If you want to test the effects of this, attempt to log in to an account the number of times you specified in step three above. The account should then become locked.

To unlock an account at any time, perform the following steps:

1. Select the user name in User Manager.

2. Choose User, Properties.

3. To unlock the account, clear the Account Locked Out check box.

Exercise 6.2: Adding a User or Group to a Rights List

To add a user or group to the rights list for a particular right, perform the following steps:

1. In User Manager, select Policies, User Rights. The User Rights Policy dialog box appears.

2. From the Right drop-down list, choose the action for which you want to control the rights. Then click the Add button. The Add Users and Groups dialog box appears.

3. Select the name of a user or group from the Names list. (By default, only group names appear in the Names list; click the Show Users button to include individual users in the list.) Click the Add button, and the name you selected appears in the Add Names list in the lower frame.

6

4. Click the OK button to add the selected user or group to the list of accounts assigned to the right. The name then appears in the list in the User Rights Policy dialog box.

5. Click the OK button to exit.

Exercise 6.3: Configuring a Mandatory Profile

To configure a mandatory profile for an account, perform the following steps:

1. Select the account in User Manager and choose User, Properties. The User Properties dialog box appears.

2. Click the Profile button. The User Environment Profile dialog box appears.

3. In the User Profiles area, specify the user profile path and a logon script name. Click OK.

> **Note** If the directory does not exist, Windows NT creates it when the roaming profile is created. Note, however, that the local machine must have access to the roaming profile directory by way of a network share.

4. Open the Control Panel's System application and choose the User Profiles tab.

5. Click the Change Type button to access the Change Type dialog box. Choose the Roaming Profile option and click OK.

6. Back on the User Profiles tab, click the Copy To button to open the Copy To dialog box, which enables you to copy the user profile to another directory or to another computer on the network.

7. Copy the profile to the subdirectory you specified for the user profile path (in step 3). Change the extension from .DAT to .MAN.

8. Close the Copy To dialog box and exit the System application.

6

TEST DAY FAST FACTS

Here are some fast facts about networking and Windows NT Workstation that you need to know to pass the exam. Each bullet point below can be considered a short answer version of a main point explored elsewhere in the chapter.

- Installing and configuring Windows NT Workstation 4.0 networking components can be a very simple process. When you first install Workstation, the installation process examines your system for a network card; if it finds one, services are installed at that time.

- If you add a card after installation or choose to change your services, use the wizard for easy installation and configuration.

- The Network Device Interface Specification (NDIS) controls how network adapter card drivers need to be written. Windows NT 4.0 supports NDIS 3.0 and 4.0.

- Although the names seem similar, don't make the common mistake of confusing the NetBEUI transport protocol with the NetBIOS API. NetBIOS and NetBEUI serve different functions in the networking components of Windows NT.

Day 7

Introduction to Networking Concepts

This chapter examines the basics of networking from an inexperienced user's point of view. If you are a network administrator or a user with networking experience, review this chapter quickly, study the objective coverage in section 7.5, and then move to the next chapter. If you are less experienced, the concepts in this chapter are crucial to helping you understand all networking discussions in later chapters.

Objective

This chapter will cover one subobjective of the
Connectivity objective:

- Adding and configuring the network components
  of Windows NT Workstation

This specific subobjective is covered in section 7.5.

7.1. Defining a Network

A network can be thought of as any collection of computers communicating with each other. Windows NT Workstation can communicate on two types of networks:

- Those without servers (workgroups), also known as *peer-to-peer networking* environments.
- Those with servers (domains), also known as *distributed application* environments.

In a workgroup, the member computers communicate with one another and share their resources (such as files and printers) with one another. A Windows NT Workstation computer can be a member of a workgroup and share a portion of its hard drive (anywhere from some to all of it) and printer with other users. It can also be a part of a workgroup but share none of its resources and only access those made available by other computers on the network. You learned about sharing resources in Chapter 5.

In a domain, one or more servers are responsible for controlling access to resources. All workstations or clients (whether they are running Windows NT Workstation, Windows 95, Windows for Workgroups, or another operating system) access the PDCs and BDCs for security information instead of accessing other workstations.

Windows NT Workstation 4.0 can participate in networks (workgroups or domains) with servers and workstations running an endless number of operating systems, including such operating systems as Novell NetWare and UNIX-based computers.

7.2. Networking Architecture

Before you delve into the topic of components and configuration, it is important that you understand the rules for computer networking. These "rules" are known as standards, or models, and the one most referenced is the OSI model.

The OSI model breaks networking into seven layers of operation: application, presentation, session, transport, network, data link, and physical. The OSI model was developed in 1977 by the International Standards Organization for the purpose of defining networking uniformly and promoting multivendor interoperability. Figure 7.1 shows the layers of the OSI model.

Figure 7.1.

The seven layers of the OSI model.

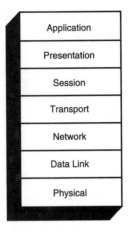

| Application |
| Presentation |
| Session |
| Transport |
| Network |
| Data Link |
| Physical |

Each layer of the model performs a specific task and also provides services to the layers beneath and above it.

The physical layer is at the bottom of the model. As the name implies, it provides a physical connection between the network wiring and the host. It specifies such things as voltage on the wire, cable pin assignments, and so on. At this layer, all data is viewed as bits.

The data link layer is responsible for packing and unpacking data that is to be sent across the network. At this layer, all data is viewed as frames.

The network layer performs the routing of the data through the network. At this layer, all data is viewed as datagrams.

Without going any further, you can see that these descriptions reveal two things. First, more work is involved at the higher levels than at the lower levels. Second, as data travels down the model, it is broken into smaller components.

The following sections look at the seven layers in detail.

7.2.1. The Physical Layer

While the OSI model does not define the media used, the physical layer is concerned with all aspects of transmitting and receiving bits on the network. Key attributes of the physical network include

- The physical structure of the network
- Electrical and mechanical specifications for using the medium
- Bit transmission encoding and timing

7

While the OSI model does not define the medium that must be used, it does define requirements that the medium must meet, and physical layer specifications differ depending on the physical medium. Physical layer specifications for Ethernet for UTP, for example, differ from specifications for Ethernet for coax.

All network connections consist of two types of building blocks:

- Multipoint connections
- Point-to-point connections

A *multipoint connection* enables one device to communicate with two or more devices. All devices attached using a multipoint connection share the same network transmission medium.

A *point-to-point connection* enables one device to communicate with one other device. When two devices are connected through a point-to-point link, they have exclusive use of the data capacity of the link.

Larger networks can be constructed by adding point-to-point links. In this case, devices rely on other devices to relay their messages. Point-to-point links can even come full circle to form a ring, enabling messages to be passed from any device to any other device on the ring.

7.2.2. The Data Link Layer

While the OSI physical layer is concerned with moving messages at the machine level, network communication is more involved than moving bits from one device to another. In fact, dozens of steps must be performed to transport a message from one device to another.

Real messages consist not of single bits but of meaningful groups of bits. The data link layer receives messages called *frames* from upper layers (recall the description of OSI layer-to-layer communication in the earlier section on the OSI reference model). A primary function of the data link layer is to disassemble these frames into bits for transmission and then to reconstruct frames from the bits that are received.

The data link layer has other functions as well (although all functions might not be performed by a given network protocol stack). This layer performs the following tasks:

- Identifies devices on the network
- Controls (and possibly corrects) errors
- Controls access to the network medium
- Defines the logical topology of the network
- Controls data flow

The data link layer is conventionally divided into two sublayers:

- *Logical Link Control (LLC).* This sublayer establishes and maintains links between communicating devices.
- *Media Access Control (MAC).* This sublayer controls the means by which multiple devices share the same media channel. There are several methods of performing this operation, the most popular of which are contention, token passing, and polling. Table 7.1 summarizes the benefits and considerations of each access control method.

Table 7.1. Advantages and considerations of access control methods.

Access control method	Advantages	Considerations
Contention	Simple software. Once access is gained, a device has complete control of the medium. No priority mechanism.	Access is probabilistic (not guaranteed). Collisions increase geometrically with demand.
Token passing	Each device is guaranteed media access (deterministic). Priorities might be assigned. Collisions are eliminated.	More complex software and hardware. Might require a central control device. High throughput under heavy load.
Polling	Each device is guaranteed media access (deterministic). Priorities might be assigned. Collisions are eliminated.	Uses a significant portion of network bandwidth. Requires bandwidth overhead even for devices that have nothing to transmit.

7

7.2.3. The Network Layer

The network layer involves communication with devices on logically separate networks connected to form internetworks. Because internetworks can be large and can be constructed of different types of networks, the network layer utilizes routing algorithms to guide packets from their source to their destination networks.

A key fact about the network layer is that each network in the internetwork is assigned a network address that can be used to route packets. The nature of those addresses and how they're used to route packets constitute the topics of addressing and switching.

7.2.4. The Transport Layer

At the transport layer, connection-oriented communications take place. This is where error recognition and recovery take place, as well as buffering, windowing, and other mechanisms that ensure reliable data transfer.

7.2.5. The Session Layer

The session layer ensures synchronization between two machines by using checkpoints. If the network fails in some way, only the data sent after the last checkpoint has to be retransmitted.

The session layer is what enables two computers to establish, use, and end a connection. This layer implements dialog control between processes that are communicating, regulates who transmits data, and for what duration.

7.2.6. The Presentation Layer

The presentation layer determines the form used to exchange data between two networked computers. It translates the data from a format sent by the application layer into a format recognized by the two computers. The presentation layer on the other end of the network converts the data from the common format understood by the computers into the data format understood by the application layer.

The presentation layer carries out rules for data transfer, as well, and most data encryption occurs here.

7.2.7. The Application Layer

The application layer enables processes to access network services. It provides direct support for user applications, such as database access, e-mail, file transfers, and so on.

In converting the OSI model to Windows NT, the lower six layers are implemented in the kernel mode, while the application layer is in the user mode.

7.3. Windows NT Networking

The components of the Windows NT networking architecture can be organized into five categories: network adapter card drivers, protocols, transport drivers, file system drivers, and APIs.

7.3.1. Network Adapter Card Drivers

The physical component of Windows NT (which would correspond to the bottom layer of the OSI model) is the network adapter card driver. To be used with Windows NT Workstation 4.0, the driver must be 32-bit and compliant with the *Network Device Interface Specification* (NDIS) 3.0 or 4.0. Unfortunately for older machines, Windows NT cannot use 16-bit device drivers or the 32-bit NDIS 3.1-compliant drivers that were developed for Windows 95.

Because adapter card drivers and protocols are independent of each other, protocols can be substituted virtually on the fly without changing adapter card drivers.

NDIS 4.0 is an updated version, for Microsoft Windows NT 4.0, of the boundary layer that defines the interaction of network protocols and network adapter card drivers. Any network protocol compliant with NDIS 4.0 can communicate with any network card driver compliant with NDIS 4.0.

The initial connection made between each protocol being used and the network card driver is referred to as network *binding*. The actual set of networking components used is called the *protocol stack*. If you have more than one network adapter in your computer, each adapter card's protocol stack can be configured individually.

In Windows NT 4.0, NDIS 4.0 supports the following:

- An unlimited number of network adapter cards.
- An unlimited number of network protocols bound to a single network adapter card.

7

- Independence between protocols and adapter card drivers.
- Communication links between adapter cards and their drivers.
- Packet capturing without the use of promiscuous mode.

7.3.2. Protocols

The network protocols control the communications between computers on a network. Different network protocols provide varying communications services and capabilities. This section outlines the protocols Windows NT supports.

Note Windows NT Workstation 4.0 doesn't support communications with AppleTalk servers. Only Windows NT Server 4.0 can be configured with Services for Macintosh.

TCP/IP

TCP/IP (Transmission Control Protocol/Internet Protocol) is the default protocol for Windows NT 4.0 and is an industry standard suite of protocols used for wide area networks (WANs) and the Internet. TCP/IP is commonly used in wide area networks that consist of a variety of computer types.

Microsoft's implementation of TCP/IP provides a number of advantages, including the following:

- Routing support
- Connectivity with the Internet
- Interoperability with most operating systems and computer types

Implementation of TCP/IP, regardless of vendor, provides a number of advantages, including the following:

- Support for Dynamic Host Configuration Protocol (DHCP)
- Support for Windows Internet Name Service (WINS)
- Support for Simple Network Management Protocol (SNMP)

Comparing the OSI Model and TCP/IP

Remember that the OSI model carefully breaks networking into an even seven layers with definitions for each. TCP/IP is a four-layer model that predates the OSI. TCP/IP is really a combination of two protocols: TCP and IP. TCP is a transport protocol that fits into layer four of the OSI model (the transport layer). IP is a network protocol that fits into layer three of the OSI model (the network layer). Figure 7.2 illustrates the relationship between TCP/IP and the OSI model.

Figure 7.2.

Comparing the seven-layer OSI model to the four-layer TCP/IP model.

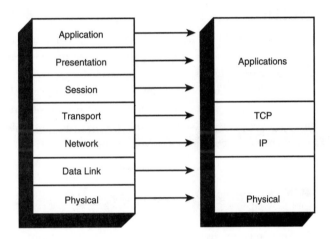

While the models and layers are different, the services are similar. But the OSI model is almost always the one used to discuss networking services.

NWLink IPX/SPX Compatible Transport

NWLink IPX/SPX Compatible Transport is Microsoft's NDIS-compliant version of Novell's *Internetwork Packet Exchange* (IPX/SPX). NWLink can be used for communications between Windows NT-based computers and MS-DOS, Windows 3.*x*, and OS/2-based computers.

The advantages of NWLink include the following:

- Routing support
- Primary support by Novell network operating systems such as NetWare
- Large installation base

7

> **Note**
>
> NWLink is only a transport protocol, and by itself, it doesn't enable a Windows NT Workstation 4.0-based computer to access files and printers on a Novell NetWare server or to act as a file and print server to NetWare clients. For a Windows NT Workstation user to access files and printers on a NetWare server, he must also use a NetWare-compatible redirector, such as Microsoft Client Services for NetWare.

NetBEUI

NetBIOS Extended User Interface (NetBEUI) was originally developed to support small departmental LANs of up to 150 users. Because it was assumed that these small departmental LANs would be connected by gateway devices, no routing support was included. Therefore, to connect two or more NetBEUI-based LANs, you must use a bridge instead of a router. Although it is possible to configure some routers to function with NetBEUI, that configuration is usually not a good choice. Only Microsoft-based computers typically use NetBEUI.

These are the main characteristics of NetBEUI:

- No routing support
- Fast performance on small LANs
- Small memory overhead
- No tuning options

DLC

Data Link Control (DLC) is not used for general networking by Windows NT Workstation 4.0. Windows NT mainly uses DLC for connectivity to printers directly attached to the network, such as Hewlett Packard JetDirect devices. Additional software is required for connectivity to Systems Network Architecture (SNA) mainframes.

7.3.3. Transport Driver Interface

The Transport Driver Interface (TDI) boundary layer (which you saw on Day 4 in Figure 4.1), provides the connection between the file system drivers and the individual transport protocols. The TDI standard enables transport protocols to be added or removed from a system independently of any file systems that might be in use. TDI is a Microsoft standard.

7.3.4. File System Drivers

File system drivers are used to access files. Whenever an application attempts to access a file, the I/O Manager determines whether the I/O request is for a local disk or for a network resource. If the request is for a network resource, a redirector passes the request to the appropriate network components. The default redirector included with Windows NT Workstation 4.0 is called the Workstation service.

It is possible for a Windows NT Workstation 4.0 to have more than one redirector to enable network communications with non-Microsoft–based servers, such as UNIX or Novell NetWare.

In addition to the Workstation service, Windows NT Workstation 4.0 also includes a component called the Server service. The Server service responds to I/O requests from other computers on the network when those requests are passed up to it by the lower network components.

7.3.5. APIs

An *application program interface* (API) is a set of routines an application program uses to request and carry out lower-level services performed by the operating system. Windows NT uses two network APIs to establish communications sessions and to transfer data to other computers in a network:

- *NetBIOS (Network Basic Input/Output System).* The original network API supported by Microsoft. IBM originally developed NetBIOS.
- *Windows Socket, also called WinSock.* A newer network API originally developed by the UNIX community (based on the Berkeley Sockets standard). Microsoft now also supports it.

7.4. How Sharing Really Works

The sequence of actions that takes place when a computer requests to share the resources of another computer can be outlined like this:

1. A client initiates a File Open command (via a program option or from a command prompt).
2. The I/O Manager at the client determines that the file is located remotely.
3. The Workstation service at the client passes the I/O request to the lower-level networking layers, which send the request to the remote server.

7

4. The Server service at the server receives the I/O request asking to open a file that resides at the server.

5. The Server service at the server passes the I/O request to the I/O Manager.

6. The I/O Manager at the server passes the I/O request to the local file system driver.

7. The local file system driver at the server performs the desired action.

8. An acknowledgment is sent back to the requesting client.

In this process, either computer could be Windows NT Workstation 4.0 or Windows NT Server 4.0.

7.5. Add and Configure the Network Components of Windows NT Workstation

You can configure all your network components when you first install Windows NT Workstation 4.0. If you want to examine how your network components are configured, or if you want to make changes to your network configuration, double-click the Network program in Control Panel to open the Network dialog box. You must be an administrator to make changes to the network settings on your computer.

7.5.1. Identification Options

Figure 7.3 shows the Identification tab of the Network dialog box. Here you can view your computer name and your workgroup or domain name. Click the Change button to change your computer name (maximum length for a computer name is 15 characters) or to join a workgroup or domain (maximum length for a workgroup or domain name is 15 characters).

The Windows NT security system requires that all Windows NT computers in a domain have accounts. Only domain administrators and other users that have been granted the user right of Add Workstations to Domain by a domain administrator can create computer accounts in a Windows NT domain.

If you are a domain administrator, you can give any user or group the user right of Add Workstations to Domain. First, open User Manager for Domains. In the Policies menu, choose User Rights. Make sure that you check the Show Advanced User Rights box. Then grant the user rights as you learned on Day 6.

Figure 7.3.

The Identification tab of the Network service.

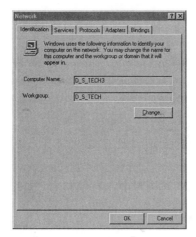

The following two methods enable you to change your domain name:

■ If a domain administrator has already created a computer account for your computer, type the domain name into the Domain box and click OK.

■ Alternatively, you can create your computer account in the domain. To create your own computer account, the user name specified must be that of a domain administrator or a user who has been granted the user right of Add Workstations to Domain by a domain administrator.

Regardless of which method you use to join a domain, you should see a status message welcoming you to your new domain. You must then restart your computer to complete the process of joining the new domain.

To join a domain, you must have network connectivity to the primary domain controller (PDC) in the domain you want to join. Also, make sure that you do not have a network session open with that PDC. If you must have open network sessions with that PDC, close all open files. Then join that domain, restart your computer, and reopen the files.

7.5.2. Services Options

Use the Services tab in the Network dialog box to view and modify the network services for your computer. Figure 7.4 shows a standard Services tab.

7

Figure 7.4.

The Services tab of the Network service.

You might want to add some of the following network services to Windows NT Workstation 4.0:

- *Client Services for NetWare (CSNW).* Enables you to access files and printers on a NetWare server.

- *Microsoft Peer Web Services.* Installs an intranet web server on your computer. It can also be used over the Internet but is very limited for that purpose.

- *Microsoft TCP/IP Printing.* Configures your computer to act as a print server to which TCP/IP-based clients, such as UNIX systems, can submit print jobs. This also allows the workstation to be a client of UNIX-based printers.

- *Remote Access Service.* Enables your computer to connect to remote networks via telephone lines or the Internet.

- *SNMP service.* Enables your computer to transmit status information via TCP/IP to network management stations.

7.5.3. Protocols Options

Use the Protocols tab in the Network Properties sheet to view and modify the transport protocols for your computer. Figure 7.5 gives an example of a Protocols tab.

Windows NT Workstation 4.0 allows an unlimited number of network transport protocols. You might want to add some of the following network transport protocols to a Windows NT Workstation 4.0:

- *TCP/IP.* The default protocol for Windows NT Workstation 4.0. It is required for Internet connectivity.

- *NWLink IPX/SPX Compatible Transport.* Required for connectivity to NetWare servers.
- *NetBEUI.* Typically allows connectivity only to other Microsoft-based computers and does not support routing.

Figure 7.5.

The Protocols tab of the Network service.

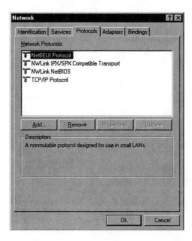

You can also add third-party transport protocols compatible with TDI and NDIS, which have not been developed by Microsoft.

7.5.4. Adapters Options

You can use the Adapters tab in the Network Properties sheet to add, remove, view properties of, or update your network adapter drivers. Windows NT Workstation 4.0 allows an unlimited number of network adapters. Figure 7.6 shows the dialog box from which you can add an adapter to Workstation after it is started.

Figure 7.6.

Adding an adapter through the Adapters tab of the Network service.

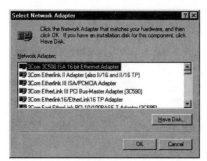

7

Even if you don't have a network adapter, you can still practice installing some of the network services that will not install without a network adapter. Select MS Loopback Adapter from the Network Adapter list.

7.5.5. Bindings Options

Network bindings are the connections between network services, transport protocols, and adapter card drivers. You can use the Bindings tab in the Network Properties sheet to view, enable, disable, and change the order of the bindings on your computer. The current default protocol for each network service appears at the top of each section in the display. The default protocol for the Server service is TCP/IP. Figure 7.7 shows an example of the Bindings tab.

Figure 7.7.

The Bindings tab of the Network service.

If the binding from the Server service to the NetBEUI protocol is disabled, client computers that are configured only with the NetBEUI protocol cannot establish network sessions with this computer. However, this computer can still establish network sessions with servers configured only with the NetBEUI protocol because the Workstation service is still bound to the NetBEUI protocol.

For maximum performance, remove any unnecessary protocols and always make sure that your most frequently used protocol is configured to be your default protocol.

Lab

The following review questions will test your knowledge on the topics covered in this chapter.

Review Questions

1. What is the maximum length allowed for a computer name?

    A. 8 characters

    B. 8.3 characters

    C. 15 characters

    D. 255 characters

2. To make changes to network settings, what is the minimum security logon required?

    A. User

    B. Administrator

    C. Guest

    D. Domain user

3. Which tab in the Network Properties sheet is used to view and modify the network services for your computer?

    A. System

    B. Connectivity

    C. Protocols

    D. Services

4. Which tab in the Network Properties sheet is used to view and modify the transport protocols for your computer?

    A. System

    B. Connectivity

    C. Protocols

    D. Services

7

5. Which of the following protocols are included with Windows NT Workstation 4.0?

   A. NetBEUI

   B. TCP/IP

   C. AppleShare

   D. IPX/SPX-compatible

6. Which protocol is installed by default in Windows NT Workstation 4.0?

   A. NetBEUI

   B. TCP/IP

   C. AppleShare

   D. IPX/SPX-compatible

7. To join a domain, you must have network connectivity to:

   A. A member server.

   B. The backup domain controller.

   C. The primary domain controller.

   D. Another workstation.

Answers to Review Questions

1. C Maximum length for a computer name is 15 characters.

2. B You must be an administrator to make changes to the network settings on your computer.

3. D Use the Services tab in the Network Properties sheet to view and modify the network services for your computer.

4. C Use the Protocols tab in the Network Properties sheet to view and modify the transport protocols for your computer.

5. A, B, D NetBEUI, TCP/IP, and the IPX/SPX-compatible protocols ship with Windows NT Workstation.

6. B TCP/IP is installed as the default protocol.

7. C To join a domain, you must have network connectivity to the primary domain controller (PDC) in the domain you want to join.

Exercises

These exercises walk you through some of the steps discussed in this chapter.

Exercise 7.1: Add a New Network Adapter Driver

This exercise shows you the steps required to add a new network adapter driver.

Time Estimate: 10 minutes

To add a new network adapter in Windows NT Workstation, follow these steps:

1. Right-click on Network Neighborhood.
2. Click Properties in the shortcut menu.
3. Click on the Adapters tab.
4. Click Add.
5. Select MS Loopback Adapter from the Network Adapter list.
6. Click OK.
7. In the MS Loopback Adapter Card setup box, click OK.
8. Insert your Windows NT Workstation 4.0 installation CD when requested, and then click Continue.
9. Click Close in the Network Properties sheet.
10. Answer any questions having to do with any protocols that you might have installed.
11. Click Yes to restart your computer.

Exercise 7.1: Answers and Explanations

Although the MS loopback adapter enables your network services to install without errors, your computer cannot actually communicate with any other computer on your network until you configure it with a real network adapter and the appropriate driver software.

7

Day 8

Networking with Microsoft Networks

We start our eighth day by exploring some of the issues surrounding networking Windows NT Workstation into new or existing Microsoft-based networks. Specifically, you'll learn how to network with Windows 95 clients, other Windows NT Workstations, and Windows NT Server–based networks.

Objectives

This chapter will cover two subobjectives of the Connectivity objective. Specifically, these two sub-objectives are

- Using various configurations to install Windows NT Workstation as a TCP/IP client
- Using various methods to access network resources

8.1. Using Various Configurations to Install Windows NT Workstation as a TCP/IP Client

TCP/IP is the default protocol for Windows NT Workstation 4.0. It consists of a suite of protocols originally designed for the Internet, and as such, is ideally suited for use with WANs. As you learned in Day 7, TCP/IP is supported by most common operating systems and is also required for connectivity to the Internet.

You can configure TCP/IP information using either of two methods. The first is to do it manually. Manual configuration, as the name implies, requires that you walk to each machine separately and enter the key pieces of information. The problems with this are that it is very time consuming, and it leaves a great deal of room for error. The alternative to manual configuration entails using a DHCP server that issues configuration information to clients when they need it.

You will learn about both of these methods; let's look at the manual procedure first.

8.1.1. Manual TCP/IP Configuration

As stated, when you manually configure a computer as a TCP/IP host, you must enter the appropriate settings, which are required for connectivity with your network. To reach the configuration tabs, choose Network from the Control Panel, select Protocols, and then choose the TCP/IP protocol. Figure 8.1 shows the dialog box that appears. The IP Address configuration tab is displayed by default.

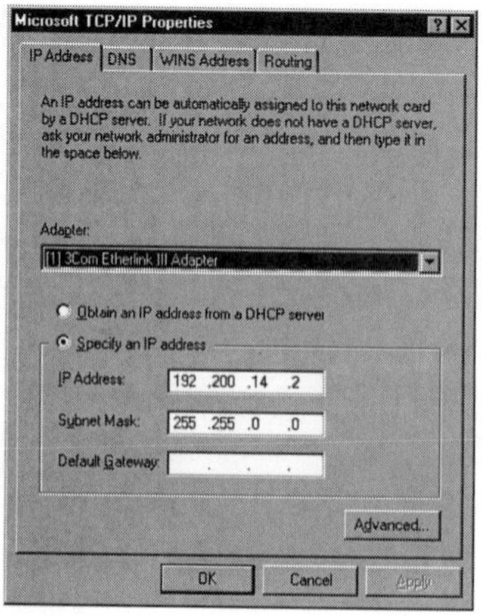

Figure 8.1.

The IP Address configuration tab.

The most common network settings are located on the IP Address, DNS, and WINS Address configuration tabs. Those settings include the following, the first two of which are required:

■ *IP Address.* A logical 32-bit address is used to identify a TCP/IP host. Each network adapter configured for TCP/IP must have a unique IP address, such as 192.14.200.4. IP address values for each octet are 1–223 for the first and 0–255 for the remaining three. The only exception to this rule is 127, which cannot be used in the first octet as it is a reserved address.

■ *Subnet Mask.* A subnet is a division of a larger network environment typically connected by routers. Whenever one TCP/IP host tries to communicate with another TCP/IP host, the subnet mask is used to determine whether the other TCP/IP host is on the same network or a different network. If the other TCP/IP host is on a different network, the message must be sent via a router that connects to the other network. A typical subnet mask is 255.255.255.0. All computers on a given subnet must have the same subnet mask.

■ *Default Gateway (Router).* This optional setting is the address of the router for this subnet, which controls communications with all other subnets. If this address is not specified, this TCP/IP host can communicate only with other TCP/IP hosts on its subnet.

> The Default Gateway must be left blank if you are not using a router but are connecting to the Internet through an Internet service provider (ISP). In that case, the ISP fills in that information upon connection.

■ *Domain Name System (DNS).* DNS is an industry standard distributed database that provides name resolution and a hierarchical naming system for identifying TCP/IP hosts on the Internet and on private networks. A DNS address must be specified to enable connectivity with the Internet or with UNIX TCP/IP hosts. You can specify more than one DNS address and, if so, the order in which those addresses should be used. Figure 8.2 shows an example of the DNS configuration tab.

Figure 8.2.

The DNS configuration tab.

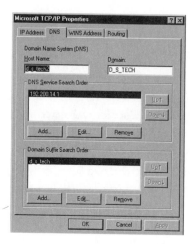

■ *Windows Internet Name Service (WINS).* Computers use IP addresses to identify one another, but users generally find it easier to use other means, such as computer names. Therefore, some method must be used to provide *name resolution*, which is the process by which references to computer names (NetBIOS) are converted into appropriate IP addresses. WINS provides name resolution for Microsoft networks. If your network uses WINS for name resolution, your computer must be configured with the IP address of a WINS server (the IP address of a secondary WINS server can also be specified). Figure 8.3 shows an example of the WINS Address configuration tab.

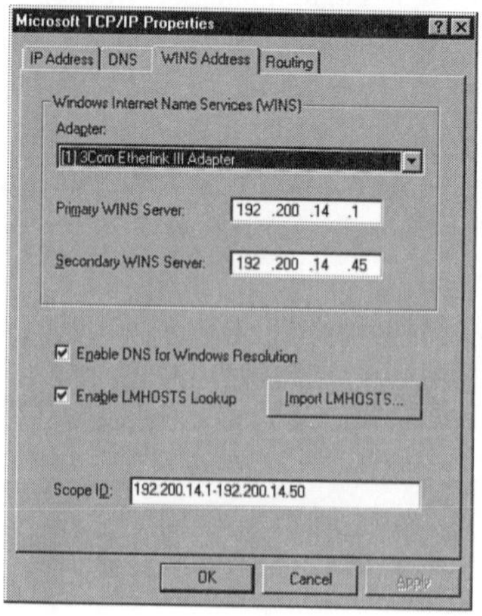

Figure 8.3.

The WINS Address configuration tab.

Name resolution is the process of translating user-friendly computer names to IP addresses. If the settings for the TCP/IP protocol are incorrectly specified, you will experience problems that keep your computer from establishing communications with other TCP/IP hosts in your network. In extreme cases, communications on your entire subnet can be disrupted.

> **Note**
>
> In the exam's section on manual configuration of TCP/IP settings, if you are asked to select two things that are required on the TCP/IP properties sheet, select IP address and Subnet mask. If you should be asked to select three required items that you must supply, select the Default Gateway as well.

8.1.2. Using DHCP for TCP/IP Configuration

As I mentioned at the beginning of the chapter, manually configuring TCP/IP creates a lot of administrative work and is not very efficient. One way to avoid the possible problems of administrative overhead and incorrect settings for the TCP/IP protocol is to set up your network so that all your clients receive their TCP/IP configuration information automatically through Dynamic Host Configuration Protocol (DHCP) Servers.

DHCP automatically centralizes and manages the allocation of the TCP/IP settings required for proper network functionality for computers that have been configured as *DHCP clients*. TCP/IP settings that the DHCP client receives from the DHCP server are only *leased* to it and must be periodically renewed. This lease and renewal sequence enables a network administrator to change client TCP/IP settings if necessary.

Using DHCP

To configure a computer as a DHCP client, all you do is select the Obtain an IP Address from a DHCP Server option on the IP Address tab of the TCP/IP properties box, as shown in Figure 8.4.

If you are moving to DHCP after having used manual configuration, you must delete the entries in the text fields or that information will override the DHCP entries. Figure 8.5 shows the warning screen that alerts you to this situation.

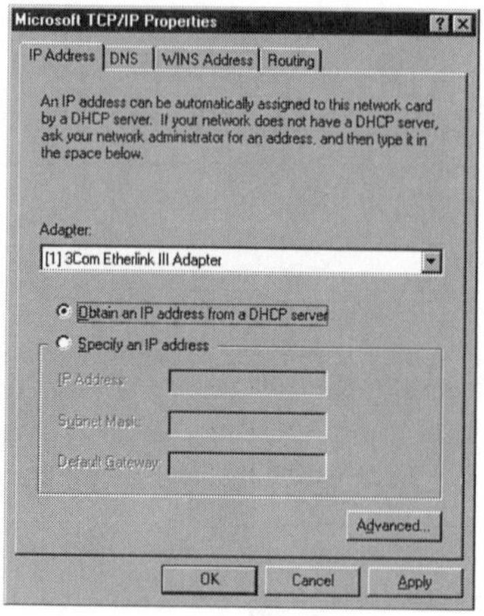

Figure 8.4.

Selecting to use DHCP services from the IP Address configuration tab.

Figure 8.5.

Although you've chosen DHCP, the IP Address configuration information has been filled in and will override DHCP settings.

Testing DHCP

To verify that DHCP is being used to obtain your configuration information, click the Advanced button on the IP Address tab. A screen similar to the one shown in Figure 8.6 appears, confirming that DHCP is enabled.

If DHCP is not enabled and information has been manually configured, a screen similar to that shown in Figure 8.7 appears when you click the Advanced button.

To determine the network settings that a DHCP server has leased to your computer, type the following command at a command prompt:

```
IPCONFIG /all
```

Figure 8.6.

The Advanced IP Addressing box indicates that DHCP is enabled.

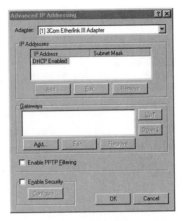

Figure 8.7.

This Advanced IP Addressing box indicates that TCP/IP information has been manually enabled.

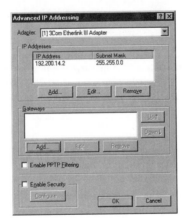

The following is sample output from the IPCONFIG program.

```
C:\>ipconfig/all:

Windows NT IP Configuration
Host Name . . . . . . . . . : TEST1
DNS Servers . . . . . . . . : 192.14.200.4
Node Type . . . . . . . . . : Hybrid
NetBIOS Scope ID. . . . . . :
IP Routing Enabled. . . . . : No
WINS Proxy Enabled. . . . . : No
NetBIOS Resolution Uses DNS : No
Ethernet adapter CE31:
Description . . . . . . . . : Xircom CE3 10/100 Ethernet Adapter
Physical Address. . . . . . : 00-10-45-81-5A-96
DHCP Enabled. . . . . . . . : Yes
```

```
IP Address. . . . . . . . . : 192.200.14.2
Subnet Mask . . . . . . . . : 255.255.255.0
Default Gateway . . . . . . : 192.200.14.1
DHCP Server . . . . . . . . : 192.200.14.16
Primary WINS Server . . . . : 192.200.14.16
Lease Obtained. . . . . . . : Saturday, August 09, 1997 12:31:29 PM
Lease Expires . . . . . . . : Sunday, August 10, 1997 6:31:29 PM
```

Note that IPCONFIG also gives you full details on the duration of your current lease. You can verify whether a DHCP client has connectivity to a DHCP server by releasing the client's IP address and then attempting to lease an IP address. You can conduct this test by typing the following sequence of commands from the DHCP client at a command prompt:

IPCONFIG /release
IPCONFIG /renew

> On Windows 95 machines (and Windows 98, as well), you can get this information from a graphical utility. Choose Run from the Start menu, and then type **WINIPCFG**. This displays the IP configuration information in an undocumented utility. Select the MORE INFO button to see additional information.

8.1.3. Static Name Resolution with TCP/IP

DNS and WINS are not the only name resolution methods available for Windows NT Workstation 4.0 TCP/IP hosts—they are simply the best. Microsoft also provides for two different lookup files, HOSTS and LMHOSTS, which enable you to use static tables to convert host names and NetBIOS names, respectively, to IP addresses. You can find both LMHOSTS and HOSTS in the \winnt_root\ SYSTEM32\DRIVERS\ETC folder.

The HOSTS File

The HOSTS file is an ASCII text file that statically maps local and remote host names and IP addresses. Prior to Windows NT 4.0 (and still in UNIX and other operating systems), the HOSTS file is case sensitive. With Windows NT 4.0 (both Server and Workstation), however, the file stopped being case sensitive.

In all operating systems and versions, the HOSTS file is limited to 255 characters per entry. It is used by PING and other utilities to resolve host names locally and remotely. One HOSTS file must reside on each host. The file is read from top to bottom until a match is found for a host name; then the file stops being read. For that reason, when there are duplicate entries, the latter ones are always ignored, and the most commonly used names should be near the top of the file.

The following is an example of the default HOSTS file:

```
# Copyright (c) 1993-1995 Microsoft Corp.
#
# This is a sample HOSTS file used by Microsoft TCP/IP for Windows NT.
#
# This file contains the mappings of IP addresses to host names. Each
# entry should be kept on an individual line. The IP address should
# be placed in the first column followed by the corresponding host name.
# The IP address and the host name should be separated by at least one
# space.
#
# Additionally, comments (such as these) may be inserted on individual
# lines or following the machine name denoted by a '#' symbol.
#
# For example:
#
#      102.54.94.97     rhino.acme.com          # source server
#      38.25.63.10      x.acme.com              # x client host

127.0.0.1       localhost
```

You should notice several things in this file. First, the pound sign (#) indicates a comment. When the system reads the file, every line beginning with a comment is ignored. And when a # appears in the middle of a line, the line is read only up to the sign. Because the file is read sequentially each time name resolution takes place, if this file were in use on a live system, you would delete the first 17 lines or move them to the end of the file to keep them from being read every time the file is referenced. Doing so would improve resolution performance by allowing the system to read the information it needs and not have to process those 17 lines that do not contribute to the process each and every time.

The second thing to note is the last entry:

```
127.0.0.1       localhost
```

This is a *loopback* address in every host. It references the internal card, regardless of the host address, and can be used for diagnostics. For example, they enable you to verify that processes are working properly internally before you begin testing to see if they are working properly down the wire.

Within the HOSTS file, fields are separated by white space that can be composed of tabs or spaces. As I mentioned earlier, a host can be referred to by more than one name. If you use multiple names, separate the entries on the same line with white space, as shown in the following example:

```
127.0.0.1          me loopback localhost
199.9.200.7        SALES7 victor
199.9.200.4        SALES4 nikki
199.9.200.3        SALES3 cole
199.9.200.2        SALES2 victoria
199.9.200.1        SALES1 nicholas
199.9.200.5        SALES5 jack
199.9.200.11       ACCT1
199.9.200.12       ACCT2
199.9.200.13       ACCT3
199.9.200.14       ACCT4
199.9.200.15       ACCT5
199.9.200.17       ACCT7
```

The aliases are other names by which the system can be referred to. In this example, me and loopback do the same as localhost, and nicholas is the same as SALES1. If an alias is used more than once, the search stops at the first match because the file is searched sequentially.

The LMHOSTS File

Whereas the HOSTS file contains the mappings of IP addresses to host names, the LMHOSTS file contains the mappings of IP addresses to Windows NT computer names. In speaking of Windows NT computer names, the inference is of NetBIOS names, or the names that would be used in conjunction with NET USE statements.

The following is an example of the default version of the LMHOSTS file.

```
# Copyright (c) 1993-1995 Microsoft Corp.
#
# This is a sample LMHOSTS file used by the Microsoft TCP/IP for Windows
# NT.
#
# This file contains the mappings of IP addresses to NT computer
# (NetBIOS) names.  Each entry should be kept on an individual line.
# The IP address should be placed in the first column followed by the
# corresponding computer name. The address and the computer name
# should be separated by at least one space or tab. The "#" character
# is generally used to denote the start of a comment (see the exceptions
# below).
#
# This file is compatible with Microsoft LAN Manager 2.x TCP/IP lmhosts
# files and offers the following extensions:
#
#       #PRE
#       #DOM:<domain>
#       #INCLUDE <filename>
#       #BEGIN_ALTERNATE
#       #END_ALTERNATE
#       \0xnn (non-printing character support)
#
# Following any entry in the file with the characters "#PRE" will cause
# the entry to be preloaded into the name cache. By default, entries are
# not preloaded, but are parsed only after dynamic name resolution fails.
#
```

```
# Following an entry with the "#DOM:<domain>" tag will associate the
# entry with the domain specified by <domain>. This affects how the
# browser and logon services behave in TCP/IP environments. To preload
# the host name associated with #DOM entry, it is necessary to also add a
# #PRE to the line. The <domain> is always preloaded although it will not
# be shown when the name cache is viewed.
#
# Specifying "#INCLUDE <filename>" will force the RFC NetBIOS (NBT)
# software to seek the specified <filename> and parse it as if it were
# local. <filename> is generally a UNC-based name, allowing a
# centralized lmhosts file to be maintained on a server.
# It is ALWAYS necessary to provide a mapping for the IP address of the
# server prior to the #INCLUDE. This mapping must use the #PRE directive.
# In addition the share "public" in the example below must be in the
# LanManServer list of "NullSessionShares" in order for client machines to
# be able to read the lmhosts file successfully. This key is under
#\machine\system\currentcontrolset\services\lanmanserver\parameters\
nullsessionshares in the registry. Simply add "public" to the list found there.
#
# The #BEGIN_ and #END_ALTERNATE keywords allow multiple #INCLUDE
# statements to be grouped together. Any single successful include
# will cause the group to succeed.
#
# Finally, non-printing characters can be embedded in mappings by
# first surrounding the NetBIOS name in quotations, then using the
# \0xnn notation to specify a hex value for a non-printing character.
#
# The following example illustrates all of these extensions:
#
# 102.54.94.97     rhino          #PRE #DOM:networking  #net group's DC
# 102.54.94.102    "appname  \0x14"                     #special app server
# 102.54.94.123    popular        #PRE                  #source server
# 102.54.94.117    localsrv       #PRE                  #needed for the include
#
# #BEGIN_ALTERNATE
# #INCLUDE \\localsrv\public\lmhosts
# #INCLUDE \\rhino\public\lmhosts
# #END_ALTERNATE
#
# In the above example, the "appname" server contains a special
# character in its name, the "popular" and "localsrv" server names are
# preloaded, and the "rhino" server name is specified so it can be used
# to later #INCLUDE a centrally maintained lmhosts file if the "localsrv"
# system is unavailable.
#
# Note that the whole file is parsed including comments on each lookup,
# so keeping the number of comments to a minimum will improve performance.
# Therefore it is not advisable to simply add lmhosts file entries onto the
# end of this file.
```

As in the HOSTS file, the pound sign (#) indicates a comment, and the file is read sequentially on each lookup, so limiting the number of comment lines at the beginning of the file is highly recommended.

You can use a number of special commands in the file to load entries into a name cache that is scanned on each lookup before the file is referenced. (By default, entries are not preloaded but are parsed only after dynamic name resolution fails.) Using these commands decreases your lookup time and increases system efficiency.

Entries in your LMHOSTS file can be imported into a WINS database if you convert to WINS by selecting the Import LMHOSTS button on the WINS Address configuration screen (see Figure 8.8).

Figure 8.8.

The Import LMHOSTS button allows WINS to convert your static file to the WINS service.

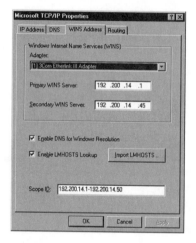

8.1.4. Other Files to Be Aware Of

Although the exam objectives specifically speak of the HOSTS and LMHOSTS files, those files work in conjunction with other files contained on a server in the `\systemroot\System32\Drivers\etc` directory, including

- SERVICES
- NETWORKS
- PROTOCOL

The next three sections provide detailed information about these files as well as a copy of each for your reference. Although you don't need to memorize them for the exam, you should be familiar with them for the real world.

SERVICES

The SERVICES file lists port numbers for services that may or may not be running. This file is important because it identifies where the services are. Moving a service to a different port is one of the easiest methods of hiding a service and preventing outsiders from running the service on your system.

```
# Copyright (c) 1993-1995 Microsoft Corp.
#
# This file contains port numbers for well-known services as defined by
# RFC 1060 (Assigned Numbers).
#
# Format:
#
# <service name>  <port number>/<protocol>  [aliases...]   [#<comment>]
#

echo            7/tcp
echo            7/udp
discard         9/tcp      sink null
discard         9/udp      sink null
systat         11/tcp
systat         11/tcp      users
daytime        13/tcp
daytime        13/udp
netstat        15/tcp
qotd           17/tcp      quote
qotd           17/udp      quote
chargen        19/tcp      ttytst source
chargen        19/udp      ttytst source
ftp-data       20/tcp
ftp            21/tcp
telnet         23/tcp
smtp           25/tcp      mail
time           37/tcp      timserver
time           37/udp      timserver
rlp            39/udp      resource       # resource location
name           42/tcp      nameserver
name           42/udp      nameserver
whois          43/tcp      nicname        # usually to sri-nic
domain         53/tcp      nameserver     # name-domain server
domain         53/udp      nameserver
nameserver     53/tcp      domain         # name-domain server
nameserver     53/udp      domain
mtp            57/tcp                     # deprecated
bootp          67/udp                     # boot program server
tftp           69/udp
rje            77/tcp      netrjs
finger         79/tcp
link           87/tcp      ttylink
supdup         95/tcp
hostnames     101/tcp      hostname       # usually from sri-nic
iso-tsap      102/tcp
```

```
dictionary      103/tcp     webster
x400            103/tcp                 # ISO Mail
x400-snd        104/tcp
csnet-ns        105/tcp
pop             109/tcp     postoffice
pop2            109/tcp                 # Post Office
pop3            110/tcp     postoffice
portmap         111/tcp
portmap         111/udp
sunrpc          111/tcp
sunrpc          111/udp
auth            113/tcp     authentication
sftp            115/tcp
path            117/tcp
uucp-path       117/tcp
nntp            119/tcp     usenet      # Network News Transfer
ntp             123/udp     ntpd ntp    # network time protocol (exp)
nbname          137/udp
nbdatagram      138/udp
nbsession       139/tcp
NeWS            144/tcp     news
sgmp            153/udp     sgmp
tcprepo         158/tcp     repository  # PCMAIL
snmp            161/udp     snmp
snmp-trap       162/udp     snmp
print-srv       170/tcp                 # network PostScript
vmnet           175/tcp
load            315/udp
vmnet0          400/tcp
sytek           500/udp
biff            512/udp     comsat
exec            512/tcp
login           513/tcp
who             513/udp     whod
shell           514/tcp     cmd         # no passwords used
syslog          514/udp
printer         515/tcp     spooler     # line printer spooler
talk            517/udp
ntalk           518/udp
efs             520/tcp                 # for LucasFilm
route           520/udp     router routed
timed           525/udp     timeserver
tempo           526/tcp     newdate
courier         530/tcp     rpc
conference      531/tcp     chat
rvd-control     531/udp     MIT disk
netnews         532/tcp     readnews
netwall         533/udp                 # -for emergency broadcasts
uucp            540/tcp     uucpd       # uucp daemon
klogin          543/tcp                 # Kerberos authenticated rlogin
kshell          544/tcp     cmd         # and remote shell
new-rwho        550/udp     new-who     # experimental
remotefs        556/tcp     rfs_server rfs# Brunhoff remote filesystem
```

```
rmonitor          560/udp     rmonitord   # experimental
monitor           561/udp                 # experimental
garcon            600/tcp
maitrd            601/tcp
busboy            602/tcp
acctmaster        700/udp
acctslave         701/udp
acct              702/udp
acctlogin         703/udp
acctprinter       704/udp
elcsd             704/udp                 # errlog
acctinfo          705/udp
acctslave2        706/udp
acctdisk          707/udp
kerberos          750/tcp     kdc         # Kerberos authentication--tcp
kerberos          750/udp     kdc         # Kerberos authentication--udp
kerberos_master   751/tcp                 # Kerberos authentication
kerberos_master   751/udp                 # Kerberos authentication
passwd_server     752/udp                 # Kerberos passwd server
userreg_server    753/udp                 # Kerberos userreg server
krb_prop          754/tcp                 # Kerberos slave propagation
erlogin           888/tcp                 # Login and environment passing
kpop              1109/tcp                # Pop with Kerberos
phone             1167/udp
ingreslock        1524/tcp
maze              1666/udp
nfs               2049/udp                # sun nfs
knetd             2053/tcp                # Kerberos de-multiplexor
eklogin           2105/tcp                # Kerberos encrypted rlogin
rmt               5555/tcp     rmtd
mtb               5556/tcp     mtbd        # mtb backup
man               9535/tcp                # remote man server
w                 9536/tcp
mantst            9537/tcp                # remote man server, testing
bnews             10000/tcp
rscs0             10000/udp
queue             10001/tcp
rscs1             10001/udp
poker             10002/tcp
rscs2             10002/udp
gateway           10003/tcp
rscs3             10003/udp
remp              10004/tcp
rscs4             10004/udp
rscs5             10005/udp
rscs6             10006/udp
rscs7             10007/udp
rscs8             10008/udp
rscs9             10009/udp
rscsa             10010/udp
rscsb             10011/udp
qmaster           10012/tcp
qmaster           10012/udp
```

NETWORKS

The NETWORKS file gives network names and number mappings for the local network and provides network name and ID resolution for TCP/IP management utilities.

```
# Copyright (c) 1993-1995 Microsoft Corp.
#
# This file contains network name/network number mappings for
# local networks. Network numbers are recognized in dotted decimal form.
#
# Format:
#
# <network name>  <network number>    [aliases...] [#<comment>]
#
# For example:
#
#    loopback     127
#    campus       284.122.107
#    london       284.122.108

loopback                 127
```

PROTOCOL

The PROTOCOL file lists the protocols and their assigned numbers. This file is used by Windows Sockets applications.

```
# Copyright (c) 1993-1995 Microsoft Corp.
#
# This file contains the Internet protocols as defined by RFC 1060
# (Assigned Numbers).
#
# Format:
#
# <protocol name>  <assigned number>  [aliases...]   [#<comment>]

ip        0     IP        # Internet protocol
icmp      1     ICMP      # Internet control message protocol
ggp       3     GGP       # Gateway-gateway protocol
tcp       6     TCP       # Transmission control protocol
egp       8     EGP       # Exterior gateway protocol
pup       12    PUP       # PARC universal packet protocol
udp       17    UDP       # User datagram protocol
hmp       20    HMP       # Host monitoring protocol
xns-idp   22    XNS-IDP   # Xerox NS IDP
rdp       27    RDP       # "reliable datagram" protocol
rvd       66    RVD       # MIT remote virtual disk
```

8.2. Using Various Methods to Access Network Resources

Windows NT Workstation 4.0 provides for several methods of working with network resources—each of which offers different ways of determining what network resources are available to you and the types of connections you can make to those network resources.

8.2.1. Universal Naming Convention

The *Universal Naming Convention* (UNC) is a standardized way of specifying a share name on a specific computer. Share names can refer to folders or to printers. The UNC path takes the form of \\computer_name\share_name. Commonly, the share names (as with computer names) are limited to fifteen characters in length.

It is important to note that connections made via UNC paths take place immediately and do not require the use of a drive letter. It is also important to note that if a dollar sign ($) is placed at the end of a share name, the name becomes "hidden" and does not show up in listings. However, the share can still be accessed if a user enters the complete UNC name.

You can also use UNC connections to connect to network printers. For example, \\ACCTSERVER\ACCTPRINT would be the UNC path to a printer named ACCTPRINT on a server named ACCTSERVER.

> **Note**
>
> Many 16-bit applications do not work with UNC paths. If you need to work with a 16-bit application that doesn't support UNC paths, you must map a drive letter to the shared folder or connect a port to the network printer.

The limitation on the length of share names is not related to limitations for long filenames. Rather, it is the result of limitations on NetBIOS names, which can contain no more than 15 characters and cannot contain embedded blanks. The actual folder name under Windows NT can still be a long filename, but the share name must be short. For example, a share named MYDOCS$ might be a folder on your desktop workstation that's named "My documents where I keep information on service contracts."

Note Some older clients (DOS and possibly Windows 3.x) might have trouble with share names longer than 8 characters.

8.2.2. Network Neighborhood

If your Windows NT Workstation 4.0 computer has a network card or the DialUp Adapter installed, the Network Neighborhood icon appears on your desktop. When you double-click the Network Neighborhood icon, the list of all computers in your workgroup or domain appears. By double-clicking the Entire Network icon, you can view all computers connected to your network that are not members of your workgroup or domain.

When you view lists of computers in Network Neighborhood, you are actually viewing a graphical representation of what is called a *browse list*. The browse list is maintained by a computer that has been designated as a Browse Master. All computers in the network (those that have an active Server service) periodically announce their presence to the Browse Master to keep the browse list current.

The *Browse Master* in a Microsoft network receives periodic broadcasts from all servers on the network and maintains the browse list, which lists all available servers.

Note that if a workgroup contains a Windows 95 computer that has the same name as a Windows NT domain, the two are listed together in the browse list.

Net View Command

You can also access the current browse list from the command prompt by using the Net View command. This displays the current browse list on your screen. A sample browse list looks like this:

```
C:\>Net View
Server Name          Remark

-------------------------------------------------
\\TEST1
\\TEST2
\\TESTPDC
The command completed successfully.
```

8

Net Use **Command**

You can assign network resources to drive letters from the command prompt by using the Net Use command and the UNC path of the resource. For example, to connect drive letter X: to a share called Kristin on a server named SERVER1, you would type the following command at a command prompt:

Net Use X: \\SERVER1\Kristin

You can also use the Net Use command to connect clients to network printers. For instance, if you wanted to connect port Lpt1: to a network printer named HP5 on a server named SERVER1, you would use the following command:

Net Use Lpt1: \\SERVER1\HP5

To disconnect the network resources, use the Delete or /d parameter with the Net Use command. For the previous two examples given, you would use the following two commands:

Net Use X: /d

Net Use Lpt1: /d

Other parameters you can use with the Net Use command include

/HOME	Connects a user to his or her home directory.
/PERSISTENT	Controls the use of persistent network connections. The default is the setting used last.
/USER	Specifies a different user name with which the connection is made.

Note | The TCP/IP Properties sheet associated with the protocol actually contains four tabs. You've already learned about the three you need to know of for the exam. The fourth tab is the Routing tab, shown in Figure 8.9. It contains the option for enabling IP forwarding.

Figure 8.9.

On the Routing tab, you can enable IP forwarding for TCP/IP.

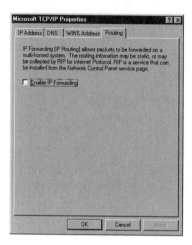

Lab

The following review questions will test your knowledge on the topics covered in this chapter.

Review Questions

1. What is the default protocol for Windows NT Workstation 4.0?

    A. IPX/SPX

    B. NCP

    C. TCP/IP

    D. NetBEUI

2. Which of the following is the UNC path for a file named ANN on the server MICHAEL in the share SCOTT?

    A. \\MICHAEL\SCOTT\ANN

    B. \\ANN\SCOTT\MICHAEL

    C. //ANN/SCOTT/MICHAEL

    D. //MICHAEL/SCOTT/ANN

3. Which of the following are valid TCP/IP addresses?

    A. 192.200.14.7

    B. 1.1.1.200

    C. 34.56.76.256

    D. 127.120.200.14

4. A share name is traditionally limited to how many characters?

    A. 8.3 characters

    B. 10 characters

    C. 15 characters

    D. 256 characters

5. Which of the following is defined as a value used to determine whether a host is on the same network or a different network?

   A. Default Gateway

   B. Subnet mask

   C. IP address

   D. DNS server address

6. To make a share hidden so that it doesn't appear in browse lists, you add what character to its name?

   A. #

   B. $

   C. ;

   D. <backspace>

7. Which transport protocol provides connectivity with the Internet?

   A. DLC

   B. NetBEUI

   C. NWLink IPX/SPX Compatible Transport

   D. TCP/IP

8. IP addresses given to clients from a DHCP server are said to be

   A. Issued

   B. In use

   C. Leased

   D. Reserved

9. Name resolution is commonly performed to which of the following?

   A. Default Gateway

   B. Subnet mask

   C. IP address

   D. DNS server

8

10. Which of the following is defined as a unique logical 32-bit address used to identify a TCP/IP host?

   A. Default Gateway

   B. Subnet mask

   C. IP address

   D. DNS server address

11. Which of the following is defined as the optional setting that identifies the router?

   A. Default Gateway

   B. Subnet mask

   C. IP address

   D. DNS server address

12. What command can you use to view your computer's IP address?

   A. IPCONFIG

   B. DHCP

   C. IPX

   D. NETCONFIG

13. Which of the following is not a valid IPCONFIG command?

   A. IPCONFIG /ALL

   B. IPCONFIG /RENEW

   C. IPCONFIG /RELEASE

   D. IPCONFIG /CACHE

14. A computer name is traditionally limited to how many characters?

   A. 8.3 characters

   B. 10 characters

   C. 15 characters

   D. 256 characters

15. UNC names are supported by what percent of Windows NT Workstation functions?

    A. 50%

    B. 75%

    C. 78%

    D. 100%

16. Which of the following is the UNC path for a file named SPENCER.DAT in a directory named EVAN in a share named KRISTIN on a server named KAREN?

    A. \\KRISTIN\KAREN\EVAN\SPENCER.DAT

    B. \\SPENCER.DAT\EVAN\KRISTIN\KAREN

    C. \\KAREN\KRISTIN\EVAN\SPENCER.DAT

    D. //SPENCER.DAT/EVAN/KRISTIN/KAREN

17. Which two of the following are used for name resolution?

    A. DHCP

    B. WINS

    C. IPCONFIG

    D. DNS

18. Which of the following are host name lookup files provided by Microsoft for Windows NT Workstation?

    A. Services

    B. Networks

    C. HOSTS

    D. LMHOSTS

19. Which of the following network settings are required when manually configuring a Windows NT Workstation 4.0 to communicate in a routed WAN configuration? (Choose all that apply.)

    A. IP address

    B. Subnet mask

    C. DHCP server address

    D. Address of the Default Gateway

8

20. To hide a share so that it doesn't appear in browse lists, you add a special character at what location in the name?

    A. At the beginning

    B. Anywhere within the name

    C. At the end of the name

    D. Within quotation marks anywhere in the name

21. UNC names can be used to access which two of the following?

    A. Windows NT servers

    B. Routers

    C. Gateways

    D. NetWare servers

22. The files Windows NT uses to look up host names are located in which of the following directories?

    A. `\winnt_root\SYSTEM32\DRIVERS\ETC`

    B. `\winnt_root\`

    C. `\winnt_root\ETC`

    D. `\winnt_root\SYSTEM32`

23. The UNC path takes the form of:

    A. `\\computername\sharename [\optional path]`

    B. `\\sharename\computername [\optional path]`

    C. `\\sharename [\optional path]`

    D. `\\computername [\optional path]`

24. Which of the following bits of information does not show up in IPCONFIG information?

    A. NIC card physical address

    B. ARP cache location

    C. Subnet mask

    D. Date of lease expiration

Answers to Review Questions

1. C The default protocol for Windows NT Workstation 4.0 is TCP/IP.

2. A `\\MICHAEL\SCOTT\ANN` is the correct UNC path.

3. A, B IP addresses take the form of `0-223.0-255.0-255.0-255`, with the exception of 127, which cannot be used as a class address.

4. C The share name is usually limited to 15 characters.

5. B A value used to determine whether a host is on the same or a different network is the subnet mask.

6. B If a dollar sign (\$) is added to the end of the share name, the share name will not be visible to another computer through a browse list such as Network Neighborhood.

7. D The TCP/IP protocol provides connectivity with the Internet.

8. C TCP/IP settings issued through DHCP are leased.

9. D The DNS server is used for name resolution, identifying TCP/IP hosts on the Internet.

10. C The IP address is a unique logical 32-bit address used to identify a TCP/IP host.

11. A The optional setting that identifies the router is the Default Gateway.

12. A `IPCONFIG` shows the local computer's TCP/IP configuration information.

13. D `IPCONFIG /CACHE` is not a valid command.

14. C The computer name is limited to 15 characters.

15. D All Windows NT Workstation functions support using a UNC name, including the Run option on the Start menu and the command prompt.

16. C `\\KAREN\KRISTIN\EVAN\SPENCER.DAT` is the correct UNC path.

17. B, D WINS and DNS are used for name resolution.

18. C, D Host name lookup files provided for Windows NT Workstation by Microsoft include HOSTS and LMHOSTS.

19. A, B, D You must always configure the IP address and Subnet mask during manual configuration. In addition, you need to configure the Default Gateway in order to enable TCP/IP connectivity in a WAN.

20. C If a dollar sign (\$) is added to the end of the share name, the share name will not be visible to another computer through a browse list, such as Network Neighborhood.

8

21. A, D NetWare servers and Windows NT servers can be accessed through a UNC name.

22. A The lookup files referred to in question 18 are located in the `\winnt_root\SYSTEM32\DRIVERS\ETC` directory.

23. A The UNC path takes the form of `\\computername\sharename [\optional path]`.

24. B IPCONFIG does not show ARP Cache information.

Day 9

Networking with NetWare Networks

We start Day 9 by exploring the issues involved with networking Windows NT Workstation into NetWare-based networks. Specifically, you'll learn how to network with Novell NetWare 2.*x*-, 3.*x*-, and 4.*x*-based networks.

Objective

This chapter will cover one subobjective of the
Connectivity objective:

■ Implementing Windows NT Workstation as a
client in a NetWare environment

9.1. Implementing Windows NT Workstation as a Client in a NetWare Environment

Windows NT Workstation 4.0 can run NetWare connectivity services and access NetWare networks quite easily. Depending upon your connections and needs, you may need only to install the NWLink IPX/SPX-compatible transport protocol. To enable a Windows NT Workstation 4.0 computer to access resources on a NetWare server, however, it may be necessary to install additional software besides the NWLink protocol on the Windows NT Workstation 4.0 computers.

The type of access you are trying to establish determines whether additional software must to be installed. NWLink can establish client/server connections but does not provide access to files and printers on NetWare servers.

> Novell NetWare traditionally uses a proprietary protocol known as IPX/SPX. This is not an open protocol or one that can be included freely in products. In order to use that protocol elsewhere, one must pay a royalty to Novell. In order to make Windows NT (Server and Workstation) as compatible with NetWare as possible, Microsoft created a new protocol called NWLink.
>
> NWLink is a reengineered version of IPX/SPX created and wholly owned by Microsoft. Whenever you see NWLink listed, it is always denoted as being IPX/SPX-compatible. This is an issue of semantics indicating that it works with Novell NetWare networks, but no royalty is paid to Novell on its use.

You install the NWLink protocol by adding it to the protocols loaded on your workstation. To do so, simply select Network from the Control Panel, and then choose the Protocols tab (see Figure 9.1).

If you want to be able to access files or printers on a NetWare server, you must go one step further and install the Microsoft Client Service for NetWare (CSNW), which is included with Windows NT Workstation 4.0. CSNW enables Windows NT Workstation 4.0 to access files and printers at NetWare servers running NetWare 2.15 or later (including NetWare 4.*x* servers running NDS). CSNW installs an additional network redirector on the workstation.

Figure 9.1.

The Protocols tab of the Network dialog box enables you to load NWLink on the workstation.

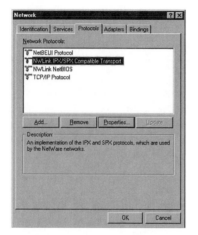

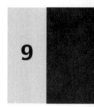

Windows NT Workstation 4.0 computers that have NWLink and CSNW installed gain the following:

■ A network redirector compatible with NetWare Core Protocol (NCP). NCP is the standard Novell protocol for file and print sharing.

■ The capability to work with long filenames when the NetWare server is configured to support long filenames.

It is important to note that long filename support is automatic in Workstation, but those names are not saved on the NetWare server unless the administrator has enabled long filename support there by loading the OS/2 Name Space module, OS2.NAM. In addition to loading the name space module (OS2.NAM), you also have to explicitly add the name space to the individual NetWare volumes. When attempting to do this, be aware that several problems can occur and be ready to deal with them.

■ Large Internetwork Packet protocol (LIP), which enables automatic negotiation and determination of the largest possible frame size that can communicate with NetWare servers.

In brief, the Microsoft *Client Service for NetWare* (CSNW) enables Windows NT Workstation 4.0 to access files and printers on NetWare servers. CSNW is ideal if you have a primarily NetWare-based network with a few Windows NT

Workstations. If you have a primarily Windows NT–based network with a few NetWare servers, CSNW is not the best solution.

Even if you have not added CSNW, Windows NT Workstation 4.0 can access files and printers on a NetWare server by connecting through a Windows NT Server configured with Gateway (and Client) Services for NetWare (GSNW). GSNW, which can be installed only on Windows NT Server, is the best approach to take if you have a few NetWare servers in a mostly Windows NT–based network.

Although NWLink and CSNW enables a Windows NT Workstation 4.0 to access files and printers on a NetWare server running NDS, it does not support administration of NDS trees. It also works in only one direction: Windows NT Workstations can access files and printers on a NetWare server, but NetWare clients cannot access files and printers on a Windows NT Workstation 4.0.

If you need for NetWare clients to be able to access files and printers on a Windows NT 4.0 computer, you must install Microsoft File and Print Services for NetWare (FPNW), available separately from Microsoft, on a Windows NT Server 4.0.

9.1.1. Installing Client Services for NetWare (CSNW)

To install Client Services for NetWare, select the Network program from the Control Panel. Then choose the Services tab shown in Figure 9.2.

Figure 9.2.

To add the Client Services for NetWare, access the Services tab of the Network dialog box.

Click the Add button, and a list of available services appears. Choose Client Service for NetWare, and a number of files will be loaded (you may even be prompted for the original Windows NT Workstation 4.0 CD or disk). If the service has already been loaded on your machine, an error message similar to the one shown in Figure 9.3 appears.

Figure 9.3.

If Client Service for NetWare has already been loaded, an error message prevents you from continuing.

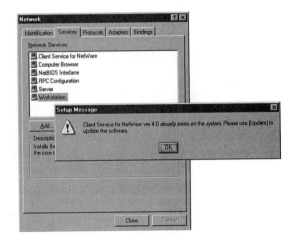

After the service is installed, you are prompted to reboot the workstation. Upon reboot, a configuration screen like that shown in Figure 9.4 appears. From here you can choose the NetWare server to be automatically connected to at login (and authenticated, as well), and you can choose to run the login script if it exists. You'll learn more about this configuration in the next section, "Configuring Client Services for NetWare (CSNW)."

Figure 9.4.

Upon reboot, you are prompted to enter the NetWare server information.

You should be aware of a few other changes after you install CSNW, as well. The first is a change in the Services tab of the Network program. Compare Figure 9.5 with Figure 9.2 to see the difference.

Figure 9.5.

After you add the Client Service for NetWare, a Network Access Order button appears on the Services tab.

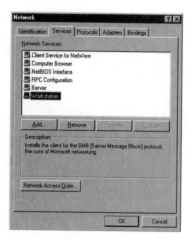

The Network Access Order button enables you to configure which network is your primary network if you are connected to more than one (such as a Windows NT network and a NetWare network). You can change the ordering, as Figure 9.6 shows, to increase your efficiency. The network you access the most should be at the top of the order, and the one you access the least should be at the bottom.

Figure 9.6.

Changing the network access order can increase the efficiency of your network operations.

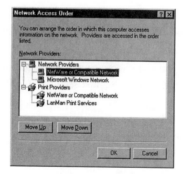

To change the order, select a network and use the Move Up and Move Down buttons at the bottom of the frame, or right-click a network listing and choose Move Up or Move Down.

The second change to be aware of after installing CSNW is a new CSNW program that's listed in the Control Panel (see Figure 9.7). This icon gives you access to the configuration dialog box shown in Figure 9.8, in which you can configure the connection information.

Figure 9.7.

The CSNW program now appears in the Control Panel.

Figure 9.8.

From the CSNW program, you can configure your NetWare connection information.

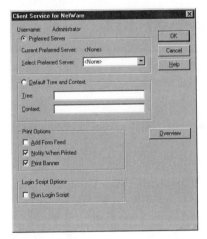

9

9.1.2. Configuring Client Services for NetWare (CSNW)

As I mentioned earlier, after CSNW is installed and the computer is rebooted, when a user logs on next, he receives a prompt to enter the details of his NetWare accounts. The user can enter a preferred server for NetWare 2.15 or above or 3.x, he can enter his default trees and context for NDS (the default in NetWare 4.x), or he can specify <None> if he does not have NetWare accounts. From then on, each time that particular user logs on to that computer, the user automatically connects to the specified NetWare account in addition to the Windows NT account.

Each user enters the NetWare account information only once. The only way to change a user's recorded NetWare account information is through the CSNW program in Control Panel. You can also use the CSNW program in Control Panel to modify your print options for NetWare printers—adding form feeds or print banners, for example (refer to Figure 9.8).

Even though Windows NT Workstation 4.0 attempts to automatically connect you to your NetWare system, there is no direct link between the two account databases. If you change either network password, the other password does not change automatically to match your new network password. To make that change, press Ctrl+Alt+Del, choose Change Password, and select NetWare or Compatible Network in the Domain field. There you can change the NetWare password. (On NetWare servers running in bindery mode, you can also use the Setpass utility.)

9.1.3. Connecting to NetWare Resources

After you install NWLink and CSNW, you access the NetWare servers in your network using the same methods that you use to connect to any Windows NT Server. You can also connect to files and printers on the NetWare servers without any special procedures:

- *Browsing.* After you install NWLink and CSNW, when you double-click Network Neighborhood and then double-click Entire Network, you can choose to browse either the Microsoft Windows Network or the NetWare or Compatible Network.

- *Map Command.* After you install NWLink and CSNW, right-click on Network Neighborhood and choose Map Network Drive from the menu. You can then assign any drive letter to any directory on a NetWare server for which you have appropriate permissions. Alternatively, you can browse to the appropriate resource, right-click, and select Map Network Drive.

- *Other Commands.* The Capture, Login, Logout, and Attach commands, all from NetWare, can cause problems if they are run from Windows NT Workstation. These four utilities should be avoided to prevent execution failures; however, their functionality is available from other utilities supplied with Workstation.

If after you install NWLink and CSNW you cannot establish connectivity to your NetWare servers, you should check to see what IPX Ethernet frame type the servers are configured for. Windows NT Workstation 4.0 attempts to automatically determine the correct frame type, but you might have to manually specify the frame type to make the connection work.

You can manually change the frame type by following these steps:

1. Choose Network from the Control Panel.

2. Select the Protocols tab.

3. Highlight the NWLink protocol and click the Properties button.

4. Change from Auto Detect to the correct frame type for your network.

Figure 9.9 shows the protocol's Properties sheet.

Figure 9.9.

If connectivity cannot be established, change the frame type to that used by your NetWare network.

9

In this chapter, I spoke of changing the network access order to increase networking efficiency on your workstation. You can also change the order in which protocols are bound to the adapter cards if you are using more than one protocol (and virtually every workstation is). The order in which they are bound is very important: The most frequently used protocol should be bound first, and the least frequently bound protocol should be loaded last.

For example, in a predominantly Windows NT 4.0 network, TCP/IP should be loaded first. In a predominantly NetWare network, NWLink IPX/SPX-compatible transport protocol should be loaded first.

To make such a change, choose Network from the Control Panel, and then choose the Bindings tab. You can then move bindings up and down in the load order in the same way you changed the network access order. Figure 9.10 shows a sample screen.

Figure 9.10.

Changing the binding order can increase networking performance of your workstation substantially.

Lab

The following review questions test your knowledge on configuring Windows NT to access a NetWare network.

Review Questions

1. If you want to be able to access files or printers on a NetWare Server, which of the following must you install in addition to NWLink?

   A. Gateway (and Client) Services for NetWare

   B. Microsoft Client Service for NetWare Networks

   C. Microsoft File and Print Services for NetWare

   D. IPX/SPX

2. To enable NetWare clients to access files on a Windows NT 4.0 computer, you must install which of the following (in addition to NWLink) on a Windows NT Server?

   A. Gateway (and Client) Services for NetWare

   B. Microsoft Client Service for NetWare Networks

   C. Microsoft File and Print Services for NetWare

   D. IPX/SPX

3. Which of the following is the standard Novell protocol for file and print sharing?

   A. IPX

   B. SPX

   C. NCP

   D. LIP

4. The protocol used to negotiate and determine the largest possible frame size that can be used to communicate with NetWare servers is which of the following?

   A. IPX

   B. SPX

   C. NCP

   D. LIP

9

5. A Windows NT Workstation can access NetWare servers via a Windows NT Server if the server is running which of the following?

   A. Gateway (and Client) Services for NetWare

   B. Microsoft Client Service for NetWare Networks

   C. Microsoft File and Print Services for NetWare

   D. IPX/SPX

6. CSNW is installed from which Control Panel applet?

   A. Network

   B. System

   C. Services

   D. User Manager for Domains

7. Which two of the following Ethernet frame types are used by NetWare and detected by CSNW?

   A. 802.1

   B. 802.2

   C. 802.3

   D. 802.4

   E. 802.5

Answers to Review Questions

1. B Microsoft Client Service for NetWare Networks (CSNW) must be installed with Windows NT Workstation for users to access files or printers on a NetWare network.

2. C If you need for NetWare clients to be able to access files and printers on a Windows NT 4.0 computer, you must install Microsoft File and Print Services for NetWare (FPNW), available separately from Microsoft, on a Windows NT Server 4.0.

3. C While IPX/SPX is the standard networking protocol, NCP is the standard Novell protocol for file and print sharing.

4. D The protocol used to determine the largest possible frame size that can be used to communicate with NetWare servers is Large Internetwork Packet protocol (LIP).

5. **A** A Windows NT Workstation can access NetWare servers via a Windows NT Server if the server is running Gateway (and Client) Services for NetWare.

6. **A** CSNW is installed the same way as any other network service: through the Network program in the Control Panel.

7. **B, C** 802.2 and 802.3 are the two NetWare frame types CSNW detects.

Exercises

These exercises are meant to allow you to practice what you've learned today.

Exercise 9.1: Installing Client Service for NetWare (CSNW)

This exercise shows you how to enable your computer to access files and printers on a NetWare server. To install the Client Service for NetWare, follow the steps outlined here:

1. Double-click the Network program in Control Panel.

2. Click the Services tab.

3. Click Add.

4. Select Client Service for NetWare in the Network Service list, and then click OK.

5. Insert your Windows NT Workstation 4.0 installation CD when prompted, and then click Continue.

6. Click Close and wait while the bindings are reset.

7. Click Yes to restart your computer.

8. Press Ctrl+Alt+Delete and log on to your computer.

9. When the Select NetWare Logon box appears, select your NetWare 3.x preferred server or your NetWare 4.x default tree and context. Then click OK.

10. When your desktop appears, right-click Network Neighborhood.

11. In the Network Neighborhood menu, choose Who Am I. Your NetWare user information appears.

Exercise 9.1: Answers and Explanations

Although CSNW enables a Windows NT Workstation 4.0 user to access files and printers located on a NetWare server, you must install the Microsoft File and Print for NetWare (FPNW) service if you need for NetWare clients to be able to access files and printers located on Windows NT Workstation 4.0.

9

Exercise 9.2: Changing the Frame Type of the NWLink Protocol

This exercise shows you how to adjust the properties of the NWLink protocol to change the frame type from autodetect to 802.2. To change the NWLink's Protocol Frame Type, follow the steps given here. Do note, however, that changing your frame type might sever your NetWare server, so do not do so unless you can afford the time to correct it if necessary.

1. Double-click the Network program in Control Panel.
2. Click the Protocols tab in the Network properties box.
3. Select the NWLink IPX/SPX Compatible Transport protocol.
4. Click Properties.
5. In the Frame Type drop-down box, select Ethernet 802.2.
6. Click OK.
7. In the Network properties box, click Close.
8. Restart your computer when prompted.

Exercise 9.2: Answers and Explanations

The default setting for the NWLink frame type in Windows NT Workstation 4.0 is automatic. You must change this setting if you are using more than one frame type.

Exercise 9.3: Connecting to a NetWare Print Server

This exercise shows you how to connect your computer to a NetWare print server. To implement Windows NT Workstation as a client in a NetWare environment, follow these steps:

1. Double-click the Printers program in My Computer.
2. Double-click Add Printer.
3. In the Add Printer wizard, select Network Printer Server, and then click Next.
4. In the Connect to Printer box, select the desired network printer, and then click OK. (Note that you can double-click the desired print server to see a list of the printers available on that print server.)
5. In the Connect to Printer box, click OK.
6. Select the proper printer from the list and click OK.
7. Insert your installation CD when prompted, and then click OK.

8. Specify whether you want this new printer to be your default Windows print-
    er, and then click Next.

9. Click Finish.

Exercise 9.3: Answers and Explanations

After you install CSNW, connecting to a printer on a NetWare server is just as easy
as connecting to printers on a Windows NT Server. This exercise illustrated that and
walked you through the steps for establishing such a connection.

9

Day 10

Dial-Up Networking and RAS

We start our tenth day by exploring some of the issues surrounding dial-up networking with Windows NT Workstation and remote access services. As networks become more diverse and as more users and administrators are required to log in remotely, the importance of remote access to resources increases every day.

Objective

This chapter will cover one subobjective of the Connectivity objective:

- Configuring and installing Dial-Up Networking in a given situation

TEST DAY
FAST FACTS

- Each RAS communications device has three settings. They are Dial Out Only (the default), Receive Calls Only, and Dial Out and Receive Calls.

- Dial-Up Networking supports most protocols, with the exception of XNS.

- Authentication and encryption settings are set individually for each phonebook entry.

10.1. Configuring and Installing Dial-Up Networking

Remote Access Service (RAS) and Dial-Up Networking (DUN) enable you to extend your network to unlimited locations. RAS servers and DUN clients enable remote clients to make connections to your LAN either via ordinary telephone lines or through higher-speed techniques such as ISDN or X.25. The incoming connections can also be made via the industry standard Point-to-Point Protocol (PPP) or the newer Point-to-Point Tunneling Protocol (PPTP) that makes use of the Internet. DUN also supports the use of Serial Line Internet Protocol (SLIP) to initiate dial-up connections with SLIP servers.

You enable Dial-Up Networking services on your workstation by selecting the Dial-Up Networking program from My Computer (see Figure 10.1).

Figure 10.1.

Choose the Dial-Up Networking program in My Computer to install Dial-Up Networking on your workstation.

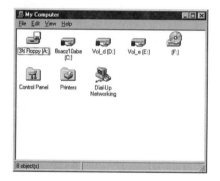

Windows NT Workstation 4.0 is limited to one inbound RAS session at a time. If you need to support multiple simultaneous RAS sessions, you should purchase Windows NT Server 4.0.

10.1.1. Installing the Dial-Up Networking Client

You can install DUN, which uses TAPI settings, either when you install Windows NT Workstation 4.0 or later. If you select Remote Access to the Network during setup, both RAS and DUN are installed. However, either or both services can be installed separately after installation of Windows NT Workstation 4.0.

To install DUN after you've installed Windows NT Workstation 4.0, you double-click the Dial-Up Networking icon in My Computer and click Install to start the Installation wizard shown in Figure 10.2. Then you follow the wizard's instructions.

Figure 10.2.

The Dial-Up Networking wizard walks you through the installation process.

During installation, files are copied to the System32 directory, and you will probably be prompted for the installation CD. You will need to specify a minimum of one RAS device, and that can be either a modem or an X.25 device. Figure 10.3 shows the configuration dialog box; Figure 10.4 shows the completed information in the setup window.

10

Figure 10.3.

You must configure at least one device to complete Dial-Up Networking installation.

Figure 10.4.

Device configuration information is displayed in the Remote Access Setup dialog box.

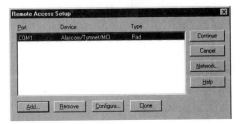

Note

If you have a recognizable modem, you will be prompted to use that as the dial-up device. When you click Yes to start the Modem Installer, the Install New Modem wizard appears.

You can allow the Install New Modem wizard to automatically detect your modem, or you can select your modem from a list, or you can supply a manufacturer's installation disk. The next step in the installation process is to add the modem as a RAS device. After you add the modem as a RAS device, you must configure it.

continues

After you configure your modem, you specify how RAS should use the phone line. You have the following options:

- Dial Out Only (the default setting for Microsoft Windows NT Workstation 4.0)
- Receive Calls Only
- Dial Out and Receive Calls

You must reboot your workstation in order to continue with the setup. After rebooting, select Dial-Up Networking from My Computer again, and the Location Information screen shown in Figure 10.5 appears.

Figure 10.5.

*Location informa-
tion must be filled in
for Dial-Up
Networking setup to
be completed.*

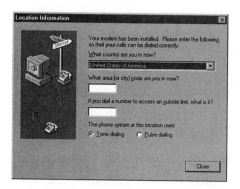

Having entered the location information, you are ready to begin adding phonebook entries.

Creating a Phonebook Entry

During DUN installation, you are prompted to create a phonebook entry. Following the first time through, you can create new phonebook entries at any time by starting Dial-Up Networking and clicking New. The New Phonebook Entry wizard then appears, as shown in Figure 10.6.

Check the I Know All About Phonebook Entries and Would Rather Edit the Properties Directly check box. The New Phonebook Entry properties sheet appears. Each user on a computer has a unique phonebook that's stored as part of his or her user profile.

Figure 10.6.

The New Phonebook Entry wizard walks you through the steps for creating an entry.

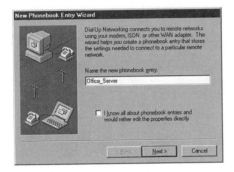

 Note

If you choose to create a manual phonebook entry, the wizard will not bother you again. However, if you selected this in error and want to be able to use the New Phonebook Entry wizard again, follow these steps:

1. Double-click the Dial-Up Networking icon in My Computer.
2. Click on More.
3. Click on User Preferences.
4. Click the Appearance tab.
5. Click Use wizard to Create New Phonebook Entries.

The New Phonebook Entry wizard automatically starts the next time you run Dial-Up Networking.

10

After naming the location to which you want to connect, choose the methods by which you are going to connect (see Figure 10.7) and enter the phone number of the server you are calling (see Figure 10.8).

Figure 10.7.

You specify how you intend to connect to the phoneboook entry.

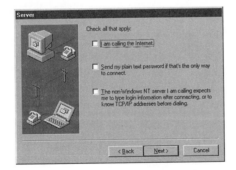

Figure 10.8.

Enter a phone number for the server and specify an alternative if necessary.

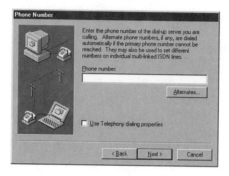

Editing Phonebook Entries

After you create a phonebook entry, you can change the values associated with it by changing any of the three lines of information that appear when the entry comes up (as shown in Figure 10.9). You can also select the More button and choose from the options that appear.

Figure 10.9.

To edit phonebook entries, select the More button.

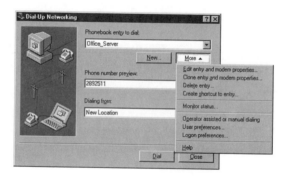

For example, if you choose Edit Entry and Modem Properties, the Edit Phonebook Entry dialog box appears. It contains the following five tabs:

- *Basic.* This allows you to change the name of the entry, the phone number, or the device used.

- *Server.* Shown in Figure 10.10, this tab enables you to change the line protocol or network protocol used.

- *Script.* This tab lets you define a script to run upon establishing a connection.

- *Security.* Discussed in detail in the next section, this tab provides options with which you can define the level of security used.

- *X.25.* This tab enables you to define the X.25 parameters, if applicable.

Figure 10.10.

Line protocols and network protocols are defined on the Server tab.

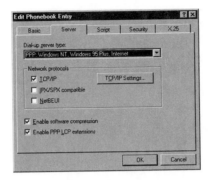

Authentication

Security is a major consideration in the design of DUN. From the Security tab shown in Figure 10.11, you can choose from the security settings described here:

- *Accept Any Authentication Method Including Clear Text.* Use this setting when you're not concerned whether the line you're using will be tapped.

- *Accept Only Encrypted Authentication.* RAS supports several industry standard encrypted authentication procedures to support connections to non-Microsoft remote networks, including RSA, DES, and Shiva.

- *Accept Only Microsoft Encrypted Authentication.* If you select this option, you will be given the option of having your entire session with the remote network encrypted—not just your logon. This setting is available only if you are connecting to a Windows NT RAS server.

Figure 10.11.

On the Security tab, you can choose from three types of authentication.

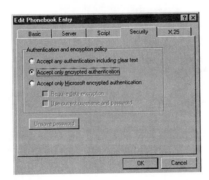

You set the authentication and encryption settings individually for each phonebook entry.

10.1.2. Changing and Adding Locations

If you double-click the Telephony applet in Control Panel, the Dialing Properties dialog box appears (see Figure 10.12). You can enter calling-card information by clicking the Dial Using Calling Card check box and then clicking Change to access the dialog box shown in Figure 10.13.

Figure 10.12.

From the Dialing Properties sheet you can change or create new location information.

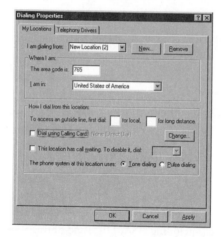

Figure 10.13.

You can enter calling-card information once here so you don't have to enter it each time you establish a connection.

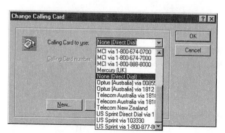

10.2. Line Protocols

The network transport protocols (NetBEUI, NWLink, and TCP/IP) were designed for the characteristics of LANs and are not suitable for use in phone-based connections. To make the network transport protocols function properly in phone-based connections, it is necessary to encapsulate them in a line protocol. Windows NT Workstation 4.0 supports two line protocols: SLIP and PPP.

10.2.1. Serial Line Internet Protocol (SLIP)

SLIP is an industry standard that supports TCP/IP connections made over serial lines. Unfortunately, SLIP has several limitations, as outlined here:

- SLIP supports TCP/IP only; it provides no support for IPX or NetBEUI.
- SLIP requires static IP addresses; it provides no support for DHCP.
- SLIP transmits authentication passwords as clear text; it provides no support for encryption.
- SLIP usually requires a scripting system for the logon process.

Windows NT Workstation 4.0 supports SLIP client functionality only; SLIP server functionality is not supported. For the most part, SLIP has been replaced in the world and is seldom implemented anymore.

10.2.2. Point-to-Point Protocol (PPP)

The limitations of SLIP prompted the development of a newer industry standard protocol called Point-to-Point Protocol (PPP). Some of the advantages of PPP include the following:

- PPP supports TCP/IP, IPX, NetBEUI, PPTP, and others.
- PPP has support for DHCP or static addresses.
- PPP supports encryption for authentication.
- PPP doesn't require a scripting system for the logon process.

New to Windows NT Workstation 4.0 is support for PPP multilink, which enables you to combine multiple physical links into one logical connection. A client with two ordinary phone lines and two 28.8Kbps modems, for example, could establish a PPP multilink session with a RAS server with an effective throughput of up to 57.6Kbps. The two modems do not have to be the same type or speed, but both the RAS server and the DUN client must have PPP multilink enabled.

10.2.3. Point-to-Point Tunneling Protocol

New to Windows NT Workstation 4.0 is an extension to PPP called Point-to-Point Tunneling Protocol (PPTP). The *Point-to-Point Tunneling Protocol* (PPTP) enables clients to connect to remote servers over the Internet.

PPTP enables a DUN client to establish a communications session with a RAS server over the Internet. PPTP enables multiprotocol virtual private networks (VPNs) so

10

that remote users can gain secure encrypted access to their corporate networks over the Internet. Because PPTP encapsulates TCP/IP, NWLink, and NetBEUI, it enables the Internet to be used as a backbone for NWLink and NetBEUI.

To use PPTP, first establish a connection from the DUN client to the Internet. Then establish a connection to the RAS server over the Internet.

> After you have made a connection to the remote network, you can select which of the network transport protocols (TCP/IP, IPX, or NetBEUI) you want to use. Follow these steps to change your RAS configuration after you finish the installation process:
>
> 1. Double-click the Network program in Control Panel.
> 2. Click the Services tab.
> 3. Double-click the Remote Access Service in the list.
> 4. In the Remote Access Setup box, either click Configure to config ure port usage or click Network to select dial-out protocols.
>
> You must restart your computer after you change your RAS configuration.

Whether using PPP or PPTP, after clients establish a connection to a RAS server, they are registered into the local network and can take advantage of the same network services and data that they could if they were actually physically connected to the local network. The only difference clients might notice is that a WAN connection is much slower than a direct physical connection to one's own LAN.

Lab

The following review questions will test your knowledge on the topics covered in this chapter.

Review Questions

1. Which of the following is an extension of PPP that enables clients to connect to remote servers over the Internet?

   A. SLIP

   B. POP

   C. PPTP

   D. PPP+

2. Windows NT Workstation 4.0 supports which two line protocols?

   A. SLIP

   B. PPP

   C. PPTP

   D. TCP/IP

3. Which of the following is an industry standard that supports only TCP/IP connections made over serial lines?

   A. SLIP

   B. PPP

   C. PPTP

   D. TCP/IP

4. Which of the following protocols work with SLIP?

   A. TCP/IP

   B. NetBEUI

   C. IPX/SPX

   D. PPTP

10

5. How does Windows NT Workstation support SLIP functionality?

    A. As a server

    B. As a client

    C. As a client and a server

    D. Windows NT Workstation does not support SLIP

6. Which of the following networking protocols works with PPP?

    A. TCP/IP

    B. NetBEUI

    C. IPX/SPX

    D. PPTP

7. Which of the following line protocols supports DHCP addresses?

    A. SLIP

    B. PPP

    C. IPX/SPX

    D. TCP/IP

8. Which of the following is the protocol used to create virtual private networks over the Internet?

    A. SLIP

    B. PPP

    C. POP

    D. PPTP

9. How many inbound RAS sessions can Windows NT Workstation serve at a time?

    A. 1

    B. 2

    C. 5

    D. 255

10. RAS can be configured in which three of the following ways?

   A. Dial Out Only

   B. Receive Calls Only

   C. Dial Out and Receive Calls

   D. Manual

11. Which of the following configuration settings is the default for RAS?

   A. Dial Out Only

   B. Receive Calls Only

   C. Dial Out and Receive Calls

   D. Manual

12. Authentication and encryption settings are set

   A. For each workstation

   B. For each domain

   C. For each phonebook entry

   D. For each user

13. The Dialing Properties dialog box is accessed from which Control Panel applet?

   A. System

   B. Services

   C. RAS

   D. Telephony

14. Which of the following are limitations of SLIP for Dial-Up Networking (DUN) clients?

   A. DUN doesn't support use as a SLIP client.

   B. SLIP doesn't support NWLink or NetBEUI.

   C. SLIP doesn't support DHCP.

   D. SLIP doesn't support encrypted authentication.

10

15. What methods are supported by Dial-Up Networking to establish sessions with remote networks?

    A. ISDN

    B. X.25

    C. Dial-up with modems and ordinary phone lines

    D. XNS

Answers to Review Questions

1. C The *Point-to-Point Tunneling Protocol* (PPTP) is an extension to PPP that enables clients to connect to remote servers over the Internet.

2. A, B Windows NT Workstation 4.0 supports two line protocols: SLIP and PPP.

3. A SLIP is an industry standard that supports TCP/IP connections made over serial lines.

4. A SLIP supports only TCP/IP.

5. B Windows NT Workstation supports only SLIP client functionality.

6. A, B, C PPP supports TCP/IP, NetBEUI, and IPX/SPX, among others.

7. B TCP/IP and IPX/SPX are not line protocols. SLIP does not support DHCP addressing—only static addressing. PPP supports DHCP addressing.

8. D PPTP is used to create virtual private networks over the Internet.

9. A Windows NT Workstation is limited to one RAS session at a time.

10. A, B, C Dial Out Only, Receive Calls Only, and Dial Out and Receive Calls are the three settings for RAS.

11. A Dial Out Only is the default RAS setting.

12. C Authentication and encryption settings are set individually for each phone-book entry.

13. D Telephony is the Control Panel applet that gives access to Dialing Properties.

14. B, C, D Windows NT Workstation 4.0 supports usage as a SLIP client but not as a SLIP server.

15. A, B, C DUN doesn't support XNS.

Exercises

These exercises walk you through some of the steps discussed in this chapter.

Exercise 10.1: Adding a New Dial-Up Networking (DUN) Phonebook Entry

This exercise leads you though the steps of adding a new DUN phonebook entry. To configure and install Dial-Up Networking in a given situation, follow these steps:

1. Double-click the Dial-Up Networking program in My Computer.
2. Click New.
3. Enter **New Server** for the name of the new phonebook entry, and then click Next.
4. Click Next for the Server settings.
5. Enter the phone number **555-5555**, and then click Next.
6. Click Finish.
7. Click the Phonebook Entry to Dial drop-down arrow to see how you can choose which phone number you want to use.
8. Click Close.

Exercise 10.1: Answers and Explanations

This exercise led you though the steps of adding a new DUN phonebook entry. Each user of a Windows NT Workstation 4.0 computer has her own phonebook and can add to it any entries she wants to in order to personalize it for herself.

Exercise 10.2: Adding a New Dial-Up Networking (DUN) Dialing Location

This exercise shows you how to add a new dialing location so that you can use your DUN client from a new location. To understand the methodology behind configuring and installing Dial-Up Networking, follow these steps:

1. Double-click the Telephony program in Control Panel.
2. Click New.
3. Click OK in the dialog box that tells you a new location was created.
4. Change the area code to your new area code.
5. Specify Dial 9 for an Outside Line and Dial 8 for Long Distance.

10

6. Check the Dial Using Calling Card check box, and then click Change.

7. Select your calling card from the list, and then click OK.

8. Click OK to close the Dialing Properties box.

Exercise 10.2: Answers and Explanations

This exercise showed you how to add a new dialing location so that you can use your DUN client from a new location. Multiple dialing locations can be useful for mobile users who need to initiate remote network sessions from multiple locations.

Day 11

Peer Web Services

Welcome to Day 11! Today we're going to talk about Peer Web Services. Peer Web Services (PWS) is the Windows NT Workstation component that corresponds to Windows NT Server's Internet Information Server (IIS). In fact, Peer Web Services was designed specifically to allow people to develop applications for IIS without having to have a Windows NT Server present at all times.

Objective

Today we cover the final subobjective of the Connectivity objective:

- Configuring Microsoft Peer Web Services in a given situation

11.1. Similarities and Differences Between PWS and IIS

When Microsoft decided to include the Internet Information Server (IIS) as a part of the Windows NT Server operating system, it took the computer industry by storm. When faced with the decision to buy a Web server or use the one that was included free of charge with the operating system, most users found that the choice was clear. Everyone started using the free Web server.

However, one problem cropped up. For someone to develop for IIS, she needed an IIS server. This meant an organization had to have two Windows NT servers: one to run the production Web site on and another one for the developer to work with. The problem got worse if there was more than one developer because each developer would want her own IIS server to work on.

To combat this problem, Microsoft started including Peer Web Services (PWS) with Windows NT Workstation. Peer Web Services includes almost all of the support for extended features that IIS has. From a development standpoint, it is essentially identical. This enables organizations to deploy Windows NT Server as the Web server and to allow developers to test Web sites by using Peer Web Services on the Windows NT Workstation. Thus, the developer no longer needs a separate IIS.

Although PWS is almost identical to IIS, there are a few differences:

- Peer Web Services doesn't support access control by IP address. This effectively prevents it from being used as an Internet server when security is a concern.
- Peer Web Services doesn't support virtual servers. This means that it can't be used to host more than one Web site.
- Peer Web Services can't log access to an ODBC datasource. This makes it harder to get statistics on utilization.
- Peer Web Services can't limit the amount of network bandwidth used.
- Peer Web Services has a 40-bit key encryption as opposed to the 40-bit or 128-bit security of IIS. 128-bit security is available only in the United States and Canada.
- Peer Web Services can't scale by using multiple threads across more than one CPU.

If we review these limitations, we see that they are aimed squarely at preventing PWS from being used in a production environment that involves many sites or users. However, the limitations of PWS don't in any way impact its capability to be used for development purposes.

11.2. Install Peer Web Services (PWS)

The first step to using PWS is installing it. Like other Windows NT network services, it is installed from the Services tab in the Network applet of the Control Panel (as shown in Figure 11.1).

Figure 11.1.

The Services tab of the Network Control Panel applet.

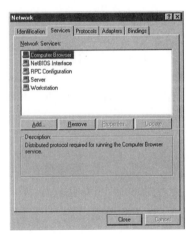

11

To add Peer Web Services to your system, perform the following steps:

1. Start the Network Control Panel applet by selecting Start, Settings, Control Panel and then double-clicking the Network icon.

2. Select the Services tab.

3. Click the Add button.

4. Select the Microsoft Peer Web Services and click OK.

5. Insert the Windows NT CD-ROM as requested.

6. Click OK and reboot the computer as prompted.

When Peer Web Services has been installed, you see a Start menu group that contains the Internet Service Manager. You use the Service Manager to configure Peer Web Services.

11.3. Configure Peer Web Services (PWS)

PWS is easy to configure because there aren't many options to be set up in order for Peer Web Services to operate.

Table 11.1 outlines the most common options used with Peer Web Services. All are configured by double-clicking the WWW service in the Internet Service Manager.

Table 11.1. Peer Web Services options.

Option	Description
TCP Port	The port that the Web server will listen to. Web servers are generally located on port 80. That is the default value.
Connection Timeout	How long PWS will keep a connection open that hasn't been closed. The default is 900 seconds.
Maximum Connections	The maximum number of connections that PWS will support. The default value is 100,000.
Anonymous Login	The login used by PWS for all connections that aren't specifically logged in.
Password Authentication: Allow Anonymous	Specifies whether PWS should accept connections without requiring logins. By default, this option is on.
Password Authentication: Basic Clear Text	This allows users to log in via clear text. This is not recommended. Any clear-text password can be seen in transit to the server and isn't secure. By default, this option is off.
Password Authentication: Windows NT Challenge/Response	This secure form of password transmission allows users to log in to the PWS server without the password being visible during transmission. By default, this option is on.
Enable Logging	Specifies whether PWS should maintain activity logs. The default is on.
Log Format	Specifies the format of the logging file. You can select NCSA format or Standard format. Standard format is the default.

Option	Description
Automatically Open New Log	Specifies the frequency to open a new log. This is useful when you want to analyze the data in the log file. If the logs are never closed, you'll never be able to review the information they contain. The default is Daily frequency, but you can set it to Weekly, Monthly, or when the file reaches a certain size.
Enable Default Document	This option specifies that PWS will search any directory specified for a certain document and send the document instead of the directory if the document exists. The default is on, with a default document of DEFAULT.HTM.
Directory Browsing Allowed	This option specifies whether PWS should allow the user to see the directory of files for any directory he specifies. This option is normally turned off to prevent people from finding files that they aren't supposed to find. The default is off.

In addition to the preceding options, there are also options regarding which directories are used to serve WWW pages. Open the WWW Service Properties dialog box and select the Directories tab to access the settings for the directories (see Figure 11.2).

11

Figure 11.2.

The Directories tab of the WWW Service Properties dialog box is used to change which directories are served.

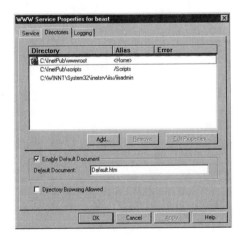

You can add a new directory by clicking the Add button. The Directory Properties dialog box, shown in Figure 11.3, appears.

Figure 11.3.

The Directory Properties dialog box is used to change the properties of the directories that are used on the server.

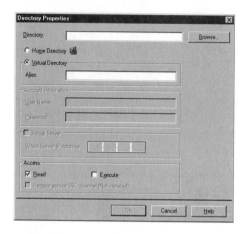

By entering a directory and an alias, you can create a virtual directory on the PWS server. This directory then appears as if it is under the home directory, even though it's actually located in another directory on your hard drive.

For instance, suppose you're using the default settings, your home directory is C:\INETPUB\WWWROOT, and you have a set of Web pages already installed in D:\MYAPPS\WEB\ORDERENTRY. You can create a virtual directory called ORDERENTRY under the root, which actually points to the D:\MYAPPS\WEB\ORDERENTRY directory.

For every directory, you can also specify whether the files can be read or executed or both. This is important because you don't want your scripts to be read by other people, and you want to isolate the programs that can be run.

If you allow files to be read from a directory, you're allowing PWS to send the file to a user wanting to see Web pages, text files, or any other file that's readable in a browser. If you allow files to be executed, you're allowing scripts to be placed in and run from the directory. This is important because the advanced features are available only through the use of scripts and CGI-BIN programs. It's generally not acceptable to permit both Read and Execute access to the same directory.

Lab

PWS is a powerful Web server that was designed as a developer platform for IIS. The following sections test your comprehension of the material we've just covered. The answers are found at the end of the section.

Review Questions

1. Which Web server is Peer Web Services modeled after?

   A. Netscape

   B. Apache

   C. NCSA Mosaic

   D. Microsoft Internet Information Server

2. Which of the following are valid logging options for PWS?

   A. Standard format

   B. NCSA format

   C. ODBC datasource

   D. Access databases

3. Which of the following are supported features of PWS?

   A. Virtual servers

   B. Secure Socket Layer (SSL)

   C. ODBC database login

   D. IIS APIs

4. You're starting an Internet service provider (ISP) and need to host multiple company Web sites from their own domains. You also need to minimize your costs but provide the database access via ODBC database sources. Which Web server should you use?

   A. Internet Information Server

   B. Peer Web Services

   C. Netscape

   D. Apache

11

5. What is the default Web server port?

   A. 80

   B. 1180

   C. 81

   D. 453

Answers to Review Questions

1. D PWS is a limited version of IIS.

2. A, B Both Standard format and NCSA format are file types supported by PWS. ODBC logging is a feature of IIS that isn't present in PWS. Access databases can be logged to by IIS through an ODBC datasource.

3. B, D PWS supports 40-bit versions of SSL and all IIS APIs. Virtual servers and ODBC database login are seen as production system needs and aren't supported from PWS.

4. A Peer Web Services doesn't support virtual servers, which would be required to host multiple company Web sites on the same machine. Netscape and Apache are incorrect because they would require additional purchases—which doesn't fit with attempting to minimize costs.

5. A Web servers generally function on port 80.

Exercises

Exercise 11.1: Creating a Web Page

Time Estimate: 5 minutes

For this exercise, you'll need Word for Windows 97. To start, open Word for Windows 97 and perform the following steps:

1. Select File, New to display the New File dialog box.

2. Select the Web Pages tab, and then select the Web Page wizard.

3. Select the type of page from the Web Page Wizard dialog box and click Next.

4. Select the visual style you want to use and click Finish.

5. Edit the document with your personal information.

6. Select File, Save.

7. Create a new directory and save the Web page in it as DEFAULT.HTM.

You've completed your Web page. You might have noticed several other files in your Web page directory. These files are the graphics used by your Web page and were inserted automatically by Word.

Exercise 11.2: Adding a Virtual Directory

Time Estimate: 5 minutes

In this exercise, you'll add the directory you just created for your Web page in Exercise 11.1.

1. Select Start, Programs, Peer Web Services (Common), Internet Service Manager.
2. Double-click the WWW Service.
3. Select the Directories tab.
4. Click the Add button.
5. Enter the path to the directory you want to add (in this case, the directory in which you created your Web page).
6. Enter an alias for the virtual directory (in this case, enter **/MyPage** as the alias).
7. Make sure that Read access is enabled and Execute access is not enabled.
8. Click OK to return to the Directory Properties dialog box.
9. Click OK to close the WWW Service Properties dialog box.
10. Close the Internet Service Manager.

You've just created a new virtual directory called /MyPage on your server.

Exercise 11.3: Browsing a Local Web Page

Time Estimate: 5 minutes

In this exercise, you use Peer Web Services to view the page that you created in Exercise 11.1.

For this exercise to work, you must:

■ Be on the same machine you created the home page on.
■ Have completed Exercises 11.1 and 11.2.

11

To view your Web page, follow these steps:

1. Start Internet Explorer.

2. Enter the URL `http://localhost/MyPage/default.htm` and press Enter. Your Web page should appear.

3. Enter the URL `http://localhost/MyPage` and press Enter. If the default document was left at its default setting, you should also see your Web page.

You can browse other files and directories in the same way. The `localhost` identifier always identifies the local host and can be used on any system on which TCP/IP is installed.

Day 12

Running Applications

Welcome to Day 12! Just three days to go until you're done studying for your Microsoft Workstation Test.

Objectives

Today we're going to cover the Running Applications objective. This objective has two subobjectives:

- Starting applications on Intel and RISC platforms in various operating system environments
- Starting applications at various priority levels

12.1. Start Applications on Intel and RISC Platforms in Various Operating System Environments

When Microsoft was designing Windows NT, it recognized that it couldn't abandon the hundreds of thousands of applications that had been written for DOS and Windows 3.11. As a result, it created a modular architecture that would allow applications of different types to run under the Windows NT operating system.

Since its initial release (version 3.1), Windows NT has offered support for:

- 32-bit Windows applications
- 16-bit Windows applications
- DOS applications
- OS/2 1.3 character mode applications
- POSIX applications (POSIX stands for Portable Operating System Interface based on UNIX)

These can be broken down into two groups. The first group contains those application standards designed for future compatibility, which include 32-bit Windows applications and POSIX applications.

32-bit Windows applications use Microsoft's new structure for applications that don't have the same memory constraints as the older 16-bit Windows applications. The 32-bit applications also have full access to a more complete API set. 32-bit Windows applications have direct access to all of Windows NT's resources. Because of that, they are the fastest applications that can be run on Windows NT.

POSIX support was also included so that applications written to the POSIX standard would run on Windows NT. POSIX is a source code–compatible operating environment that allows a single source code to be compiled for multiple systems. The POSIX standard was supposed to revolutionize the way in which UNIX applications were built, reducing the amount of time that had to be spent porting an application from one hardware platform to another. (*Porting* refers to the energy and effort spent making a program work on a platform other than the one for which it was originally written. Porting is one of the biggest limitations to the UNIX market.)

The second group of applications Windows NT supports includes applications from three legacy operating environments. These are 16-bit Windows applications, DOS applications, and OS/2 applications.

At the time Microsoft was developing Windows NT, 16-bit Windows applications were all the craze. Despite their memory limitations and seemingly inherent instability, they were the most popular applications of the day. Windows 3.1 had taken hold, and people wanted the graphical interface and the freedom to run multiple programs.

In addition to the those people running 16-bit Windows applications, many people were still running DOS applications. Microsoft knew from their experience with OS/2 and Windows 3.1 that DOS support was critical to Windows NT's success.

Finally, Microsoft included support for OS/2 applications. Although Microsoft was abandoning OS/2, they didn't want the developers and customers who had invested in OS/2 to feel like Microsoft had deserted them.

In the following sections, we look at each of these subsystems in detail, discussing how to start applications, how the applications will run, and what you can do to control them.

12.1.1. 32-Bit Windows Applications

In Windows NT, 32-bit Windows applications are the king of the hill. In fact, the Win32 subsystem from which all 32-bit Windows applications run is the native subsystem for Windows NT and controls all input and output to other subsystems.

32-bit Windows applications run directly in the Win32 subsystem and have access to the complete system. Each application always runs within its own protected memory space and is preemptively multitasked with other applications running on Windows NT. This means that no other application—whether it is a 16-bit Windows application, an OS/2 application, or a POSIX application—can interfere with a 32-bit Windows application.

Each 32-bit Windows applications has the capability to access up to 2GB of memory (the operating system reserves another 2GB). In addition, every application has one thread of execution and can have multiple threads.

12

Note | Windows NT Server Enterprise Edition allows applications to use as much as 3GB of memory each. The upper 1GB is still retained for Windows NT's use.

A *thread* is a string of commands that are executed in succession. DOS applications and 16-bit Windows applications have only one thread; thus, items are always processed in order, one at a time. In a multithreaded application, however, one thread can handle user input, while another thread prints a document in the background and another thread queries a database for results. Think of threads as separate programs that share the same memory space and work together.

Because all applications are preemptively multitasked, Windows NT retains control of the system. Even if a single application or thread locks up, it will not prevent the other applications or threads from running.

32-bit Windows applications perform better than any other programs when running on Windows NT because the 32-bit applications have full access to resources and because no translation is necessary between the native Win32 subsystem and the program. The caveat to using 32-bit Windows applications is that they must be compiled for each environment. An application that is compiled for an Intel platform will not run on an Alpha without being recompiled. For this reason, 32-bit Windows applications are said to be *source compatible*, which means that the source code for the program remains the same, but the program must be recompiled for the specific platform.

| Note | Digital has released a product called FX!32 that allows some Intel-compiled 32-bit applications to be installed and run on Digital Alpha systems. However, this doesn't work for every application and isn't recommended when an Alpha-compiled version is available. As far as the test is concerned, FX!32 doesn't exist. |

12.1.2. 16-Bit Windows Applications

While working on OS/2, Microsoft developed several techniques to allow 16-bit applications to run in a 32-bit environment. The most common method was called *thunking*. Thunking converts 16-bit calls to 32-bit calls on-the-fly. This is primarily done by converting references, or memory addresses, from a 16-bit segmented format to a 32-bit revised format.

Note

16-bit addresses and 32-bit addresses are very different from one another. This is because Intel used some trickery to allow a 16-bit processor to run with up to 1MB of RAM. To access 1MB of RAM, you must have 20 bits. Instead of using a 20-bit number to refer to addresses, Intel developed a segmented memory structure.

Each address in memory is referred to via the combination of a 16-bit segment and a 16-bit offset. Intel shifted the segment four bits to the left, making the segment refer to lines 20–5 and making the offset refer to lines 1–16. Although the addressing of the segment and the offset overlap, it's possible to refer to any memory address in the entire 1MB memory structure.

Working with 16-bit addresses is complicated because there's no easy way to process information greater than 64KB in size; that's all that the offset can manipulate. If more than 64KB of memory must be manipulated, code must be written that progressively increases the segment and reduces the offset accordingly. This code slows down the operation, though, because many cycles are wasted converting offsets into segment changes.

32-bit addressing doesn't have these limitations. 32-bit addressing isn't segmented, and there's no distinction between the upper 16 bits and the lower 16 bits. A 32-bit address is just a representation of how many bytes the particular location is away from the start of memory.

16-bit addresses can be converted to 32-bit addresses by clearing a memory space, placing the segment in the memory, rotating it to the left four positions, and adding the offset. The result is a 32-bit address that specifies the exact same location as the 16-bit address.

32-bit addresses can be converted to 16-bit addresses by placing the last four bits in the offset, rotating the number to the right four places, and placing the result in the segment. This results in a 16-bit address that is the same as the 32-bit address. However, this works only if the 32-bit address isn't beyond 1MB.

12

Microsoft used the thunking process to allow Windows NT to run 16-bit Windows applications. Using the thunking method, Microsoft developed a subsystem called WOW, which is short for Windows on Windows (or 16-bit Windows on 32-bit Windows). The WOW subsystem converts 16-bit API calls to 32-bit API calls and handles cooperative multitasking for any 16-bit applications run within it.

By default, Windows creates one WOW session when the first 16-bit application is started. This is where all 16-bit Windows applications will be run, unless Windows NT is instructed to start them in separate memory spaces.

When more than one 16-bit application is running in a WOW session, the applications are not protected from each other. The WOW system cooperatively multitasks more than one application in a single WOW session. This means that Windows NT doesn't prevent any 16-bit Windows application from taking up all of the WOW session's processor time—some of which rightfully belongs to the other 16-bit applications. In addition, Windows NT doesn't protect an application's memory from being written over by another application.

This is why Windows NT provides the option to run each 16-bit Windows application in its own WOW session. This is called running a program in a *separate memory space*. It allows the applications to be preemptively multitasked yet also be protected from other 16-bit applications.

You might think that you would want to run every 16-bit Windows application in its own memory space. However, this does have its drawbacks. First, each WOW session takes about 4–5MB of RAM. For every 16-bit Windows application you want to start in a separate memory space, the system requires an additional 4–5MB of RAM. The second drawback is that some applications (most notably Schedule 1.0 and Microsoft Mail for Windows) communicate by directly modifying memory in other applications. This doesn't work when Windows NT is running applications in separate memory spaces because applications are protected from other applications modifying their memory.

To run a Windows 16-bit application in a separate memory space, you perform three general steps:

1. Select Run in Separate Memory Space in the Run dialog box (see Figure 12.1).
2. Include the /SEPARATE option in the START command (which you'll learn more about in the upcoming section "The START Command").
3. Select the Run in Separate Memory Space option on the Shortcut tab of the program's properties sheet (see Figure 12.2).

Figure 12.1.

The Run dialog box enables you to run 16-bit applications in a separate memory space.

Figure 12.2.

The properties for a shortcut allow you to specify whether the application will be run in a separate memory space.

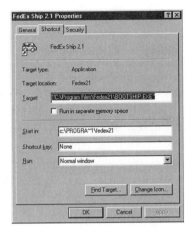

One of the key limitations to Windows NT's support of 16-bit Windows applications is that the applications cannot directly modify hardware. This limitation especially affects programs such as fax programs and specialized hardware control applications because they won't work correctly in Windows NT.

In Windows NT, every device is controlled by the operating system. If applications are allowed access to a device, it is either through virtualized device drivers that emulate the hardware device or via Windows API calls. In either case, 16-bit Windows applications are not allowed to communicate directly with hardware. This limitation caused a lot of problems when Windows NT was introduced because fax programs and other programs on which people had begun to depend wouldn't run in the NT environment.

One advantage of using 16-bit Windows applications is that you can run them on any platform. They are said to be *binary compatible*, which means that they can run on an Alpha or an Intel without having to be recompiled. This is a great feature, but not without its price. Because every instruction in a 16-bit Windows application has to be translated to the instruction or instructions of the RISC platform, 16-bit applications often run slowly even on high-performance RISC platforms.

12.1.3. DOS Applications

DOS has always been the wicked stepchild in Windows. Even back to Windows 3.1, DOS applications could be run from Windows, but the support often caused Windows 3.1 to crash. Even in Windows 95, an errant DOS application can bring the system to its knees.

12

Just as Windows NT has a translation system for 16-bit Windows applications, DOS applications have their own translation subsystem that converts 16-bit calls to 32-bit calls. However, this subsystem is rarely referred to separately.

In Windows NT, all character-based programs are run from the CMD.EXE program, which is similar to DOS's COMMAND.COM file. CMD.EXE determines whether the command you are running is a 32-bit console application or a DOS application. If the application is a DOS application, COMMAND.EXE spawns a separate Windows NT Virtual Device Manager (NTVDM) session. This is a separate memory space that is protected from the rest of the operating system. In fact, each WOW session that is used to support 16-bit applications actually runs in an NTVDM session. This is why 16-bit Windows applications can't affect programs that aren't running in the same WOW session.

One thing that's difficult for people to understand is that not every program with a character interface is a DOS application. Some OS/2 applications and 32-bit console applications also have the character interface. 32-bit console applications are character-based applications that have been compiled to run as 32-bit applications in Windows 95 or Windows NT. Whereas every DOS application will run on any hardware platform without being recompiled, 32-bit console applications must be specifically recompiled for the platform.

12.1.4. OS/2

When Microsoft started working on advanced operating systems, it partnered with IBM to develop OS/2. OS/2 was supposed to be the second-generation operating system, designed from the ground up to run multiple programs at the same time (as opposed to Microsoft's current Windows offerings, which allowed multiple programs to run by way of some trickery).

OS/2 had requirements that, at the time of its release, seemed excessive. When it was released, OS/2 required a 286 with 2MB of RAM. Although those requirements seem almost silly today, 10 years ago they were a high bar to set.

When Microsoft decided to turn over the development of OS/2 to IBM, it also decided that its next operating system must provide some support for the platform that Microsoft was abandoning. Microsoft wanted to cushion the blow as much as possible.

> **Note**
>
> There was a lot of speculation as to why the Microsoft and IBM alliance broke up and Microsoft allowed IBM to keep OS/2. One camp believes that Microsoft realized its mistake in developing for a 80286 processor because OS/2 didn't handle switching out of 32-bit protected mode well (read: at all!). Another possible reason was the desire to be processor independent. Another camp believes it was because IBM's productivity measurements were set up to measure lines of code, not feature points. Thus when Microsoft engineers would rework a routine to improve performance and would delete lines of code, they would have negative productivity.
>
> Whatever the reason, it's clear that many of the concepts of OS/2 appear in Windows NT.

Microsoft decided to include OS/2 support in Windows NT. Although the OS/2 support is limited to character-based applications and doesn't include applications written to use the Presentation Manager interface, it still enabled Microsoft to provide support for some of the early OS/2 applications that had been written.

Unfortunately, OS/2 applications can't be run on non-Intel platforms. Although Windows NT runs on multiple platforms, OS/2 applications have the same problem that other 32-bit applications have: They are source code compatible, not binary compatible. Because there is no OS/2 compiler for RISC systems, OS/2 applications can't be run on RISC systems.

The one exception to this is that some OS/2 applications contain both the OS/2 executable and a DOS executable. These are called *bound* applications. These bound applications can be run on non-Intel platforms because they can run in DOS mode.

12.1.5. Portable Operating System Interface Based on UNIX (POSIX)

POSIX is the standard that never was. Its purpose was to reduce the fragmentation in the UNIX market by allowing a single set of source code to run on multiple platforms. POSIX is a C-level source code and API definition. Even though POSIX support is source code compatible only, it was thought to be a major accomplishment because previously each version of UNIX required specific source code to handle the peculiarities of that hardware.

At the time Microsoft was developing Windows NT, POSIX support was required by the federal government for all systems being implemented. That is probably the largest contributing factor to why Windows NT has POSIX support.

12

To get NT's full support for POSIX.1, the NTFS file system must be used on all file systems the POSIX applications are going to access. This allows for the following three components of POSIX systems:

- *Case-sensitive files.* POSIX files are case sensitive.
- *Hard links.* The same file can have two different names.
- *Last-accessed time.* POSIX requires a last-accessed time stamp, which FAT doesn't support. The last-accessed time defaults to the last-modified time on FAT file systems.

Because POSIX is source compatible only, each POSIX application must be compiled for the specific hardware platform on which it will be run.

12.2. Start Applications at Various Priority Levels

One of the key features of Windows NT is its Task Scheduler. The Task Scheduler for Windows NT determines when each application will run and how long it will be allowed to run. Unlike Windows 3.1, which cooperatively multitasked, Windows NT preemptively multitasks programs.

Cooperative multitasking requires that each application give up the processor after a reasonable amount of time. This works fine when all of the applications are well-behaved. However, it doesn't work well when an application doesn't release the processor. With *preemptive multitasking,* the operating system maintains control of the processor (or processors) and arbitrates when a program gets to use the processor and for how long.

For a multitasking system to be robust enough to support mission-critical applications and to allow applications to be responsive enough to the user, a somewhat complex priority scheme must be developed. Windows NT has just such a complex priority scheme. However, it hides the complexities of its scheduling system from you by establishing four priority levels that can be assigned to any program or thread. These priorities are:

- LOW: For applications that need to be completed sometime but that you don't want to interfere with other applications.
- NORMAL: For most applications. This is the default priority.

■ HIGH: For applications that must be completed quickly, when you don't want other applications to interfere with this application's performance.

■ REALTIME: For applications that must have the processor's undivided attention to handle time-critical tasks. Only members of the Administrators group can run applications at the REALTIME priority level.

These mnemonic priorities actually fit within the framework of Windows NT's numeric scheduling system. The numeric scheduling system that NT uses has a total of 32 priorities. Table 12.1 lists the mnemonic priority and its numeric equivalent.

Table 12.1. Priorities and equivalents.

Mnemonic Priority	Numeric Equivalent
LOW	4
NORMAL	8
HIGH	13
REALTIME	24

In addition to a process's base priority, Windows NT also assigns and schedules based on a dynamic priority. NT decrements and increments a process's dynamic priority from its base priority based on specific circumstances. Table 12.2 indicates some of the reasons why a priority might be incremented or decremented. Windows NT will never decrement a dynamic priority to less than the base priority, and Windows NT always schedules off of the dynamic priority.

Table 12.2. Priorities.

Operation	Result
Receive keyboard input	+5
Receive COM port data	+1
Wait for disk IO to complete	+1
Complete cycle use	−1
Foreground application	+2, +1, or 0, based on user settings

Programs can be started with different priorities via the START command. After a program is running, you can change its priority only by using the Task Manager. These two methods of changing priority are discussed in the following sections.

12

12.2.1. The START Command

The START command is a command-line utility that allows you to specify every possible option for starting a program. The only other way to access some of the options that START gives you is to write a program to make the specific Win32 API call to start running an application. Regardless of what kind of program you want to run, START can be used to start it.

The START command has the following format:

```
START ["title"] [/Dpath] [/I] [/MIN ¦ /MAX] [/SEPARATE ¦ /SHARED] [/LOW ¦ /NORMAL
    ➡¦ /HIGH ¦ /REALTIME] [/WAIT] [/B] Program [Program arguments]
```

The "title" option enables you to specify a title for the resulting window. This option is useful when you want to be able to identify any special options used when starting the program. This option has no effect for Windows-based applications.

The /Dpath option enables you to specify the directory in which the application will start. By default, the application starts in the current directory.

The /I option specifies that the environment received by the application that is started will be a copy of the default environment—as opposed to a copy of the current environment from which the command is being run.

The /MIN option specifies that the window will be opened minimized. This option is good for programs that should be running but don't require interaction with the user. The /MAX option specifies that the window will be opened maximized. This forces the application to take up the entire screen.

The /SEPARATE option starts each 16-bit Windows application in a separate memory space. This protects the applications from interference from other errant 16-bit Windows applications. (This option is ignored if the application isn't a 16-bit Windows application.) The /SHARED option starts a 16-bit Windows application in a shared memory space. Although this option is the default, it is ignored if the application isn't a 16-bit Windows application.

The /LOW option specifies that the application should start at the LOW priority. The /NORMAL option specifies that the application should start at the NORMAL priority. (This is the default option.) The /HIGH option specifies that the application should start at the HIGH priority. The /REALTIME option, available only to administrators, specifies that the application should start at the REALTIME priority level.

Do not run applications at the REALTIME priority level unless they were specifically designed to be run at the REALTIME priority level. REALTIME applications run at a higher level than some components of Windows NT, which can cause the system to lock up or become so slow that it's unusable.

The /WAIT option specifies that the START command won't be executed until the application startup is complete. This option is used to synchronize operations in batch files.

The /B option prevents START from creating a new window and disables Ctrl+C. However, Ctrl+Break will still work.

Program and *Program arguments* represent the program you want to run and its parameters.

The START command is a key component to creating installation batch files and controlling how applications are started.

12.2.2. Task Manager

After a program has been started, there is only one way to change its priority without adding utilities. You must use the Task Manager. The Task Manager is much different in Windows NT than it was in Windows 3.1. Windows NT's Task Manager has three tabs with which you control applications, control processes, and review performance.

To start the Task Manager, either start the security manager by pressing Ctrl+Alt+Del and then select Task Manager, or right-click on an open area of the Taskbar and select Task Manager.

The Applications tab, shown in Figure 12.3, shows all the applications currently running on the system. From this tab, you can switch to a task, bring a window to the front, end the application, or go to the main process of the application.

To see how this works, right-click any application in the Task list and select the Go to Process option from the shortcut menu that appears. You are taken to the Processes tab, where the process for the application you selected is highlighted (see Figure 12.4).

12

Figure 12.3.

The Applications tab shows the running applications.

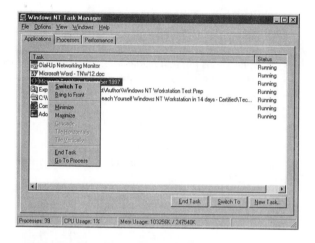

Figure 12.4.

The Processes tab shows details about the processes, including those that don't have windows.

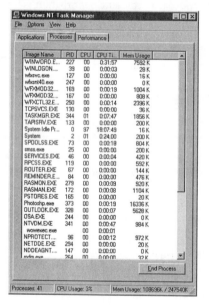

Right-click a process, and the shortcut menu shown in Figure 12.5 appears. If you select the Set Priority option, you can change the priority of an application.

If you tell Windows NT to change the priority of an application, NT displays a warning like the one shown in Figure 12.6, telling you that changing the priority of an application might make it unstable. You can generally ignore this option when changing the priority to LOW, NORMAL, or HIGH, but you should heed this warning when changing applications to REALTIME priority.

Figure 12.5.

The Processes tab allows you to change the priority of a process.

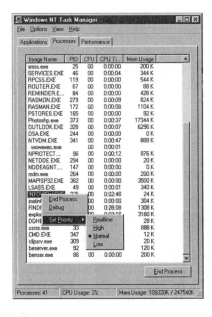

Figure 12.6.

Windows NT warns you that changing a priority can make the program unstable.

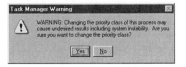

The priority change remains in effect as long as the program is running. During that time, no other application can change this application's priority, and the program itself doesn't attempt to modify its own priority.

12

Lab

In today's labs, you'll review how Windows NT runs programs and which platforms can run different application types. Answers to review questions appear at the end of the section.

Review Questions

1. You have a Windows NT Workstation running on an Intel server. You want to run a 32-bit Windows application that you got from someone running Windows NT Workstation on an Alpha system. What must you do in order to run this program?

   A. Install Alpha 32-bit Windows support from the Control Panel.

   B. Get the source code for the program and a compiler, and recompile the program for Intel.

   C. Load the 32-bit Alpha emulator on your machine, and then start the program.

   D. Nothing. The program will run fine.

2. You have an OS/2 character-based application that you've been told is a bound application. You have a Digital Alpha system. What must you do to run this program?

   A. Install OS/2 support from the Add/Remove Programs applet in the Control Panel.

   B. Nothing. The program will run fine as is.

   C. Nothing. You will not be able to run the program.

   D. Get the source code and purchase an OS/2 compiler for the Alpha.

3. You have three 16-bit Windows applications. One of them is an accounting program, which can't be allowed to crash. The other programs are a communications program and a word processor. How can you start the programs so that the accounting application will be protected from the other applications?

   A. Run the accounting program in a separate memory space, and run the other two programs in the shared memory space.

   B. Run the communications program in a separate memory space, and run the accounting program and word processor in the shared memory space.

C. Run the communications program and word processor in separate memory spaces, and run the accounting program in the shared memory space.

D. Run all programs in separate memory spaces.

4. You receive a POSIX program from a UNIX buddy of yours. What must you do to run the program?

A. Compile the source code for the system that you're running on.

B. Purchase the POSIX subsystem add-in.

C. Start the POSIX emulator.

D. Nothing. The program will run as is.

5. You just received a 32-bit OS/2 Presentation Manager application from a friend. What must you do to be able to run it?

A. Install OS/2 support through the Add/Remove Programs applet in the Control Panel.

B. Nothing. The application will run as is.

C. Nothing. The application won't run.

D. Get the source code and recompile it for your hardware platform.

6. You have a DOS program that directly modifies hardware. How do you allow this program to run in Windows NT?

A. Do nothing. The program will run just fine.

B. Use the System applet in the Control Panel to enable direct hardware access.

C. Do nothing. The program will not run in Windows NT.

D. Go to the Properties tab of the program and select Direct Access.

7. You want to run a spreadsheet program called MYSS.EXE at high priority so it will be completed quickly. How can you start the program?

A. Open the Start menu, choose the Run option, and enter MYSS.EXE /HIGH.

B. From the Task Manager, click the New Task button and enter MYSS.EXE /HIGH.

12

C. From a command prompt, enter `START /HIGH MYSS.EXE`.

D. From a command prompt, enter `START MYSS.EXE /HIGH`.

8. Which of the following are valid Windows NT priorities?

A. IDLE

B. NORMAL

C. QUICK

D. HIGH

9. Joe is trying to start an application with a REALTIME priority, but he keeps getting an unspecified error. What are the potential causes of this error?

A. Joe isn't an administrator; therefore, he can't start an application at high priority.

B. The application wasn't designed to be run at a high priority, and running it at the REALTIME priority level has caused an internal error.

C. Joe doesn't have a REALTIME-compatible system.

D. Joe is running a Windows application, and Windows applications can't be run at the REALTIME priority level.

10. You need to change the priority of a complex math program to LOW so that the user can continue working in the foreground. Which application do you use to change the priority?

A. The System applet in the Control Panel

B. The START command

C. The Task Manager

D. User Manager

11. You're considering purchasing a Digital Alpha–based system for speed, but you're concerned about the types of applications you'd be able to run. Which of the following types of applications would you be able to run?

A. OS/2 1.3 character-mode applications

B. DOS applications

C. POSIX applications

D. 32-bit Windows applications compiled for Intel systems

12. You have installed Windows NT Workstation on an Intel-based system and are about to upgrade your memory from the minimum 12MB of RAM to something that can more efficiently handle the applications you're running. You frequently run three relatively small 16-bit Windows applications (two of which are started in a separate memory space) and a 32-bit Windows application that takes about 4MB of RAM. How much RAM should you configure for your system so that it doesn't page often?

   A. 24MB

   B. 32MB

   C. 48MB

   D. 64MB

13. You have three 16-bit Windows applications (a communications program, a word processor, and a spreadsheet) installed and running on your computer. You also have your 32-bit Windows accounting system running. What must you do to protect the accounting system from the 16-bit applications?

   A. Start each 16-bit Windows application in a separate memory space.

   B. Start two of the 16-bit applications in separate memory spaces, and start the final 16-bit application in the shared memory space.

   C. Start the accounting system in a separate memory space.

   D. Nothing. The application is already protected.

Answers to Review Questions

1. B 32-bit Windows applications are source code compatible, which means that the source code must be compiled for each hardware platform.

2. B Although non-Intel systems can't run native OS/2 programs, they can run bound programs because bound programs contain a DOS version of the executable. OS/2 support cannot be added or removed from the Control Panel, and there is no compiler for OS/2 that supports an Alpha processor.

3. A, C, D To protect the accounting application from the other applications, you must run the accounting application in its own memory space, whether that is in the shared memory space by itself or in a specifically separate memory space. Options A and D are correct because they put the accounting application in a separate memory space. Option C is valid because no other 16-bit Windows applications are running in the shared space with the accounting program.

4. A POSIX compatibility is, by definition, source code compatibility. This means that the source code must be recompiled for the specific platform on which it's going to be run.

5. C Windows NT has support for OS/2 applications only up to version 1.3 without Presentation Manager support.

6. C Windows NT will not run DOS applications that attempt to directly access hardware.

7. C The only way to change the starting priority of an application is to use the START command. When using the START command, you enter any necessary START command options before the application name.

8. B, D The valid Windows NT priorities for both Task Manager and the START command are LOW, NORMAL, HIGH, and REALTIME.

9. A, B An administrator privilege is required to run programs at REALTIME priority. In addition, some applications aren't designed to run at REALTIME priority. There are no special restrictions on the type of hardware that can run applications at REALTIME priority, nor are Windows programs restricted from running at REALTIME priority.

10. C The Task Manager is used to change the priority of an application that is already running. Neither the System applet in the Control Panel nor User Manager can be used to change the priority of an application.

11. B, C OS/2 is supported only on Intel systems. 32-bit Windows applications must be compiled for Alpha to run on an Alpha system. DOS applications are supported natively by Windows NT running on an Alpha. POSIX applications are compatible if they are compiled for the Alpha system.

12. B You should configure for 32MB of RAM. Windows NT requires a little less than 12MB for itself, and you have three 16-bit Windows applications that will take about 4–5MB of RAM each plus a 32-bit Windows application that needs another 4MB. You end up with a total memory usage of about 28–31MB of RAM. Any more would probably be wasted, and less would cause paging to occur.

13. D Because the accounting application is already a 32-bit application, it is automatically protected from all other applications, including 16-bit Windows applications.

Exercises

Exercise 12.1: Starting a High-Priority Command Prompt

Time Estimate: 5 minutes

In this exercise, you'll start a high-priority command prompt. This command prompt should remain responsive even if other applications and command prompts don't.

Here's what you do:

1. Start a command prompt by opening the Start menu and choosing Programs.

2. Type **START** and press the Spacebar, but don't press Enter.

3. Type the title for the command prompt between quotes, followed by a space. For example, type **"High Priority Command Prompt"** and press the Spacebar. Don't press Enter.

4. Type the command line option **/HIGH** and press the Spacebar. Do not press Enter.

5. Type the program name for the command prompt: **CMD.EXE**. Your completed line should look like this:

   ```
   START "High Priority Command Prompt" /HIGH CMD.EXE
   ```

6. Press Enter, and a new command prompt titled "High Priority Command Prompt" appears.

The command prompt that you've started will have a HIGH priority, which means that no NORMAL priority applications can prevent it from running.

Exercise 12.2: Changing the Priority of an Application

Time Estimate: 5 minutes

In this exercise, you'll change the priority of a command prompt that is already running to make it a high-priority command prompt.

Here's what you do:

1. Start a command prompt by opening the Start menu and choosing Programs.

2. Start the Task Manager by right-clicking on a blank area of the Taskbar and selecting Task Manager.

3. Select the Applications tab of the Task Manager.

12

4. From the list of tasks, select the command prompt that you started in step one and right-click it.

5. Select Go To Process from the shortcut menu.

6. With the process still selected, right-click again and select Set Priority. Click HIGH.

The command prompt that you changed to high priority cannot be blocked by NORMAL-priority processes.

TEST DAY FAST FACTS

Here are the fast facts about this chapter that you may want to know ahead of time. These facts provide great last-minute study material as well. Each bullet point below can be considered a short answer version of a main point explored elsewhere in this chapter.

- Task Manager is a quick, simple, and easily accessible tool for performing basic monitoring functions.

- Performance Monitor is a flexible and complex monitoring tool that can assess almost any situation.

- Task Manager provides information on processor(s) and memory only. It doesn't monitor any other resources.

- Performance Monitor has four views: Chart, Report, Alert, and Log. The Chart view can display line graphs or bar charts of current and historical data. The Report view provides a snapshot of the last values recorded. The Alert view is used to notify you of performance criteria you specify, even if you're not at your computer. The Log view is used to record performance information for later analysis.

- A *baseline* is a log of the performance data recorded when the system was operating normally. A baseline is intended as a reference for use when there are problems.

- Performance Monitor uses objects, which have counters, which can have instances.

Day 13

Monitoring and Optimizing Windows NT Workstation

Welcome to Day 13! You're almost done. However, after a few days of taking it easy, we're going to step it up a notch or two. We've got a lot of ground to cover in these last two days, so let's get started.

Objectives

Today we're going to cover the Monitoring and Optimization objective. Monitoring and Optimization has three subobjectives, listed here:

- Monitoring system performance by using various tools
- Identifying and resolving a given performance problem
- Optimizing system performance in various areas

Most understanding of how to optimize a system comes from understanding what to monitor and what the results mean. We'll explore these two concepts throughout the chapter.

- The Log view of Performance Monitor uses only objects (not counters and instances). All counters and instances are recorded for the log.

- Performance Monitor logs can be used with the Chart and Report views.

- Data from the Chart and Report views of Performance Monitor can be exported in tab- or comma-delimited text file formats.

- To monitor hard disk performance, you must enter the command DISKPERF -Y from a command prompt and reboot the machine.

- When a system needs more memory, the Pages/Sec counter will exceed 100, or the committed bytes will exceed the RAM.

- When a system needs more memory, the system might appear to have a disk problem because paging will consume all of the hard drive's time.

- When a system needs more or better disks, the % Disk Time counter in either the LogicalDisk or PhysicalDisk object will approach 100%.

- When a system needs a faster processor, either the % Total Processor Time in the System object or the % Processor Time counter(s) in the Processor object will approach 100%.

- When optimizing disks, try to put the paging file on a disk other than that used by the system or application programs.

13.1. Monitor System Performance by Using Various Tools

Windows NT Workstation provides two key applications that can be used to monitor performance:

- Task Manager
- Performance Monitor

You can use the Task Manager to get the basic performance information from a system. It's like taking your car to a gas station: It's a form of preventative maintenance, but it probably won't fix any major problems.

Performance Monitor, on the other hand, is very powerful and complex. Using this tool is like hiring one of the designers of your car to come help you work on it. Performance Monitor can tell you almost everything about your computer—much like the designer of the car could for your car.

Task Manager is used to get quick information on how Windows NT is doing and to fix minor problems. Performance Monitor helps solve more serious problems.

13.1.1. Task Manager

Task Manager is one of those little utilities that you would have coveted in Windows 3.1. As you learned in Chapter 12, it allows you to control applications and processes, even to the point of changing their priority. But Task Manager can do much more.

Task Manager can give you a quick indication of how much processor time is being used and how memory is being used, for example. These are two of the three main indicators that are used in performance tuning or *optimizing* a system. By looking at the way in which Windows NT uses memory and processor time, you can tell which component needs to be upgraded.

To start the Task Manager, right-click on a blank area of the Taskbar and select the Task Manager option. (Alternatively, you can press Ctrl+Alt+Del and select Task Manager from the Security dialog box.) The Task Manager appears, as shown in Figure 13.1. If the Performance tab isn't selected, select it now.

Figure 13.1.

The Task Manager can display the most important system performance information.

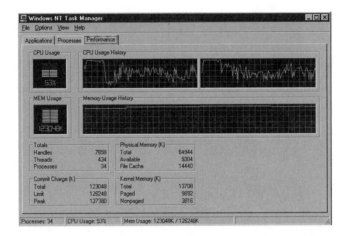

The Task Manager window displays two graphs and two audio level–type displays. The top audio level–type display shows the current processor usage, while the bottom one shows the current memory usage. The graphs offer a historic perspective of these values on the system. These graphs are great tools for determining how much memory and how much processor time has been used in the last few minutes.

If you have two processors, like the system shown in Figure 13.1, the processor graph will be divided into two graphs. Each one shows the processor activity history for one of the processors.

In addition to the graphical displays are a set of numeric counters that are important to learning how the system is performing. Table 13.1 provides an overview of these counters and their functions.

Table 13.1. Numeric counters.

Counter	Description
Totals: Handles	This counter tells you the total number of object handles and which handles are in use by the system. (Handles generally refer to files or devices.)
Totals: Threads	This counter tells you how many threads are currently running. Each process has at least one thread, so this number will always be greater than the number in Totals: Processes.

continues

13

Table 13.1. continued

Counter	Description
Totals: Processes	This counter tells you how many processes are currently running. This includes applications you are running as well as system services.
Physical Memory (K): Total	This counter displays the total amount of physical RAM that is installed in the system. This number will never change during Windows NT operation. It changes only when you change the amount of memory that is installed in the computer.
Physical Memory (K): Available	This counter displays the amount of memory that is available for use either by programs or by the file cache. It is possible to have more memory in use than physical memory and still have available memory. In this case, the paging file contains at least as much memory as there is available.
Physical Memory (K): File Cache	This counter displays how much physical memory is being used to cache file requests. This is a dynamic number that grows and shrinks as Windows NT reallocates resources to accommodate changing resource needs. This number tends to increase rapidly if there is available memory and heavy disk access.
Commit Charge (K): Total	This is the total amount of memory that is in use or committed, including physical memory and that used by the paging file. This number grows as programs use more memory and shrinks as programs use less memory. This counter doesn't change as a result of allocations to file caching.
Commit Charge (K): Limit	This is the limit of paging file space and physical memory that can be used by the system without extending the paging file.
Commit Charge (K): Peak	This shows the most memory the system has used since it was started. This counter generally reports a value close to that of the Commit Charge: Total counter, unless large applications have been opened and then closed.

Counter	Description
Kernel Memory (K): Total	The total amount of memory that is being used by the Windows NT kernel. In practical terms, this is the absolute minimum amount of memory you must have to start Windows NT.
Kernel Memory (K): Paged	The amount of memory that is being used by the Windows NT Kernel, which can be paged to disk to accommodate other programs if necessary.
Kernel Memory (K): Nonpaged	The amount of memory used by the kernel that cannot be paged under any circumstances. (This includes the reference table that indicates which memory pages are in memory and which ones are on disk.) It grows as the amount of used space in the paging file grows.

In the upcoming section "Identify and Resolve a Given Performance Problem," we'll discuss how you can use these counters to gain an understanding of what the problem is.

In addition to the counters on the Performance tab, you can also get useful information from the Processes tab. The Processes tab shows how much memory is currently in use by the application and how much processor time the program has used. This is important when you are trying to determine which program is responsible for a performance problem.

13.1.2. Performance Monitor

The Performance Monitor is the most comprehensive performance monitoring tool that Windows NT has, and it's quite complete in its capability to monitor different aspects of the system. However, it can seem a little complex at first.

Performance Monitor is based around objects and counters. Each *object* has one or more *counters*, which might have one or more *instances*.

Some of the common objects are

- Processor
- Memory
- Physical Disk
- System

13

Each of these objects has several counters. The following list shows the same objects with some of their common counters:

- **Processor**

   % Processor Time

   % Privileged Time

   % User Time

- **Memory**

   % Committed Bytes in Use

   Pages/Sec

   Available Bytes

- **Physical Disk**

   % Disk Time

   Avg. Disk Queue Length

   Disk Bytes/Sec

   Disk Transfers/Sec

- **System**

   % Total Processor Time

   % Total Privileged Time

   % Total User Time

   % Registry Quota in Use

Each of the counters relates to the object of which it is a part. You'll also notice that some objects contain counters similar to those of other objects. In particular, the System object contains some counters similar to those of the Processor object. However, there are differences. In the Processor counter, the processors are tracked individually. If a system has two processors, you will be given the opportunity to choose which processor to monitor. The System object, on the other hand, monitors only the total processor time.

Figure 13.2 shows the results of the System object's % Total Processor Time counter, as well as both instances of the Processor object's % Processor Time counter in a dual processor system. You will see that the System object's % Processor Time tracks the average usage of the two processors.

Figure 13.2.

The Processor object enables you to track specific instances of counters.

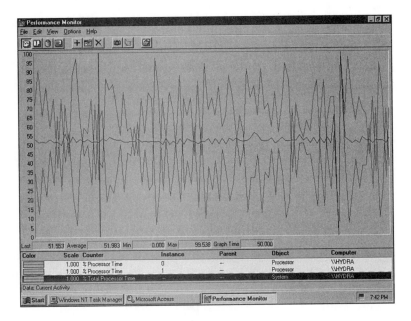

Performance Monitor has four views: Chart, Report, Alert, and Log. We'll cover these modes of operation in the next few sections.

Chart

Chart view is probably the most widely used view for people just getting acquainted with Performance Monitor. This is the view that comes up when you first start Performance Monitor, and it provides the quickest visual feedback.

In chart view, Performance Monitor can display information in one of two ways: as a line chart or as a histogram. The default display of Chart view is a line chart. In this mode, Performance Monitor records data points from each object, counter, and instance at regular intervals on the chart. In addition, if you specify that you want it to, Performance Monitor draws a line between these points. The top part of the screen shown in Figure 13.2 is an example of a line chart.

The other display mode in Chart view is a histogram. In this mode, Performance Monitor shows the last value measured from each object, counter, and instance. The result looks like a bar chart that is constantly changing. Figure 13.3 shows an example of a histogram.

13

Figure 13.3.

Histograms look like bar charts.

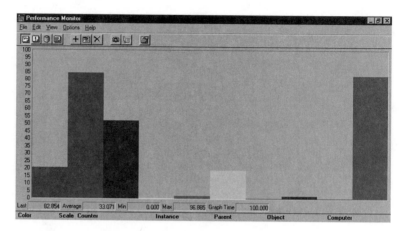

You can choose which view you would like and set other options by selecting Options, Chart. The Chart Options dialog box shown in Figure 13.4 appears.

Figure 13.4.

The Chart Options dialog box controls the view, update interval, and other details of how the chart looks.

Table 13.2 outlines the options of the Chart Options dialog box.

Table 13.2. Chart Options.

Option	Description
Legend	Determines whether or not Performance Monitor will display a legend indicating which lines represent which counters. This option should generally be left on.
Value Bar	Controls whether the Value bar is turned on or off. The Value bar is the bar at the bottom of the graph that indicates the last, minimum, maximum, and average values. The Value bar shows the values for the currently selected object, counter, and instance.
Vertical Grid	Adds vertical gridlines to the graph.

Option	Description
Horizontal Grid	Adds a horizontal grid.
Vertical Labels	Controls whether the Vertical Labels feature is turned on or off. Vertical Labels are the scale on the left side of the graph. This option should generally be left on.
Vertical Maximum	Defines the maximum value shown on the y-axis. Scaling factors are used on the objects, counters, and instances to get them within this range.
Update Time	Controls whether Performance Monitor automatically updates the graph at periodic intervals or waits for you to manually update the graph. The default is automatic update every second.

When you finish setting the chart options, you can add objects, counters, and instances you want displayed on the graph by selecting Edit, Add to Chart or by clicking the Add to Chart button on the toolbar. The Add to Chart dialog box appears, as shown in Figure 13.5.

Figure 13.5.

The Add to Chart dialog box enables you to add items to the current chart.

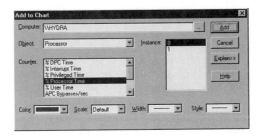

Table 13.3 describes the options in the Add Chart dialog box:

Table 13.3. Add Chart dialog box options.

Option	Description
Computer	The computer for which the object and counters will be displayed. The local system is the default; however, you can also specify any other system to which you have administrator privileges.
Object	The object that you want to monitor. This is a grouping of similar counters, such as System.

continues

13

Table 13.3. continued

Option	Description
Counter	The counter that you want to monitor. This is the specific item that you want to monitor.
Instance	The instance, or occurrence, that you want to watch. Some counters, such as the Physical Disk object's % Disk Time counter, can have more than one instance if there is more than one physical disk drive in the system. This determines which instance is being monitored.
Color	The color in which the line will be displayed on the screen. You use this setting to differentiate one graph line from another.
Scale	The scale used to represent the object, counter, and instance. For counters that deal with percentages, the default is 1.0. For other counters, such as Number of Bytes Transferred, the default may be 0.0001. This is the number that is multiplied with the actual result to obtain the value that is graphed. The scale is designed to allow all of the counters to fit in the same vertical scale.
Width	A value representing how wide the line is. It's also a way of differentiating lines on the graph.
Style	A value indicating how the line is drawn: for example, with or without dashes and what kind of dashes (if they're included). This further differentiates the lines.

You'll also note that the Add to Chart dialog box has an Explain button. You can click the Explain button to see a short description of the counter. Figure 13.6 shows the expanded Add to Chart dialog box with the explanation of the Processor object's % Processor Time counter.

Although Microsoft doesn't ask you specifically which counters do what, you might want to review the explanations for the objects and counters discussed here. Understanding the main objects and counters will improve your chances for success on this portion of the exam.

Figure 13.6.

The Explain button offers details about what the counter actually shows.

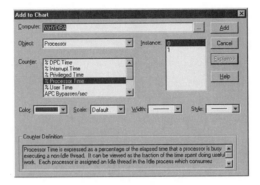

After you select the options you want to monitor, click the Add button to have the line added to your current chart. You see the line immediately, but the Add to Chart dialog box remains open so you can add more lines to the chart.

When you're finished adding objects, counters, and instances you want to track, click the Cancel button. This returns you to the Chart view, where the lines track your counters each second (if you didn't change the default update interval).

You can save your chart settings or export the chart if you want. You might want to save your settings and use them when you want to monitor a specific set of counters at different times. To save the chart settings, select File, Save Chart Settings. Performance Monitor saves all the objects, counters, and instances that you added, as well as their line colors, widths, styles, and scales.

Exporting the chart enables you to export the data that makes up the chart in either a tab-delimited value file or a comma-delimited value file. Microsoft Excel and Microsoft Access can read such files and use them for further analysis or to create more visually appealing graphs for presentations.

Report

Whereas Chart view is Performance Monitor's way of displaying data in a graphical format, Report view is its way of displaying numeric data. Report view is almost identical to Chart view when Chart view is in histogram display mode.

The Performance Monitor report shows the last value from every object, counter, and instance selected. The Add to Report dialog box offers no fancy options for selecting color, width, style, or scale. However, in all other respects, the Add to Report dialog box is the same as the Add to Chart dialog box.

To display the Report view, select View, Report. This opens a blank page like the one shown in Figure 13.7.

13

Figure 13.7.

Initially, Performance Monitor's Report mode is like a blank sheet of paper.

You can add counters to the blank page by selecting Edit, Add to Report or by clicking the Add to Report button on the toolbar. Figure 13.8 shows the result of adding the Processor object's % Processor Time counter for two processors as well as the System object's % Total Processor Time counter.

Figure 13.8.

In Report mode, Performance Monitor displays counters as raw numbers.

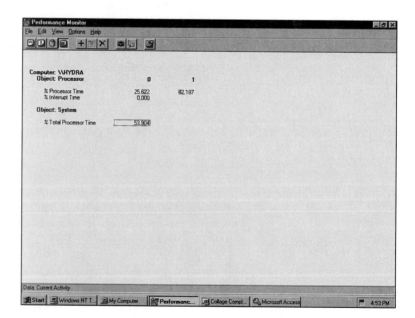

You can save your report settings or export the report just as you could save and export the chart. As you learned earlier, you can export the report in a tab-delimited or comma-delimited file format.

Alert

So far we've discussed how to view data as it happens. You've seen both a graphical and a textual means of reviewing performance data as it happens. However, this only goes so far. What happens when you're not there? How can you be informed of performance problems when you're not sitting next to the computer?

Performance Monitor's Alert view was designed for just this purpose. It enables you to leave Performance Monitor running when you're not there, and it can log the condition or notify you.

To display the Alert view of Performance Monitor, select View, Alert. Performance Monitor changes to the view shown in Figure 13.9.

Figure 13.9.

In Alert mode, you can be notified when a specified condition occurs.

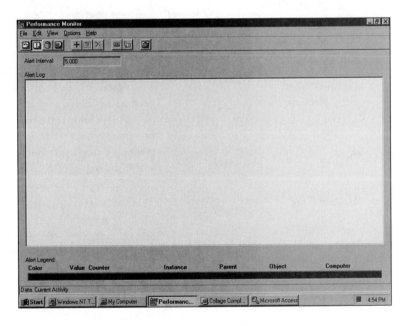

The first thing to do when setting up Alert view is to go to the options and set them to your preferences. To do so, select Options, Alert. The Alert Options dialog box shown in Figure 13.10 appears.

Figure 13.10.

With the Alert Options you can configure how the program as a whole runs.

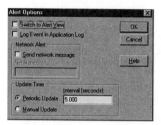

Table 13.4 describes each of the options in the Alert Options dialog box.

Table 13.4. Alert Options.

Option	Description
Switch to Alert View	This causes Performance Monitor to switch to Alert view when an alert is triggered.
Log Event in Application Log	This causes Performance Monitor to register an event in the Application log when an alert is triggered. This is useful when you have utility programs that monitor the Event log and notify you, or if you just want to log the problems.
Network Alert: Send Network Message	This option causes Performance Monitor to send a network broadcast message to the name specified in the Net Name text box. This option is useful if you aren't always around the server but want to make sure that you're notified of an alert no matter where you're logged in. The net name can be either a computer name or a user name.
Update Time	These options control whether Performance Monitor checks the Alert rules automatically or only at your command. If you choose the automatic periodic update option, you also set the update interval in seconds. This option should generally not be set lower than 5 seconds. A more typical update interval is 1 minute (60 seconds) or 5 minutes (300 seconds).

After you set up these global settings, you can start to add alerts to Performance Monitor by selecting Edit, Add to Alert or by pressing the Add to Alert button. The Add to Alert dialog box shown in Figure 13.11 appears.

Figure 13.11.

The Add to Alert dialog box enables you to control which objects, counters, and instances are monitored.

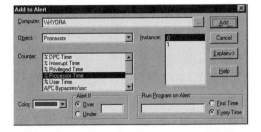

The Add to Alert dialog box is the same as the Add to Chart and Add to Report dialog boxes that you learned about in earlier sections of this chapter. However, this one has two new option groups, which are outlined in Table 13.5.

Table 13.5. The Add to Alert dialog box's unique options.

Option	Description
Alert If	Determines whether the alert is to occur if the value is over (in excess of) the number to the right, or whether the alert is to occur if the value is under (less than) the number specified.
Run Program on Alert	Enables Performance Monitor to run a program when the alert occurs. The program might be any batch file or executable program that Windows NT can run. This option is often used to run programs to send electronic mail or to page the administrator.
Run Program on Alert: First Time or Every Time	This option determines whether the program is run only the first time that the alert occurs or every time it occurs. If you use this option to send pages or mail, it's often best to run the program only once. This will notify you of the problem without driving you nuts with additional notifications.

If you set up an alert that becomes true, it will be listed in the Alert Log portion of the window, as shown in Figure 13.12. All of the alerts in the log can be exported to a tab- or comma-delimited text file, and the alert options can be saved for future use.

13

Figure 13.12.

Alerts appear in the Alert Log portion of the window.

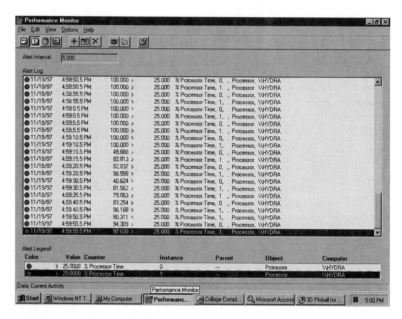

Log

The Chart and Report views of Performance Monitor enable you to see in real-time how the system is performing. The Alert view enables you to log and notify people of certain conditions on the system. The final view, Log view, provides a means of generating a system baseline or comparing a baseline to the current performance levels.

One of the fundamental rules of performance analysis is that you must measure a *baseline* for your system. That is, you must record performance data when your system is operating normally so that you can refer to this when you have a problem. You'll be able to compare object by object, counter by counter, and instance by instance which activities are the same and which activities are well beyond or below the performance levels of the original configuration.

In Log view, the Performance Monitor captures all the information for selected objects and writes it to a file that can be used later by the Chart or Report views. Figure 13.13 shows Performance Monitor's Log view.

Before specifying the log file and interval, you must select the objects you want to monitor. Unlike in other views where you can select an object, counter, and instance, you can specify only objects in Log view. All counters and instances for that object will automatically be recorded.

Figure 13.13.

Performance Monitor's Log view enables you to record performance measurements.

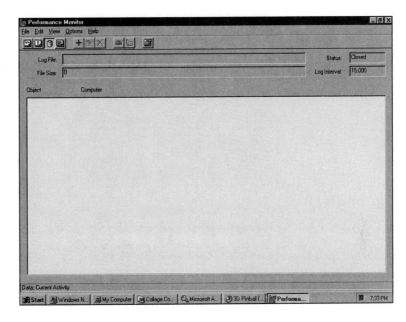

Warning

If you choose to log all the objects, the log file will grow very rapidly. Try to select only those objects that you definitely need to watch the first time you log data. This will minimize the amount of disk space the log consumes.

To add objects to be logged, select Edit, Add to Log or click the Add to Log button. The Add to Log dialog box shown in Figure 13.14 appears.

Figure 13.14.

The Add to Log dialog box enables you to add objects you want logged.

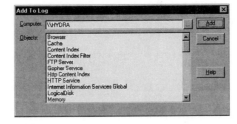

13

First you select the objects you want to monitor. Then you need to set up the log itself. To do so, select Options, Log. The Log Options dialog box shown in Figure 13.15 appears.

Figure 13.15.

In the Log Options dialog box, you set the options so Performance Monitor can start logging.

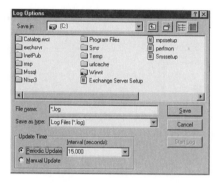

In addition to specifying the file to log to, you must indicate how the log will be updated. As in other views, you can have Performance Monitor do this automatically at specified intervals or manually at your command.

Generally, a log file is not updated as often as other views because all the data for all the objects is saved each time. This can cause a log file to grow rapidly if many objects are selected. The interval is also longer because log files generally are used to analyze trends and problems on a long-term basis, whereas the other modes of operation focus on more instant and real-time analysis. With a log, the momentary changes aren't as important as the long-term changes are.

Good intervals of time are 30 seconds, 1 minute, 5 minutes, or even 10 minutes. With intervals of 30 seconds or 1 minute, you can still see a lot of detail about the activity, and you'll have six times less or twelve times less detail (respectively) than if your interval were 5 seconds.

To start a log, you specify the name of the log and click Start Log. Performance Monitor closes the dialog box, and you're returned to the log screen that shows which objects are being logged. In the lower-right corner, you'll see an indicator of how much space the log has already used.

The value of making a log is dependent on how you use it later. When you want to use a log, choose the Option, Data From command in either Chart or Report view. The Data From dialog box appears (see Figure 13.16). Click the Log File option, specify the log you want to use, and click OK.

Having selected the file from which to retrieve the information, you can chart the data in the same way that you chart real-time data. However, only the objects that you selected when you recorded the log file will be available.

Figure 13.16.

The Data From dialog box enables you to retrieve data from a log file.

Figure 13.17 shows the result of charting the Processor object's % Processor Time counter and the System object's % Total Processor Time counter. Because the data collection was short, only a few data points are displayed.

Figure 13.17.

Performance Monitor can graph logged information the same way it can real-time data.

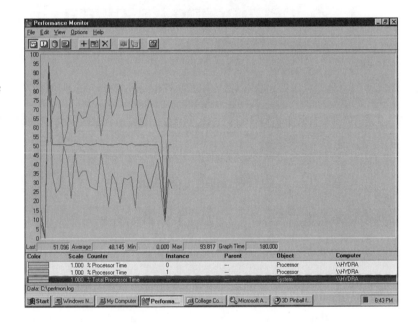

In some log files, particularly baseline log files, you might have to select a certain portion of the time to view instead of viewing the entire file. To select only a portion of time, choose the Edit, Time Window command. The Input Log File Timeframe dialog box shown in Figure 13.18 appears.

13

Figure 13.18.

In the Input Log File Timeframe dialog box, you can select the portion of a log file that you want to review.

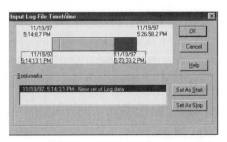

When you select a range of time in the time window, Performance Monitor expands the detail for that portion of time. While you're changing the times in the time window, you'll also see black vertical lines that represent the new beginning and end of the time window, so you can visually isolate the section for which you want to see more detail.

You'll need to be comfortable using all the views and features of Performance Monitor to be able to meet the next objective.

13.2. Identify and Resolve a Given Performance Problem

In section 13.1, you learned how to use Windows NT's tools for monitoring performance. In this section, you'll put those tools to practical use.

The Windows NT Workstation test requires you to identify a system problem given a set of performance information. Because you aren't given a baseline, you normally need to know only the tell-tale signs for particular problems.

13.2.1. Generating a Baseline

Before we begin identifying specific problems, let us stress again the importance of creating a baseline performance log file. The test emphasizes that the baseline is necessary, even if it doesn't provide you a baseline for reference in the questions.

The baseline performance log is designed to give you an understanding of what is "normal" for your particular system. You can create a baseline by selecting critical objects to monitor and leaving Performance Monitor running for a day. Some critical objects that you should include in any Performance Monitor evaluation are

- Processor
- Memory
- Physical Disk
- System
- Server

You should include these items in any baseline so you can refer to them later.

13.2.2. Identifying Disk Performance Problems

Disk performance is one of the most often overlooked factors of performance monitoring and capacity planning. Most people define servers in terms of processor and memory and rarely quote the speed of the disk drives. This is very strange considering that disk drives are the slowest components used in a server. Poor performance from the drives can bring a server to its knees even if it has a fast processor and a lot of memory.

Before monitoring disk performance in Windows NT, you have to turn on the disk performance counters. Because the disk counters reduce performance by about 1%, Windows NT leaves them turned off by default. To turn them on, run the command DISKPERF -Y at a command prompt and reboot your system.

> I generally turn on disk performance monitors when building the system to run the baseline and never turn them off. The disk performance is then monitored without notice. Although system performance is reduced by about 1%, most users don't notice the 1%—particularly if they've never had the extra 1% performance in the first place.
>
> If you decide you want to turn the disk counters off, run the command DISKPERF -N at a command prompt. Then you'll have to reboot for the change to take effect.

Next you need to decide whether you want to track performance on physical disks or logical disks. Because Windows NT supports multiple partitions on a disk and a single partition can span more than one disk, it's important to determine ahead of time what answers you're looking for. Generally, you will want to monitor physical disks because in most cases you're looking for bottlenecks. While you can determine the same information from the Logical Disks counter, using logical disks can sometimes obscure the meaning.

One of the key counters for both the PhysicalDisk and LogicalDisk objects is the % Disk Time counter. This number is a measurement of how busy Windows NT believes the drive to be.

For example, suppose you have software-based striping set up across three drives. You have a volume set on two of those drives, and the system volume uses the remaining disk space on the other drive. Let's call the stripe set D and the volume set E. The system volume is C.

13

You've got a performance problem, but you can't figure out where it is. You decide to monitor both the PhysicalDisk and LogicalDisk objects. You see that the % Disk Time for disk 0 is 85%. The other two disks have times of about 20% each. Looking at the logical disk counters, you see that drive C's % Disk Time is about 65%, drive D's time is about 20%, and there is almost no use of drive E.

The first thing that jumps out at you from the physical disk results is that disk 0 is overworked. However, this fact is obscured when you look at the numbers from the LogicalDisk object because there's no direct correlation to indicate that a specific drive is being affected.

For the test, a correct solution to this problem would be to put the system partition on its own drive. That would eliminate the contention. The other issue the test might bring up is that the paging file should be on its own disk (see the section "Optimizing the Paging File," later in this chapter). In the described scenario, paging is most likely occurring on the system partition that is already overworked.

In addition to the % Disk Time counter, several other counters can show activity of the disk drive. However, the % Disk Time counter offers the easiest way to determine what the problem is. You can identify problem areas in the disk subsystem by reviewing the % Disk Time counter (which shouldn't remain at 100% for very long periods) or by checking the Avg. Disk Queue Length counter. This counter should remain very low, with a reading of no more than 1.

When you identify a disk problem, try to be sure that the disk performance isn't masking the greater problem of lack of memory.

13.2.3. Identifying Memory Problems

Problems related to the amount of memory that's installed are among the trickiest performance problems to identify in Windows NT. NT's memory manager is so good that it will try to make even very bad memory situations workable.

Windows NT's virtual memory manager enables NT to run more applications than it has physical RAM for. This is useful in times when you need more memory than you have and you are willing to accept the performance penalty just to be able to run the program. It's also useful if you load many applications in the morning and switch among them all day. Even though all of them are in memory, you use only one at a time.

Keeping the applications in memory, even if that memory is virtual memory on disk, speeds up access to the application because it eliminates the overhead needed to start the application. The application is already running.

In an ideal situation, Windows NT has enough RAM for the applications currently running, as well as a small amount of space left over to use for file caching. Windows NT handles file caching automatically, allocating available memory to file caching. This improves disk performance, but it works only when NT has memory that isn't being used by applications.

Identifying memory problems isn't as easy as identifying disk problems because no individual counter directly indicates a memory problem. Instead, there are a couple of key indicators to look for.

First, you should watch the Memory: Committed Bytes counter. This counter shows how much memory (virtual and physical) is in use. If this number always exceeds the physical RAM by more than a few megabytes, you probably don't have sufficient RAM. As the counter gets higher, the system will have to page memory in and out more frequently to handle both the running programs and the applications that are in memory.

The second indicator to watch is the Pages/Sec counter. This counter indicates how many pages per second are being moved to and from memory to satisfy requests. This number should be less than 100. Anything higher indicates that the system is probably RAM starved. Note, however, that the Pages/Sec counter is very sensitive and won't drop to zero even on a system that has plenty of RAM. For instance, a system that has only 80MB of committed bytes and has 128MB of RAM still reports a Pages/Sec counter in excess of 100 if an application or a large file is being loaded. What's important with this counter is that the sustained, or average, value remains under 100.

13.2.4. Identifying Processor Problems

Identifying processor problems is perhaps one of the easiest performance monitoring tasks. You don't have to turn anything on, and you don't have to decide which objects to watch. The indicators are just crystal clear.

The processor time is monitored with three main counters of the Processor object:

- % Processor Time
- % User Time
- % Privileged Time

The % Processor Time counter shows the total amount of processor time that was used on non-idle (LOW priority) threads. This includes both application processing and operating system processing.

13

The % User Time counter gives the total amount of processor time used in non-idle threads of user applications. This doesn't include system operations.

The % Privileged Time counter indicates the total amount of processor time used in non-idle threads of the operating system. The % Privileged Time value plus the % User Time value is the same as the % Processor Time value.

When determining if processing is a bottleneck, you must either include all processors in the Performance Monitor or use the counters from the System object instead of the Processor object because the System object results summarize the numbers.

Opinions vary on when to upgrade processors. Some people believe that a processor should be upgraded when its usage reaches 70–80%. I feel that the processor should be upgraded if it consistently reports usage in excess of 80%. It's clear that the processor is a bottleneck if the usage reaches and remains at 100%.

13.3. Optimize System Performance in Various Areas

Most of the time, the goal of performance monitoring is to optimize a subsystem or subsystems to improve performance. However, some people just like to do it for no reason! Sometimes you can improve performance by optimizing the resources that you already have; other times it means optimizing your purchases and additions to the system to receive the "most bang for your buck."

Once you identify the area that's causing the bottleneck (as you learned in the last few sections), it's time to focus on upgrading or reconfiguring the system to improve performance.

13.3.1. Optimizing Disk Usage

Short of buying faster disk drives or more disk drives, you can do very little to improve disk performance. However, try these suggestions for helping poorly performing disks:

- *Defragment your disks.* Fragmentation occurs when files are not stored in sequentially numbered sectors on the hard drive. This causes the disk drive to have to move the read/write head to multiple locations on the drive, which is a very slow mechanical operation. By using a defragmenter, you can reduce or eliminate fragmentation and improve performance.

- *Convert volume sets to stripe sets.* Windows NT supports volume sets, which enable a system to use multiple disks but don't improve performance, and stripe sets, which enable a system to use multiple disks and do improve performance. If possible, convert volume sets to stripe sets. This will improve performance by enabling the system to use both disks to read and write data instead of only one at a time.

- *Separate system, paging, and application activity.* There are three kinds of activity. System activity is initiated by the system reading or writing files to the system partition. Paging activity occurs when the virtual memory manager writes out memory to disk. Application activity comes from users and their applications. If possible, separate these three activities by putting them on three different drives.

When purchasing additional disks, consider the following things:

- *Disk access time.* The amount of time it takes the drive to reposition and retrieve data can significantly affect the overall throughput of the drive.

- *Maximum sustained throughput.* The more data the drive can continue to send out, the better. Burst throughput of the drive is of lesser importance because it generally refers to the speed at which the drive can transfer information from its cache.

- *Rotational speed.* This is how fast the platters spin inside the drive. The faster the platter spins, the quicker information will be under the read/write head and the faster it can be read.

When planning for additional drive space, also consider using stripe sets. Minimally, stripe sets double the performance of a drive set when compared with just the single drive. The performance improves even more as drives are added to the stripe set.

13.3.2. Optimizing the Paging File

One of the most important parts of Windows NT that can be tuned and changed is the paging file. An inappropriately sized paging file or a paging file that's not on the best partition can significantly reduce the performance of the system.

The first decision for the paging file is how big it should be initially. To determine this, boot the system and run the programs you normally run on a daily basis. Then subtract the amount of physical RAM from the peak committed bytes. This gives you a paging file that, under most circumstances, shouldn't need to be increased.

13

When Windows NT is forced to extend a paging file, it takes longer and generally creates paging files that are more fragmented. This further increases the amount of time that NT spends paging.

With regard to the maximum amount of space that the file should take up, this is normally used to prevent Windows NT from creating a very large paging file on a slow drive or a small one on a fast drive. If you have only one drive, you should set the maximum size of the paging file very large.

The next decision is where to place the paging file. The best place for a paging file is on a disk that isn't used for any other purpose. This ensures that memory requests are not queued behind application or system requests. However, this isn't always possible. The next best place to put the paging file is on the fastest drive or stripe set so the paging file can get the most possible speed. However, this must be measured against the rest of the activity on the disk. Even a very fast drive array might not be the best decision if it is heavily used.

13.3.3. Optimizing RAM Usage

RAM is a precious commodity that you can't afford to squander. Even with prices as low as they are today, it always seems that memory is in short supply.

You can do two key things to make better use of your RAM:

- *Eliminate unneeded services and programs.* Every service and utility takes up memory. If you have services installed on Windows NT that you don't need, remove them or prevent them from starting automatically. If you've got utilities running automatically in your startup group that you don't need, remove them. Reducing the amount of memory that's used even by a little bit can make a big impact on performance.

- *For the services that you do use, change the amount of memory that they use to run.*

The memory savings you'll gain by following these tips might not be a lot, but that is often the case with optimizations: You don't get huge performance increases, you just try to string together a series of small improvements.

Lab

We covered a lot of ground today. The labs will review your understanding of the monitoring and optimization topics that you need to know to pass the test. Answers to the review questions are at the end of the section.

Review Questions

1. You are having problems with performance on your computer. When you run programs, Windows NT seems to become unresponsive. You want to quickly check the activity on your system to try to identify the culprit. Which tool should you use?

   A. Performance Monitor

   B. Windows NT Diagnostics

   C. The System applet in the Control Panel

   D. Task Manager

2. You've got a problem that you can't track down. You're trying to determine why your system becomes unresponsive for a minute or so and then starts functioning normally. When it becomes unresponsive, you can't do anything, so you want to set up the program before the problem occurs. Which utility should you use?

   A. Performance Monitor

   B. Windows NT Diagnostics

   C. The System applet in the Control Panel

   D. Task Manager

3. You're trying to determine how busy drive C is in order to decide if you should buy a faster hard drive. Your system is partitioned with drives C and D on the first physical disk. Which object should you monitor?

   A. PhysicalDisk

   B. LogicalDisk

   C. Processor

   D. Memory

13

4. You're trying to determine how busy drive E is. Drive E is a stripe across three disks—disk 1, disk 2, and disk 3. Which object should you monitor to determine if you need to add another drive to the stripe?

   A. PhysicalDisk

   B. LogicalDisk

   C. Processor

   D. Memory

5. You've determined that your disk drives are a bottleneck. What else should you check before purchasing new hard drives?

   A. Memory

   B. Processor

   C. Network

   D. Nothing

6. You run a graphics program occasionally, and you notice that your processor time routinely jumps up to 100% while running it, but it doesn't stay there long. Do you need a faster processor?

   A. No, the processor is only a bottleneck if the usage indicator stays at a high level.

   B. No, you need more memory.

   C. No, you need a faster disk.

   D. Yes, the processor activity should never be allowed to reach 100%.

7. You notice that the Page/Sec counter is very high. What is the most likely bottleneck in this computer?

   A. Processor

   B. RAM

   C. Disk

   D. Network

8. You create a performance log for a system that is currently having trouble. You can't identify a value that is out of range. To what should you compare your log file?

A. The baseline that is published by your hardware manufacturer.

B. The baseline that is published by Microsoft.

C. The baseline on the first system you ever worked on.

D. The baseline taken on this system when it was running fine.

9. Bill reports performance problems with his workstation. He indicates that the problem seems to occur only when he starts his computer. What do you suspect is the problem?

A. The processor speed needs to be increased.

B. The RAM needs to be increased.

C. The disk needs to be reconfigured.

D. The paging file's initial size isn't correct.

10. What does the Processor object's % Privileged Time counter represent?

A. The total amount of processor time that was spent.

B. The total amount of time the processor spent servicing privileged users' jobs.

C. The total amount of time the processor spent servicing kernel processes.

D. The total amount of time the processor spent servicing user processes.

11. You want to look for specific problems on your system, but you don't want to sit and watch for them. Which Performance Monitor view would be best?

A. Chart

B. Report

C. Log

D. Alert

Answers to Review Questions

1. D Because you need a quick check without minute details, Task Manager is the right option. It's quick and easily accessible.

2. A The Performance Monitor is the best fit here because it enables you to log objects at periodic intervals. After the Performance Monitor is started, the problem can be reproduced to create a log file you can use to identify the problem.

3. A The PhysicalDisk counter will probably give you the best information here because you are trying to determine if you need to buy a faster drive for the system partition.

4. B Because the logical disk you're trying to monitor spans multiple physical disks, it's best to review the performance of the logical disk instead of the three physical disks that make up the logical disk.

5. A Memory problems often appear as disk bottlenecks because of the paging that occurs. Before you assume that a disk is causing the problem, you should also check the memory.

6. A Although a faster processor would improve performance, it's probably not the best upgrade because that program isn't run all the time; it's run only occasionally.

7. B A high Pages/Sec counter indicates a problem with RAM, or memory. This counter shows the total number of reads and writes made to and from the disks to service memory needs.

8. D Baselines are not published by Microsoft or hardware vendors. They are log files that you need to create for each system.

9. D If the initial paging file isn't set correctly, the computer performs slowly until Windows NT properly extends the paging file.

10. C rivileged processor time is the time spent servicing kernel processes.

11. D Alert mode can identify problems and when they occur. Log mode is a close second, but it won't pinpoint problems. Whereas logging only saves the information for later, the Alert mode can look for and alert you to specific issues.

Exercises

These exercises will walk you through a practical use for some of the topics we've discussed today.

Exercise 13.1: Generate a Baseline

Time Estimate: 1 day elapsed time, 10 minutes to set up

In this exercise, you're going to walk through creating a baseline. You can then refer to the baseline if you have problems with the system in the future.

To create a log file that can be used as a baseline, perform the following steps:

1. If disk performance hasn't been turned on, turn it on by entering **DISKPERF -Y** at a command prompt. Then reboot.

2. Start the Performance Monitor by selecting Start, Programs, Administrative Tools (Common), Performance Monitor.

3. Change to the Log view by selecting View, Log.

4. Select Edit, Add to Log to open the Add to Log dialog box.

5. Add the following objects to the log: Processor, System, Physical Disk, Logical Disk, and Memory.

6. Add other objects that you want or need in your baseline.

7. Close the Add to Log dialog box by clicking Cancel.

8. Select the Log, Options command to display the Log Options dialog box.

9. Select a file to which to save the log.

10. Set the log interval to 1 minute (or whatever you would prefer).

11. Click the Start Log button.

12. Minimize the Performance Monitor.

13. Wait approximately 24 hours, and then restore Performance Monitor. You can stop the steps sooner, but you won't have as much information.

14. Select Options, Log to display the Log Options dialog box.

15. Click the Stop Log button.

16. Click Cancel to close the dialog box.

You'll want to save the log file you've created in a place where you'll be able to find it if there is a problem. You might put it on a floppy disk and store it with the emergency repair disk for the system.

Exercise 13.2: Graph a Performance Monitor Log File

Time Estimate: 10 minutes

In this exercise, you'll review a Performance Monitor log file using the Chart view of Performance Monitor. To complete this exercise, you need a log file, such as the baseline file you created in the previous exercise.

13

To chart some objects from a log file, perform the following steps:

1. Start the Performance Monitor by selecting Start, Program, Administrative Tools (Common), Performance Monitor.

2. Select Options, Data From to retrieve the data for the chart from a log file.

3. Specify the log file that you want to read. You can browse your drive and locate the file by clicking the ellipsis button just to the right of the filename.

4. Click OK to close the Data From dialog box.

5. Select Edit, Add to Chart to add objects, counters, and instances to the chart window.

6. Select the object, counter, and instances you want to graph. If you are using the log created in the previous exercise, select the System object's % Total Processor Time counter. You might also want to select the PhysicalDisk object's % Disk Time counter for each drive that you have installed.

7. Click Cancel to close the Add to Chart dialog box and view the graph of the data collected in the log.

You can also refine the information that you see in the chart by changing the time window displayed. To refine the information displayed, perform the following steps:

1. Select the Edit, Time Window command.

2. Place your mouse pointer on the left bar in the time window dialog box and drag it to the new start time for the time period you want to view. A black vertical line moves through the graph as you move the start time. Stop your mouse pointer when the black line reaches the section for which you want to see more detail.

3. Place your mouse pointer on the right bar in the time window dialog box and drag it to the new end time. A black vertical bar appears on the right side of the screen and moves to the left as you adjust the end time.

4. Click OK to accept the new time window.

You can continue to refine the time you want to see by repeating the preceding procedure.

Exercise 13.3: Use Task Manager to Optimize Your Paging File

Time Estimate: 15 minutes

In this exercise, you'll determine an optimal initial paging file size based on the information you get from Task Manager.

To start this process, you must determine how much RAM your system normally needs. To do so, perform the following steps:

1. Restart your computer. This resets the peak amount of RAM that has been used. The peak amount of RAM is the major factor you will use to determine the correct initial size for the paging file.

2. Log in to Windows NT.

3. Start the Task Manager application.

4. Select the Performance tab.

5. Minimize the Task Manager.

6. Start the applications you run on a daily basis. You should run them simultaneously if you normally run them at the same time. Be sure to open files of about the same size as those you open on a daily basis.

7. Restore the Task Manager.

8. Subtract the amount of physical memory from the Commit Charge: Peak value. The number you get is the amount of memory you should use for the initial paging file size.

To change the initial size of the paging file, perform the following steps:

1. Run the System applet of the Control Panel by selecting Start, Settings, Control Panel, System.

2. Click the Virtual Memory button.

3. Select the first drive where the paging file exists.

4. Set the initial size so that when you've set all the paging file locations, the total initial sizes match or slightly exceed the number obtained from the previous procedure. Then click the Set button.

5. If the paging file is on more than one drive, select the next drive. Repeat step 4 for each drive.

6. Click OK to close the Virtual Memory dialog box.

7. Click OK to close the System applet of the Control Panel.

Your paging file now meets the initial memory needs of your system during your daily routine. This should improve performance by eliminating Windows NT's need to continually extend the paging file.

13

TEST DAY FAST FACTS

Here are some fast facts about troubleshooting Windows NT Workstation that you need to know to pass the exam. Each bullet point below can be considered a short-answer version of a main point explored elsewhere in the chapter.

- The `BOOT.INI` file provides the menu of operating systems shown on the boot menu.

- To hide a printer share, you add a dollar sign character to the end of the share name, as in *sharename$*.

- A print job spooled to a printer is written as a temporary file to the `%systemroot%\System32\Spool\Printers` folder.

- Spooled print job files are deleted after the printer indicates that the job has been printed.

- The most common print spool problem is a lack of available disk space.

- If an application is malfunctioning, bring up the Task Manager and close the process.

- If you need to end a 16-bit Windows application or an MS-DOS application, you must close the entire session. When you need to close a 32-bit Windows application, you have to close only that particular process or thread.

Day 14

Troubleshooting Windows NT Workstation

Welcome to your last day. If you were hoping to breeze through it without spending much time, I apologize for disappointing you. The troubleshooting section is one of the largest on the exam and contains several objectives. There are seven objectives for today, and all are fairly detailed. On the positive side, most of them have been introduced already. For example, choosing the appropriate course of action to take when the installation process fails was covered to some degree in the installation discussion in the first few chapters of this book.

Objectives

This chapter deals with the seven subobjectives of the Troubleshooting objective. Those seven subobjectives are

- Choosing the appropriate action when the boot process fails

- Choosing the appropriate action when a print job fails

- Choosing the appropriate action when the installation process fails

- Choosing the appropriate action when an application fails

- Choosing the appropriate action when a user cannot access a resource

- Modifying the Registry using the appropriate tool

- Implementing advanced techniques to resolve various problems

14.1. Choosing the Appropriate Action When the Boot Process Fails

The failure of Windows NT Workstation to start up properly and load the Windows NT shell (a problem with the boot process) is one of the most aggravating problems of all. It could be likened to trying to shut off your car alarm when you've locked the keys inside; when you don't have access to the car (or the system), your problems are compounded.

The key to troubleshooting and solving boot problems lies in understanding the logical sequence the workstation uses when starting up. When a problem occurs, Windows NT typically shows you one of several boot-sequence errors, the meaning of which should help you determine the origin of the problem. You can also examine the BOOT.INI file to determine the nature of problems, and you can use emergency repair disks to boot your system and repair common boot-process failure problems.

14.1.1. The POST Sequence

Your computer begins the operating-system boot sequence after the Power On Self Test (POST) completes itself. The first series of messages that you see when you turn on the power to your computer are hardware related and are not associated with the boot process. Your memory is tested, for example, and then your bus structure is tested. Your computer runs a series of tests that signal to peripheral devices and sense the devices' replies to check for successful I/O performance. You may see a series of messages indicating that your mouse and keyboard are detected, the presence of an IDE drive, whether a SCSI adapter is detected, responses from any devices on that SCSI chain, and so forth. Failure at this stage isn't a boot-sequence problem.

The boot sequence initiates when the hard drive Master Boot Record (MBR) is read into memory and begins to load the different portions of the Windows NT operating system. Windows NT Workstation runs on different microprocessor architectures. The exact boot sequence depends on the type of microprocessor on which you have installed Windows NT Workstation.

14.1.2. The Boot Sequence

Windows NT loads on an Intel x86 computer by reading a file called the NTLDR or NT Loader into memory from the boot sector of the startup or active partition on your boot drive. NTLDR is a hidden system file set to be read-only. NTLDR is located in the root folder of your system partition and can be viewed in the Windows NT Explorer by choosing the View All File Type option. NTLDR performs the following actions:

- Turns on the 32-bit flat memory model required by the Windows NT kernel in order to address RAM.

- Turns on the minifile system driver to access the system and boot partitions.

- Displays the Boot Loader menu on your monitor from which you select the operating system to use. These available options are contained in the BOOT.INI file in your %systemroot% directory.

Note You can install Windows NT Workstation over a previous installation of MS-DOS or Windows 95. These operating systems will appear in the menu and call the BOOTSECT.DOS file when they are loaded and executed. BOOTSECT.DOS loads and then hands off control at the end of the boot process to the operating system component that's responsible for I/O communication. In Windows 95, that file is the IO.SYS file.

The following steps round out the boot process:

- After you select an operating system, a hardware-detection routine is initiated. For Windows NT, the NTDETECT.COM program is responsible for this routine; it creates a hardware list and passes it to the NTLDR program.

- The operating system kernel is then loaded. The NTOSKRNL.EXE file located in the %systemroot%\System32 folder is called to load the kernel of Windows NT. The menu screen is replaced by the OS Loader V4.00 screen.

- A blue screen appears while the Hardware Abstraction Layer (HAL) is being loaded. To execute this function, the HAL.DLL is called with a set of routines that isolate operating-system functions from I/O.

- The HKEY_LOCAL_MACHINE\System hive of the Registry is read and the system is loaded. Registry hives are stored as files in the %systemroot%\System32\Config folder.

- The boot time drivers HKEY_LOCAL_MACHINE\System\CurrentControlSet\Control\ServiceGroupOrder are loaded. As each driver is loaded, a dot is added to the OS Loader screen.

14

> **Note** If you include the /SOS switch in the BOOT.INI file, Windows NT will list each driver's name on the OS Loader screen as Windows NT Workstation starts up. The dots that appear during normal bootup represent the drivers being loaded; the SOS switch converts these dots to the filenames.

- The list of supported hardware devices is handed off from NTDETECT.COM to NTOSKRNL.EXE.

- After NTOSKRNL.EXE executes, the computer's boot phase is finished. Then the system starts to load the software you have installed.

> **Note** A RISC computer contains the NTLDR software as part of its BIOS. Therefore, the boot phase of a RISC-based computer is both simpler and faster than the boot phase of an Intel x86 computer. A RISC computer keeps its hardware configuration in its BIOS, which obviates the need for the NTDETECT.COM file. Another item kept in firmware is the list of valid operating systems and how to access them. This means that a RISC computer also doesn't use a BOOT.INI file.
>
> A RISC computer boots by loading a file called the OSLOADER.EXE file. After reading the hardware configuration from the BIOS and executing, OSLOADER.EXE hands off the boot process to the NTOSKRNL.EXE. Then the HAL.DLL is loaded, followed by the system file, which ends the RISC Windows NT boot process.

Because BOOT.INI is an ASCII text file, you can edit this file to control aspects of the boot process. Open Windows NT Explorer and remove the read-only and system attributes from the file (which is located in the %systemroot% top-level folder) before you begin. When you open the file, you will see two sections in the BOOT.INI: the [boot loader] and [operating systems] sections shown in the following sample.

```
[boot loader]
timeout=30
default=multi(0)disk(0)rdisk(0)partition(1)\WINWKSTN
[operating systems]
multi(0)disk(0)rdisk(0)partition(1)\WINWKSTN="Windows NT Workstation Version
➥4.00"
multi(0)disk(0)rdisk(0)partition(1)\WINWKSTN="Windows NT Workstation Version 4.00
➥[VGA mode]" /basevideo /sos
```

```
multi(0)disk(0)rdisk(0)partition(1)\WINNT="Windows NT Server Version 4.00"
multi(0)disk(0)rdisk(0)partition(1)\WINNT="Windows NT Server Version 4.00 [VGA
➥mode]" /basevideo /sos
C:\="Microsoft Windows"
```

You will see parameters that control the time a user has to decide on an operating system (timeout), as well as the default location in an ARC-compliant (Advanced RISC-compliant) path nomenclature. There are two ways to change these values, one of which is performed here in the file itself. The other, which is much easier, involves changing these parameters on the Startup/Shutdown tab of the System Properties dialog box, which will be discussed momentarily.

For the test, you should know that changing the timeout parameter to 0 tells the system not to display the boot menu but to always boot the default. Making the timeout parameter -1 turns off the countdown for how long the menu is displayed forcing the system to always wait as long as is necessary for the user to make a choice.

To change system startup parameters using the System Properties dialog box, complete the following steps:

1. Right-click the My Computer icon and choose the Properties command from the shortcut menu to access the System Properties dialog box.

2. Click the Startup/Shutdown tab of the System Properties dialog box if necessary. A screen similar to that shown in Figure 14.1 appears.

Figure 14.1.

The System Properties dialog box.

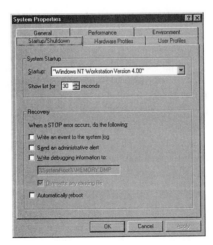

14

3. In the Startup list box, select the desired default operating system from the choices offered.

4. Change the timeout parameter in the Show List for Seconds spinner box.

Note

The spinner box enables you to choose any number up to 999 seconds. If you manually edit the file, however, you can enter virtually any number (even exceeding 999 by whatever number you desire), and the countdown will begin at that number.

5. Click the OK button to close the System Properties dialog box.

There is one major advantage to making changes in the System Properties dialog box instead of manually editing the BOOT.INI file: The dialog boxes allow you to select only valid choices. However, when you enter information into the BOOT.INI file, you run the risk of making a mistake that could cause your system to fail at boot up.

Note

If you encounter a blue-screen error, you might need to do a *memory dump* of your system for diagnostic purposes. A memory dump is a copy of the data held in RAM. To save that file, you need free disk space equal to the amount of your installed RAM plus an additional 1MB of space.

To do a memory dump, check the Write Debugging Information To and Overwrite Any Existing File check boxes in the Startup/Shutdown tab of the System Properties dialog box, as shown in Figure 14.2.

The memory dump file is written to the location displayed in the text box at the bottom of the Startup/Shutdown tab. Notice the default location for the dumps is a file called MEMORY.DMP in the %systemroot% folder. The .DMP extension indicates that the file is not ASCII readable and must be viewed with other utilities.

Close the dialog box and confirm any alerts about page-file size if necessary. Then reboot your computer.

Figure 14.2.

Selecting memory-dump options in the System Properties dialog box.

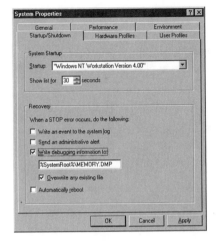

14.1.3. The Load Process

After the boot portion of the operating system loads, your device drivers are loaded, and the boot process is handed off to the operating-system kernel. In Windows NT, this portion of the startup occurs when the screen turns a blue color and the text shrinks. At that point, the kernel is initializing.

The operating system begins to read various hives in the Windows NT Registry. One of the first hives read is the CurrentControlSet, which is copied to the CloneControlSet and from which a HARDWARE key is written to RAM. The System hive is read to determine whether any other additional drivers need to be loaded into RAM and initialized. This ends the kernel-initialization phase.

The Session Manager then reads the System hive in the Registry to determine which programs must be loaded before Windows NT is loaded. Commonly, the AUTOCHK.EXE program (a stripped-down version of CHKDSK.EXE) runs and reads the file system. Other programs defined in the HKEY_LOCAL_MACHINE\SYSTEM\ CurrentControlSet\Control\SessionManager\BootExecute key are run, and a page file is then created and stored in the HKEY_LOCAL_MACHINE\SYSTEM\ CurrentControlSet\Control\Session Manager\Memory Management key.

14

Next, the Software hive is read, and then the Session Manager loads other required subsystems as defined in the HKEY_LOCAL_MACHINE\SYSTEM\CurrentControlSet\ Control\Session Manager\Subsystems\Required key. This ends the portion of the boot process in which services are loaded into RAM.

After services are loaded, the Windows WIN32 subsystem starts to load. This is where Windows NT Workstation switches into a Graphics (GUI) mode. The WINLOGON module runs, and the login dialog box appears. The Windows operating system is still loading at this point, but the user can enter his user name, domain, and password to initiate the logon process.

After the Service Controller (SERVICES.EXE) loads and initializes the Computer Browser service, Workstation service, Server service, Spooler service, and so on, the request for logon is passed to the domain controller for service.

The SERVICES.EXE program is a central program in the Windows NT operating system. It initializes various system DLL files. Should this file become damaged, you must reinstall Windows NT Workstation. The following DLLs provide operating-system services:

- *Alerter* (ALRSVC.DLL). Provides messaging services and event alerts.
- *Computer Browser* (BROWSER.DLL). Provides a way for locating resources on the network.
- *EventLog* (EVENTLOG.DLL). Notes and enters events into the three log files.
- *Messenger* (MSGSVC.DLL). Provides interapplication communications that enable one application to communicate with another.
- *Net Logon* (NETLOGON.DLL). Contains the code required to request resource validation from domain servers.
- *NT LM Security Support Provider* (NTLMSSPS.DLL). Provides security support.
- *Server* (SRVSVC.DLL). Enables Windows NT Workstation to provide limited network services to other computers.
- *TCP/IP NetBIOS Helper* (LMHSVC.DLL). Handles IP address resolution.
- *Workstation* (WKSSVC.DLL). Enables a Windows NT Workstation computer to access resources on the network. Workstation includes services that enable the computer to log on to a domain, to connect to shared resources such as printers and directories, and to participate in client/server applications running over the network.

When the boot process is completed, it's considered a successful logon. To mark the event, Windows NT Workstation updates the LastKnownGood control set key in the Registry with information about what was loaded and the current system configuration at startup.

14.1.4. Last Known Good Recovery

The Last Known Good configuration provides a method for recovering to your preceding system setup. When you create a specific configuration for Windows NT, that information is stored in a particular control set. The LastKnownGood control set enables you to recover from a boot process error—provided that you use this method immediately after discovering the error on the first bootup attempt and that you do not log on a second time. Subsequent boots (if they proceed and you log on to the system again) rule out this option as a recovery method. Every logon counts as a successful logon and becomes the point to which you can return.

The information in the LastKnownGood control set is stored in the Registry in the HKEY_LOCAL_MACHINE\SYSTEM\CurrentControlSet key. If you encounter a problem that prevents you from logging in or prevents your hardware from working, use these steps to boot to the Last Known Good configuration:

1. Reboot your system.
2. When a message appears asking you whether you want to boot the Last Known Good configuration, press the Spacebar.
3. When the Hardware Profile/Configuration Recovery menu appears, select a hardware profile and press the L key for the Last Known Good configuration.

In the event of a critical system error, Windows NT Workstation attempts to default to the Last Known Good configuration on its own accord. This doesn't always happen, but it is a frequent occurrence.

Should basic operating-system files be damaged, you must boot up using a boot floppy and then recover your system as described in the next few sections.

14.1.5. Boot-Sequence Errors

The most common cause of boot-sequence errors is that the operating-system components required for the boot process cannot be found or are corrupted. Often a modification of the BOOT.INI file leads to a failure to boot properly. If you or your client has recently made a modification to the startup files, you should suspect that first.

14

Catastrophic hardware failure is not a common problem, but it does occur—particularly in older equipment. If a hard drive stops operating, you often can tell either by the silence that remains when you can't hear the hard drive spin up and achieve its operating speed or by banshee-style screeching.

Much less obvious are hardware errors that prevent your system from starting up without noticeably altering the performance of your system. For example, if your hard drive develops a bad disk sector in the area that contains the operating system components responsible for booting your computer, the computer appears to function correctly. However, in order to boot the system, you must reestablish the boot files on another portion of your hard drive.

BOOT.INI Error Messages

One of several error messages appears when there is a problem with the BOOT.INI file. If you get one of these error messages and the Windows shell doesn't load, you should suspect the BOOT.INI file and use a Windows NT boot disk or an emergency repair disk (ERD) to repair the BOOT.INI file. (Later in this chapter, you learn how to create an ERD.)

The following message indicates that the Windows NT Loader file is either damaged or corrupted:

```
BOOT: Couldn't find NTLDR
Please insert another disk
```

Typically, the error with the NTLDR file occurs early in the boot process.

When you see a repeated sequence of error messages indicating that Windows NT Workstation is checking hardware, you have a problem with the NTDETECT.COM file. These messages look like this:

```
NTDETECT V1.0 Checking Hardware…
NTDETECT V1.0 Checking Hardware…
NTDETECT V1.0 Checking Hardware…
```

It is possible for Windows NT to load even if the BOOT.INI file is missing. If that is the case, the NTLDR starts Windows NT loading files it finds in the *default* \WINNT folder. If the operating system was installed in another location, an error message appears indicating that the NTOSKRNL.EXE file is missing or corrupt. The following error message appears when the BOOT.INI file is damaged or when it points to a location that no longer contains the Windows NT Workstation operating system files:

```
Windows NT could not start because the following file is missing or corrupt:
\winnt root\system32\ntoskrnl.exe
Please re-install a copy of the above file.
```

This message indicates that the Windows NT operating system kernel has failed to load. The problem occurs most often when someone has inadvertently renamed the folder containing the operating-system files without realizing the consequences of that action. The solution is to use your Windows NT boot disk to gain access to the system and to rename the folder back to the location specified in the BOOT.INI file. It is less common to see a change in the BOOT.INI file giving rise to this problem, as that requires a knowledgeable user's action.

Another potential explanation for the inability of the kernel to load could be that you used the Disk Administrator to create a partition with free space. If you changed the number of the partition that contains your Windows NT operating-system files, the pointer in the BOOT.INI file no longer points to the correct location. To fix this problem, you need to edit the pointer to the partition to correct the partition number so that it correctly indicates the location of your Windows NT operating-system files.

When there is a problem with the boot sector, the following error message appears during startup:

```
I/O Error accessing boot sector file
Multi(0)disk(0)rdisk(0)partition(1):\bootsect.dos
```

This error message might indicate a problem with your hard drive. You should boot from a Windows NT boot disk and run the RDISK utility.

Windows NT Workstation posts a more specific message when it can determine that the error in locating the boot sector is hardware related. The operating system checks hardware (as you have now seen) by testing it during startup. Failure to respond to one of these tests generates the following message:

```
OS Loader V4.00
Windows NT could not start because of a computer disk hardware configuration
problem. Could not read from the selected boot disk. Check boot path and disk
hardware. Please check the Windows NT documentation about hardware disk
configuration and your hardware reference manuals for additional information.
```

The preceding message indicates that the pointer in the BOOT.INI file that locates the Windows NT operating system references a damaged or nonexisting device or a partition that doesn't contain a file system that Windows NT can access with the boot loader.

Finally, you might see a STOP error if the Windows NT Loader cannot resolve the appropriate partition that contains your operating-system files. This error takes the following form:

```
STOP: 0x000007E: Inaccessible Boot Device
```

14

This error appears when the hard-disk controller has difficulty determining which is the boot device (if your computer contains a SCSI disk controller and there is an ID number conflict, for example). Another instance in which this error occurs is when the Master Boot Record (MBR) is corrupted by a virus or a disk error.

You might also see the inaccessible boot device problem if you have an internal IDE drive on the workstation and a SCSI disk drive with an ID number set to 0. On some systems, the 0 ID number is used to specify which disk is the internal disk and might conflict with a boot partition on the IDE drive. As a general rule, SCSI drives are faster than IDE drives and are preferred by the operating system. Don't mix and match these two drive types; use SCSI or don't use IDE and SCSI together. If you have a SCSI disk controller and SCSI drives, use those for your boot partition.

If your system proceeds through the load phase and boots correctly but still seems to be malfunctioning, you should check the System Event Log to see whether any system messages were written to it. The System Log might contain errors, warnings, or informational events that explain the conditions leading to the anomaly you're observing as an error in the boot sequence. To view the System Log, open the Start menu and choose Programs, Administrative Tools, Event Viewer. Then choose the System Log command from the Log menu.

14.1.6. Boot-Disk Recovery

If you create a Windows NT boot disk as a precaution, you can start up from that floppy disk if your hard-disk boot partition fails. You also can use your boot disk to start up if you have a multipartition system and have installed Windows NT in your boot partition. After you have started your system using the floppy disk, you can perform procedures to test and repair the errors that exist.

Most computers now have the capability to disable booting from the floppy disk. Often this is indicated by a Bootup Sequence option. If this setting is set to "C, A," you'll want to change it to "A, C" so that the floppy drive, the A drive, is checked before the hard drive, the C drive, is.

To create a floppy boot disk, do the following:

1. Insert a blank 1.44MB floppy disk in your floppy-disk drive.
2. Double-click My Computer on your desktop.
3. Right-click the icon for your floppy-disk drive and select the Format command from the shortcut menu.
4. Click the OK button to begin formatting, and then click the OK button to confirm that formatting occurred.

5. Open the Start menu, choose Programs, and select Windows NT Explorer.

6. In Windows NT Explorer, select the BOOT.INI, NTLDR, NTBOOTDD.SYS, and NTDETECT.COM files in the root directory of your hard drive (typically the C drive).

7. Right-click any of the selected files and drag them to the icon for your floppy-disk drive (or use the Send To option).

8. Choose the Copy Here command from the shortcut menu.

9. Restart your computer with the boot floppy disk in the floppy-disk drive to test the disk.

14.1.7. The Emergency Repair Disk (ERD)

When a portion of the Windows NT Registry becomes corrupted, your workstation can become unstable and crash. In some instances, these errors even prevent you from starting your computer and booting the Windows NT operating system itself. You can repair the Windows NT Registry by creating an ERD that contains the important system Registry information and using that disk to repair your system configuration.

An *emergency repair disk (ERD)* contains backup information about your workstation's security account manager (SAM) database, your system configuration, and important system-configuration parameters. Also copied to the ERD are the two files required to create a virtual DOS machine (NTVDM): AUTOEXEC.NT and CONFIG.NT.

You are prompted to create an ERD when you install Windows NT Workstation. If you prefer, you can create an ERD at a later time. Regardless of whether you choose to create an ERD, the appropriate files are copied to the %systemroot%\Repair directory.

Under the topic of Emergency Repair Disk in the online Help system, Windows NT Workstation's Help system walks you through the process of either creating or updating your ERD. You can also open a command-prompt window and create or update your ERD by using the RDISK.EXE command. RDISK performs the following functions:

- Copies the Registry default hive (HKEY_USERS\DEFAULT)
- Copies the Registry security hive (HKEY_LOCAL_MACHINE\Security)
- Copies the Registry software hive (HKEY_LOCAL_MACHINE\Software)

14

- Copies the Registry system hive (HKEY_LOCAL_MACHINE\System)
- Copies the workstation SAM
- Copies the AUTOEXEC.NT file
- Copies the CONFIG.NT file

These files are copied into the %systemroot%\Repair folder. After these files are copied into the Repair folder, the RDISK utility prompts you for a floppy disk on which to create an ERD. It then copies the information in the Repair folder to the disk.

The ERD is useful only if you update it on a regular basis. You should consider updating the ERD before performing any major software installations or upgrades, before making any changes to your security policy, and before changing the hardware configuration of your workstation. If the information on your ERD is not current, the restoration you are able to perform using the ERD is of limited value. Note also that the ERD doesn't take the place of a full volume backup; it saves only data that can help reestablish your system configuration based on information in the Registry.

Creating the ERD

To create an ERD, follow these steps:

1. Open the Start menu and choose Programs, Command Prompt (or choose the Run command from the Start menu).

2. Enter **RDISK /S** at the command prompt, and then press Enter. While the configuration information and files are being compressed to fit, you see the progress box shown in Figure 14.3.

Figure 14.3.

Starting RDISK begins the compression process.

3. In the Repair Disk Utility dialog box that appears, click the Create Repair Disk button.

4. Insert a formatted floppy disk (or the formatting will be done automatically for you), and then click the OK button.

5. After Windows NT Workstation creates the ERD, remove the floppy disk, write-protect it, and store it away.

6. Click the Exit button to close RDISK.

7. Click Close.

The information copied to the ERD is in compressed format. To restore a Registry key by using the Registry Editor and the ERD data, expand the files using the Windows NT Expand program. The following files are found on an ERD:

■ AUTOEXEC.NT. This file corresponds to the AUTOEXEC.BAT of MS-DOS and works in conjunction with CONFIG.NT to run a batch file and set up an environment. In addition, a it creates a small file like this one:

```
@echo off

REM AUTOEXEC.BAT is not used to initialize the MS-DOS environment.
REM AUTOEXEC.NT is used to initialize the MS-DOS environment REM unless a
different startup file is specified in an application's PIF.

REM Install CD ROM extensions
lh %SystemRoot%\system32\mscdexnt.exe

REM Install network redirector (load before dosx.exe)
lh %SystemRoot%\system32\redir

REM Install DPMI support
lh %SystemRoot%\system32\dosx
```

■ CONFIG.NT. Along with AUTOEXEC.NT, this is one of the two files responsible for a Virtual DOS Machine. This file corresponds to the CONFIG.SYS file on MS-DOS. It creates a small file something like this:

```
REM Windows NT MS-DOS Startup File
REM
REM CONFIG.SYS vs CONFIG.NT
REM CONFIG.SYS is not used to initialize the MS-DOS environment.
REM CONFIG.NT is used to initialize the MS-DOS environment unless a
REM different startup file is specified in an application's PIF.
REM
REM ECHOCONFIG
```

continues

14

```
REM By default, no information is displayed when the MS-DOS environment
REM is initialized. To display CONFIG.NT/AUTOEXEC.NT information, add
REM the command echoconfig to CONFIG.NT or other startup file.
REM
REM NTCMDPROMPT
REM When you return to the command prompt from a TSR or while running an
REM MS-DOS-based application, Windows NT runs COMMAND.COM. This allows the
REM TSR to remain active. To run CMD.EXE, the Windows NT command prompt,
REM rather than COMMAND.COM, add the command ntcmdprompt to CONFIG.NT or
REM other startup file.
REM
REM DOSONLY
REM By default, you can start any type of application when running
REM COMMAND.COM. If you start an application other than an MS-DOS-based
REM application, any running TSR may be disrupted. To ensure that only
REM MS-DOS-based applications can be started, add the command dosonly to
REM CONFIG.NT or other startup file.
REM
REM EMM
REM You can use EMM command line to configure EMM(Expanded Memory Manager).
REM The syntax is:
REM
REM EMM = [A=AltRegSets] [B=BaseSegment] [RAM]
REM
REM   AltRegSets
REM       specifies the total Alternative Mapping Register Sets you
REM       want the system to support. 1 <= AltRegSets <= 255. The
REM       default value is 8.
REM   BaseSegment
REM       specifies the starting segment address in the Dos conventional
REM       memory you want the system to allocate for EMM page frames.
REM       The value must be given in Hexdecimal.
REM       0x1000 <= BaseSegment <= 0x4000. The value is rounded down to
REM       16KB boundary. The default value is 0x4000
REM   RAM
REM       specifies that the system should only allocate 64Kb address
REM       space from the Upper Memory Block(UMB) area for EMM page frames
REM       and leave the rests(if available) to be used by DOS to support
REM       loadhigh and devicehigh commands. The system, by default, would
REM       allocate all possible and available UMB for page frames.
REM
REM   The EMM size is determined by pif file(either the one associated
REM   with your application or _default.pif). If the size from PIF file
REM   is zero, EMM will be disabled and the EMM line will be ignored.
REM
dos=high, umb
device=%SystemRoot%\system32\himem.sys
files=20
```

- DEFAULT._. The compressed copy of the System's default profile.
- NTUSER.DA_. The compressed copy of the NTUSER.DAT file, which stores user profiles.
- SAM._. The compressed copy of the SAM hive of the Registry, with a copy of the Windows NT accounts database. A workstation's SAM doesn't contain as much information as a server's SAM does (especially a domain server); missing is information about other machine and user accounts that the workstation doesn't know about.
- SECURITY._. The compressed copy of the Security hive, with SAM and security policy information for the workstation's users.
- SETUP.LOG. This text file has the names of the Windows setup and installation files, as well as checksums for each file. The file is used to determine whether essential system files are either missing or corrupt. If they are, it replaces them in a recovery operation. This file differs from most of the others in two ways: It is not compressed, and it is hidden on the floppy.
- SOFTWARE._. A compressed copy of the Software hive, with information about installed programs and associated files and configuration information for those programs.
- SYSTEM._. A compressed copy of the System hive of the Registry. This hive contains the Windows NT control set.

To update the ERD, run the RDISK program, select the Update Repair Info button, and confirm that you want to overwrite the current repair information.

The importance of using the /S switch for the RDISK program is worth noting. This switch updates the DEFAULT._, Security, and SAM changes without requiring you to first go through the Create Repair Disk dialog box. If you don't use /S, changes to your account information are not noted. If you have a lot of accounts, updating this information can take some time. In addition, your ERD will likely expand beyond the single floppy disk limit. In that case, the RDISK program asks you for additional disks, as needed.

14

For purposes of the exam, this cannot be said enough:

> The ERD is a lifesaver for fixing a damaged Windows NT Workstation.

The ERD is not bootable. You must boot from something else (the start-up floppies, a bootable floppy created earlier, or anything else). If the ERD is left in the A: drive at startup, Workstation will inform you that the ERD cannot be booted and will encourage you to start the Setup routine and then choose to restore from the ERD at the appropriate time.

Restoring Your System Using the ERD

When you use the ERD to repair a damaged Windows NT Workstation, the procedure essentially reinstalls the sections of the operating system that are required for your particular setup. The data from the Windows NT Registry that you copied to the ERD determines which files need to be replaced and how the configuration should be reestablished. The ERD does the following:

- Runs CHKDSK to determine the validity of the partition containing your Windows NT system files.

- Determines whether the individual files on a system partition are valid, as determined by the use of a checksum.

- Restores missing or corrupt files from your Windows NT installation disks.

- Replaces your default System and Security Registry hives.

- Replaces the Security Account Manager hives.

- Reinstalls the files responsible for booting your system in the boot loader: BOOT.INI, NTLDR, NTBOOTDD.SYS, and NTDETECT.COM.

Before you begin to restore your system, make sure you have your Windows NT Setup floppy disks handy. If you can't find those disks, you can create them from the installation CD by using the WINNT command with the /O or the /OX switch. You can find online documentation for the WINNT.EXE program in the Help system.

To restore Windows NT Workstation on an Intel x386 system, complete the following steps:

1. Insert the Windows NT Workstation Setup boot disk in your floppy-disk drive. (Make sure your system boots from a floppy disk first.)

2. Turn on your system and, when prompted, insert Setup Disk 2 and press the Enter key.

3. Press the R key to perform a repair.

4. Press the Enter key to mark any options that you want to restore, press Tab to move to the Continue button, and press the Enter key again.

5. Press Enter to detect devices.

6. Insert the Setup Disk 3 in your floppy-disk drive when requested.

7. If necessary, insert additional disks with device drives when the Other Disk option appears, and then replace that (those) disk(s) with Setup Disk 3 again.

8. Press Enter. When requested, insert your ERD and press Enter again.

9. Press Enter to select each Registry hive you want to restore, and then move to the Continue button and press Enter.

10. Press the A key to replace all modified system files.

11. Insert any required device driver files requested.

12. Press the Esc key to have Setup ignore the Windows NT Workstation DRVLIB disk, if you wish.

13. When the program is complete, reboot your computer.

You can choose from the following four main options during the recovery process:

- *Inspect Registry Files.* By using your ERD, you can repair corrupt portions of the Registry. You can choose to repair any or all of the following hives: `Default`, `Security/SAM`, `Software`, and `System`. Changes to the Registry do not require the use of the Windows NT installation CDs.

- *Inspect Startup Environment.* Any boot files are inspected, dissected, and potentially rejected. Because all default boot files are equivalent, you can use any ERD to replace startup files.

- *Verify Windows NT System Files.* This option compares any system file (with the system attribute) in the Windows NT directory and any subdirectories and verifies them using the checksum values in the `SETUP.LOG` file. You need your installation disks to perform this repair.

14

■ *Inspect Boot Sector.* The primary reason a boot sector becomes invalid is from upgrading MS-DOS or Windows 95 using the SYS command. Use an ERD (any ERD) and the installation disks to repair this problem.

Each ERD that you create is specific to the computer (vendor and CPU type) on which it is created. An ERD that you create on one system does not work on another system.

The process of restoring a RISC system containing the Windows NT Workstation as its operating system is similar in concept to the procedure previously described. The individual sequence differs, however, depending on the specific manufacturer of your system.

To restore a RISC-based Windows NT system, complete the following steps:

1. Start the Windows NT Setup program as your computer's manual instructs you to.

2. Insert the ERD, and then follow your computer's instructions that appear on your monitor.

When the repair is complete, remove the ERD and reboot your system.

Creating and maintaining an ERD is one of the most effective troubleshooting tools that you have in your arsenal. It cures a host of ills. It is only effective, however, if you remain diligent in updating it whenever a workstation's configuration changes.

14.2. Choosing the Appropriate Action When a Print Job Fails

One of the benefits of Windows printing is that the operating system handles all print job output in a standardized manner, regardless of the application from which you are printing. Windows NT, being a network operating system, enables you to define network printers that are available as shared resources to which other Windows NT Workstations can print. Any client or server on a network can serve as the print server to a network printer. Additionally, you can have local printers that are not shared to other network computers but that need to be managed and troubleshot by their owners.

A single standardized print model under Windows replaces the individual print models of applications under MS-DOS. Although this simplifies the process nicely, when problems do arise, they affect your entire application suite and maybe an entire workgroup.

Windows still retains the older model for printing for MS-DOS applications that run in Windows NT Workstation from the command prompt. These applications require their own printer drivers to print anything other than ASCII output. If you are using WordPerfect 5.1, for example, you must have both WordPerfect and a printer driver installed. Some MS-DOS applications might also require you to redirect a printer port to a share by using a command such as the following prior to printing:

```
NET USE LPT1: \\servername\printername
```

14.2.1. Understanding the Windows Print Subsystem

The printing subsystem is modular and works hand in hand with other subsystems to provide printing services. When an application sends a print job to a local printer, the data goes to the Graphics Device Interface (GDI) to be rendered into a print job in the printer language of the print device. (The GDI is a module that connects the printing subsystem with the application requesting the printing services.) This print job is then passed to the spooler, which is a DLL, where it is written to disk as a temporary file so that it can survive a power outage or your computer's reboot.

The client side of the print spooler is WINSPOOL.DRV. That driver makes a Remote Procedure Call (RPC) to the SPOOLSS.EXE server side of the spooler. When the printer is local (attached to the same computer), both files are located on the same computer. When the printer is attached to a Windows NT Workstation in a peer-to-peer relationship, those files are located on different computers.

SPOOLSS.EXE calls an API that sends the print job to a route (SPOOLSS.DLL). SPOOLSS.DLL then sends the print job to the computer with the local printer. Finally, the LOCALSPL.DLL library writes the file to disk as a spooled file. At this point, the printer is polled by LOCALSPL.DLL to determine whether the spooled print job is capable of being processed by the printer, and it is altered if necessary.

The print job is then turned over to a separator page processor and despooled to the print monitor. The print device receives the print job and raster image processes it to a bitmap file that is sent to the print engine to output. Rasterization occurs as the final process only if EMF was used. If the output is RAW, the file is rasterized in the first step.

14

Network Printer Process

For network printers, the process is very much the same, but client requests and server services are more clearly defined and separate. The routers found in the spooler modules (WINSPOOL.DRV, SPOOLSS.EXE, and SPOOLSS.DLL) are identical to the ones used for a local printer. A local print provider on the client LOCALSPL.DLL is matched to one of two remote print providers on the server side: WIN32SP.DLL (for Windows print servers) or NWPROVAU.DLL (for NetWare print servers). In a network printer process, the print processors and print monitors may use several different server DLLs, each of which is required by a supported operating system.

Multiple Virtual Printer Setup

You generally install a printer using the Add Printer wizard that you find in the Printer folder accessed via the Start, Settings command. Using the wizard, you create a virtual printer with a name that you provide. You can create any number of virtual (or logical, if you will) printers that use the same physical printer for a number of purposes. If you want to print to a different printer, have different security schemes, or provide different access times, having multiple virtual printers enables you to do so. You can manipulate printers using any of the following methods:

- Double-click the printer to see any spooled jobs (if you have the privilege to do so).
- Right-click a printer to view a shortcut menu that provides several options. From this menu, you can delete a printer that no longer exists, for example. Or you might use the Default Printer command to set the default printer for a Windows NT Workstation.
- Right-click a printer and select the Properties command from the shortcut menu to access the Printer Properties and modify any number of settings.

14.2.2. Using a Basic Error Checklist

Any number of things can go wrong when you attempt to print to a printer. In many cases, Windows NT alerts you to an error, and in some cases, Windows NT tells you what the error type is. Here is a standard checklist of the most common solutions to print problems. Next time your print job spools but will not print, use this check list to eliminate the following potential problems:

- ✔ The printer is turned on and all the connections are secure.
- ✔ The paper tray is full.

✔ A piece of paper is not jammed in the printer.

✔ The printer does not have an error condition that prevents print processing.

The preceding problems are so simple that many people waste precious time by overlooking them. It is amazing how many printer problems disappear when you power your printer off and back on. If that fails to work but you know your printer worked before you specified this print job, restart Windows NT Workstation.

If none of those solutions seems to work, try the following:

✔ Verify that the printer you think you printed to either is the default printer or was selected in the application from which the print job comes.

✔ Print a simple text file from Notepad. This often verifies whether the print problem is application specific. Try printing from DOS to test the DOS subsystem if that is the problem environment.

> **Note**
>
> I specifically recommend printing from DOS because it cuts out so many steps. On a PCL printer, copying the AUTOEXEC.BAT to the PRN device or a similar mapped port can help you quickly identify a problem.

✔ Print to a different printer or substitute another printer on the same printer port. This helps determine whether it's the printer that is malfunctioning.

✔ Check the amount of available hard-disk space on your system partition to see whether there was room to create the temporary spooled print file.

✔ Print to a file, and then copy that file to the printer port in question. If you can print in this manner, you should suspect the spooler or a data-transmission error. Otherwise, you are probably dealing with a hardware, device-driver, or application error.

At the very worst, you can try reinstalling the printer and supplying a new or updated printer driver. These are the usual sources of printer drivers:

■ *The Windows NT operating-system distribution disks.*

■ *The setup disks that come with your printer.*

■ *The printer manufacturer's BBS or Web site.*

14

- *Microsoft's technical support line.* You can contact Microsoft at 206-882-8080. Microsoft's current printer driver library is on the Windows NT Driver Library disk.
- *The Microsoft Web site.* Use the Search button to search for the keyword NT driver, or search for the name of your particular model of printer.
- *CompuServe.* Enter **GO WINNT** to go to that area of the service.

If you observe the problem printing to a printer immediately after you install the printer, you should probably suspect a configuration issue. Make sure you assigned the correct parallel or serial port in the Configure Port dialog box of the Add Printer wizard. You can open a printer's Properties sheet to check port settings at any time after installation.

For serial printers, make sure you have assigned the appropriate communication settings—baud rate, data bits, parity, start and stop bits, and flow control—that your printer requires. These settings should be listed in your printer's manual. Failure to configure these settings properly may result in your printer operating too slowly, improperly processing print jobs, or not working at all.

14.2.3. Printers as Shared Resources

Network printers are shared resources. In order for you to view, modify, and use a printer, you must either own the printer (have created or installed it), be an administrator, or be assigned the rights to use a printer in some way. The owner or an administrator can assign different levels of rights. You assign shared rights by selecting the Sharing command on a printer's shortcut menu to access the Sharing tab of the Printer Properties dialog box.

Multiple Printer Shares

Creating additional printer shares for the same physical printer proves useful for the following reasons:

- Each share can have different printer setups.
- It enables you to assign different access privileges to groups of users.
- Each group can have a different printing priority.
- You can control access to the printer at different times for each group.
- You can use one share for a network printer and another share name for a printer name.

If users cannot see a printer, they may not have been given the right to access that printer. An administrator should be able to view and modify the printers on any Windows NT Workstation.

If you have MS-DOS clients on the network and you want them to see a printer share, you must use a file-naming convention that DOS recognizes. Names can contain no more than 12 characters and cannot contain spaces or any of the following characters:

```
? * # ¦ \ / = > < %
```

To hide a printer share from most dialog boxes, you can add a dollar sign character to the end of the share name, as in *sharename*$. Any printer with that kind of a name will not show up in the Connect To Printer dialog box that appears during one of the steps in the Add a Printer wizard. A user must know that this printer share exists and must be able to enter both the correct name and path to the printer share name in order to connect to that printer.

14.2.4. Solving Print-Spooler Problems

Any print job spooled to a printer is written as a temporary file to the spooling directory, the default of which is `%systemroot%\System32\Spool\Printers` folder. The file is deleted after the printer indicates that the job has been printed.

The most common print-spool problem is a lack of available disk space. If you print high-resolution graphics, you might have print jobs as large as 20–80MB per file for a 32-bit image at standard page size. Not surprisingly, it doesn't take many of such print jobs to overwhelm the typical Windows NT Workstation configuration.

When you print to the spooler, two files are created for each print job: an SPL file, which is the actual print-job spool file, and an SHD file, which is a shadow file. The shadow file contains additional information about the print job that is not part of the print job itself, such as the owner, priority, and so forth.

If your computer crashes, SPL and SHD files remain in the default spool file until the service restarts and they are processed and printed. After being printed, these files are deleted from disk. Should your spooled files become corrupted, they will be orphaned and will remain in the spool folder taking up valuable space.

You can print directly to a printer from your application by turning off the print-spooling feature. Before you print, open the Scheduling tab of the Printer Properties dialog box and select the Print Directly to the Printer option button. When the printer next becomes available, your document prints. Until that point, you cannot

14

use the application that originated the print job. However, you can task-switch to another application and continue working there until your printing application becomes available.

Spooler-Performance Problems

You can solve spooler-performance problems by increasing the priority that Windows NT Workstation assigns to the Spooler service. By default, Windows NT assigns this service a rating of 7, which is consistent with other background processes. You can increase the rating to 9 to improve the performance of the spooler to the level of a foreground operation (changing the Spooler service to a rating above 9 isn't advisable, though).

Consider doing this only as a temporary measure to print a large print job, or if your workstation is used heavily as a print server. Changing this rating on a permanent basis degrades the performance of other services and applications on the workstation.

To change the priority of the Spooler service, open either the Regedit or Regedt32 application and change the value of the `PriorityClass` of type `REG_DWORD` in the following key:

`HKEY_LOCAL_MACHINE\System\CurrentControlSet\Control\Print`

Set that value to the priority class required, as illustrated in Figure 14.4.

Figure 14.4.

Changing the priority of a printer using Regedit.

If a printer is assigned a value of 0 or no value at all is entered (as is the case in Figure 14.4), it is treated as having the default value of a background process (7 for Windows NT Workstation; 9 for Windows NT Server).

Aside from changing priority classes, your main alternative is to try defragmenting your hard drive on a regular basis. It is also a simple and effective procedure that improves printer performance.

Changing the Default Spool Folder

Should you run out of room on your system partition for spooled print jobs, you can specify a different default spool folder. You make such a change on the Advanced tab of the Print Server Properties dialog box.

To change the location of spooled documents, complete the following steps:

1. Create a new spool directory.

2. Open the Start menu, choose Settings, and select Printers.

3. Choose the Server Properties command from the File menu; the Print Server Properties dialog box appears.

4. Click on the Advanced tab, and then enter the location of the spool file directory, as shown in Figure 14.5.

Figure 14.5.

Changing the location of the spool file.

5. Click the OK button and reboot when prompted.

Some possibilities to consider include creating the spool folder on an NTFS volume and setting security for the folder. You can also edit the Registry to change the value of the `DefaultSpoolDirectory` of type `REG_SZ`. You would enter the path into the following key of the Registry:

`HKEY_LOCAL_MACHINE\System\CurrentControlSet\Control\Print\Printers`

14

After you enter the new folder and its path, save the change and restart your machine for the change to take effect. Any spooled job in the original location will be lost, but it will not be deleted. You need to delete the TEMP file manually.

If you want to have individual spooled folders for each virtual printer, you can assign them. Find your printers in the following key:

```
HKEY_LOCAL_MACHINE\System\CurrentControlSet\Control\Print\~Printers\printername
```

Then enter the folder and its path as the data in the SpoolDirectory value for that key. Again, you need to restart the workstation to effect the change.

Enabling Printer Logging

You can enable event logging to your spooler by adding a check mark to the Log Spooler Error Events, Log Spooler Warning Events, and/or Log Spooler Information Events check boxes on the Advanced tab of the Print Server Properties dialog box.

You can also turn on auditing of a printer share. First, however, you must enable File and Object Access auditing in the User Manager, as shown in Figure 14.6.

Figure 14.6.

File and Object Access auditing must be enabled before printer logging can commence.

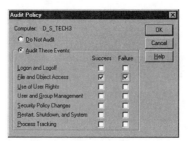

Then complete the following steps to turn on auditing of a printer share:

1. Click the printer icon in the Printers folder and press Alt+Enter to open the printer's Properties dialog box.

2. Click the Security tab of the printer's Properties dialog box, and then click the Auditing button.

3. In the Printer Auditing dialog box that appears, click the Add button.

4. In the Add Users and Groups dialog box, select a group or user to be audited and click OK.

5. Back in the Printer Auditing dialog box, select a user or group. Then click the check boxes in the Events to Audit section to select events you want to log for that user and group.

6. Click OK to close the Printer Auditing dialog box, and then click OK to close the Properties dialog box.

You use the Event Viewer utility in the Administrative Tools folder to view logged events.

Installing Print Pooling

If you have adequate printer resources and want to distribute the print queue load, you might want to install *printer pooling*. Printer pooling enables you to set up two or more identical printers so you can print to them as if they were a single printer. The print job goes to the first available printer and is managed as if there were only a single print queue.

To use printer pooling, complete the following steps:

1. Open the Start menu, choose Settings, and select Printers to display the Printers folder.

2. Right-click a printer icon and select Properties to display that printer's Properties dialog box.

3. Click on the Ports tab shown in Figure 14.7.

Figure 14.7.

You use the printer Ports tab to enable printer pooling.

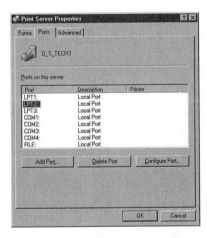

4. In the list of ports, double-click the logical printer to which you want to print.

5. On the next screen, click the Enable Print Pooling check box, and then close the printer's Properties dialog box.

14

To set up a logical printer, you can use the Add Printer wizard to add a printer to a port and use the same printer name. Although the printers need to be identical, the ports do not. You can mix and match local, serial, and parallel ports in the same logical printer.

Scheduling a Print Job

You cannot specify when a particular job will print on a printer within the current Windows NT Workstation architecture. You can control when a printer is available for printing, however, as part of a printer share's definition. You can use two differently named printer shares for the same printer and have one printer always available. Then restrict the availability of the second printer and use that printer share to schedule your print job.

To set availability times, complete the following steps:

1. Click the printer icon in the Printers folder and press Alt+Enter to open the Printer Properties dialog box.

2. Click on the Scheduling tab of the Printer Properties dialog box.

3. In the Available section, click the From radio button and then enter the starting and ending times that the printer is available (see Figure 14.8).

4. Click OK.

Figure 14.8.

The Scheduling tab.

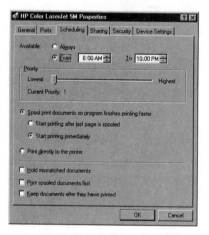

Any print job sent to the printer during its off hours is left in the print queue until the printer becomes available.

14.2.5. Using the Print Troubleshooter

To aid in solving printer problems, Windows NT comes with an interactive print-troubleshooting tool that's part of the online Help system. To access the Print Troubleshooter, follow these steps:

1. Choose the Help command from the Start menu.
2. Click the Index tab.
3. In the Type the First Few Letters text box, enter the keyword `troubleshooting`.
4. Double-click on Troubleshooting.
5. Double-click on Print Troubleshooter, and then follow the instructions in the Help system.

Printers are one of the more important network resources in many organizations. Therefore, you will be called on often to solve problems that crop up with printer shares and printer hardware. This section reviewed some of the most common problems.

14.3. Choosing the Appropriate Action When the Installation Process Fails

The Windows NT Setup program makes installation errors much less common than they were with earlier operating systems. Several types of errors might still occur after installation, but they are easier to track down and eliminate.

14.3.1. Installation Disk Errors and Upgrades

In rare cases, you might encounter a problem with the CD that you obtained to perform the Windows NT Workstation installation. Most often, a read error is posted. But once in a while, the installation is unable to complete itself, and you might not be able to determine why.

To obtain a replacement disk, contact Microsoft at 800-426-9400. Have your registration number handy; the sales and support staff requires this to process your request. New media requests under the warranty are generally sent without cost. If the upgrade is a slipstream upgrade, you may be charged postage.

14

A note about slipstream upgrades and service packs is also in order. Small problems are often repaired as part of a minor version change to the operating system. If you have a problem related to an installation, either get the latest version of the operating system from Microsoft or download any available service packs from the Microsoft Web site.

A service pack is a self-extracting and self-installing program that modifies your operating system. It isn't uncommon within the lifetime of an operating system to have two or three service packs. For example, Windows NT Server 4.0—prior to the release of beta for Windows NT Server 5—had Service Pack 3 available. You should try to install the latest service pack because it generally solves a lot more problems than it creates. (It is not unheard of, however, for a service pack to create error conditions that didn't previously exist in a workstation's configuration.)

14.3.2. Inadequate Disk Space

The Windows NT Setup program examines the partition in which you specify you want Windows NT Workstation installed for the amount of free space it contains. If there isn't adequate free space, the installation stops and fails, and you need to take corrective action to proceed with the installation.

In some respects, the Setup program is both intelligent and ignorant. It protects your files in the Recycle Bin by not deleting them, which is wise. However, it leaves any number of TEMP files scattered about your disk even though they could be safely deleted.

To free up some room on your disk, try doing any or all of the following:

- Empty your Recycle Bin.
- Delete any TEMP files you find in the various locations they are stored in (for example, the Print Cache folder).
- Delete any files you find in your Internet browser's cache folder or any other cache folder that you have.
- Uninstall any programs you no longer need.
- Compress all files that you use only on an infrequent basis.
- Go into the Disk Administrator and change the size of the system partition you want to use for your installation.
- Create a new partition with adequate room for the installation.
- Compress your NTFS partition to make more room.

Several other methods also enable you to reclaim or recover lost disk space, and it's possible to get really creative in this area. Those listed previously, however, are often sufficient to help you get over the crunch.

14.3.3. Disk-Configuration Errors

The best way to ensure that you are using hardware compatible with Windows NT Workstation is to check the Hardware Compatibility List (HCL) to see whether the device is approved for use and supported.

If you have inherited a configuration with a non-supported SCSI device adapter, you might not be able to boot your newly installed Windows NT Workstation operating system. In that case, boot to a different operating system and try starting WINNT on the installation CD. You can also use a network installation to try to rectify the problem. If none of these solutions works, you might be forced to replace the adapter with one listed on the Hardware Compatibility List.

14.3.4. Inability to Connect to a Domain Controller

The error message `Cannot Connect to a Domain Controller` is one of the more common ones you might see when you install Windows NT Workstation, change your hardware configuration, or change network settings. There are a number of explanations for this problem. Before you try anything else, though, carefully verify that you are entering the correct user name and password and that the Caps Lock key is not on.

> User Manager is used to add users and groups to a Windows NT Workstation. User Manager exists only on Windows NT Workstation.
>
> User Manager for Domains is a utility used to add users and groups to a domain. User Manager for Domains exists only on Windows NT Server.

The first thing you should check is that the account name you are using is listed in the User Manager for Domains on the primary domain controller. One of the fundamentals of security that Windows NT adheres to is that an invalid password and an invalid user name generate the same response so that a hacker can't determine when he has hit a valid account.

The second thing you should check is that the password was typed correctly: no miskeys, proper case, and so on.

14

You should also check to see whether the machine account has been added to the User Manager for the primary domain controller. You won't be able to select a domain if the machine isn't set up as a member of the domain. Next, open the Network Control Panel and verify that the network bindings are properly configured on the Bindings tab.

Some protocols such as TCP/IP require not only computer names but also IP addresses and subnet masks. If a conflict occurs between two machines on the network that have the same IP address, you get an error condition. Failure to enter the subnet mask (or entering an incorrect subnet mask) can prevent your workstation from finding and connecting to a domain controller and getting its network identity properly verified.

The failure to connect to a domain controller is such a common problem that it is really unfortunate the message isn't more descriptive of the problem.

14.3.5. Domain Name Error

If you make a mistake selecting the domain name, you get an error message when you attempt to log on. The solution, simply put, is to recognize the error and change the domain entry. Just reselect the correct domain name. Then test the system using the PING command. If you can ping your system using the loopback address and its own IP address but not its domain name, you probably have a domain name error.

Problems that can occur with name resolution and their solutions can be categorized into the following generalities:

- *The entry is misspelled.* Examine all relevant tabs and files to verify that the host name is spelled correctly.

- *Comment characters in some files prevent the entry from being read.* Verify that there is not a pound sign at the beginning of the line or anywhere on the line prior to the host name.

- *There are duplicate entries in the file.* Because the files are read in linear fashion, if there is any duplication, only the first entry is read; all others are ignored. Verify that all host names are unique.

- *A host other than the one you want is contacted.* Verify that the IP address in the file(s) is valid and corresponds to the host name.

14.4. Choosing the Appropriate Action When an Application Fails

Unlike in MS-DOS and earlier versions of Windows, an application failure in Windows NT Workstation 4.0 won't bring your system to a complete halt. Most application failures are recoverable, and in many cases, you won't even need to reboot your computer to reestablish a working configuration. That is not to say that a system crash is impossible, only that it happens very infrequently.

Most often, the worst culprits are applications written for MS-DOS or 16-bit Windows applications. These programs tend to crash more frequently than 32-bit Windows applications (one good reason to upgrade).

If an application is malfunctioning, bring up the Task Manager and close the process down. You can access the Task Manager using either your mouse or your keyboard (which is especially convenient if either is hung up by a malfunction).

To close an application, complete the following steps:

1. Using your keyboard, press Ctrl+Alt+Delete to open the Windows NT Security dialog box, and then click the Task Manager button to open the Task Manager.

    Using your mouse, right-click over the status bar and select the Task Manager command.

2. Click the Applications tab to see the screen shown in Figure 14.9.

Figure 14.9.

The Task Manager shows all active applications and their status.

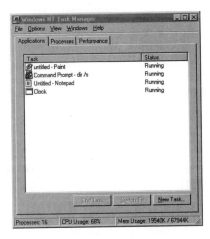

14

3. Select the offending application and click the End Task button.

4. Close the Task Manager.

If you need to end a 16-bit Windows application or an MS-DOS application, you must close the entire session. However, if you need to close a 32-bit Windows application, you need only close that particular process or thread.

14.4.1. Using the Application Log

Many errors are logged in the Application log for native Windows NT applications. The developer of the application determines the events that will be logged, their codes, and meanings. Often an application's manual or online Help system contains documentation about the events listed in the Application log (which you can view with Event Viewer). You might also find details about your ability to control the events that are logged.

14.4.2. Service Failures

Many applications run as services on Windows NT Workstation. Internet Information Server's three applications, WWW, FTP, and Gopher, for example, all are services. Services are started, stopped, and paused either from within their central administrative tool (for IIS that tool is the Internet Service Manager) or from within the Services Control Panel. If you want to configure a service so that it runs automatically when your workstation boots, more often than not you will use the settings in the Services Control Panel.

Though it's sad to say, sooner or later you will see the following infamous error message after the load phase of Windows NT Workstation startup:

```
One or more services failed to start. Please see the Event Viewer for details.
```

You can use the Event Viewer to examine the System Log, which it displays by default (see Figure 14.10).

In the Event column of the Event Viewer, look for the event code that has a value of 6005 (notice the one at approximately the middle of Figure 14.9). That event is an informational message that indicates the EventLog service started up. Any event prior to that is a boot event and should be resolved. To get more information on the event that caused the EventLog service to be started, open the View menu and choose Detail, or select the event message and press Enter, or simply double-click the event message. This displays an Event Detail dialog box. Figure 14.11 shows the Event Detail dialog box for the event error message that was logged at 8:56:56 on 11/5/97 (listed in the middle of the Event Viewer in Figure 14.10).

Figure 14.10.

The Event Viewer lets you examine the System Log for errors.

Date	Time	Source	Category	Event	User	Computer
11/17/97	4:07:29 PM	EventLog	None	6005	N/A	D_S_TECH3
11/17/97	4:05:27 PM	BROWSER	None	8033	N/A	D_S_TECH3
11/17/97	4:05:26 PM	BROWSER	None	8033	N/A	D_S_TECH3
11/17/97	4:05:26 PM	BROWSER	None	8033	N/A	D_S_TECH3
11/17/97	3:18:32 PM	EventLog	None	6005	N/A	D_S_TECH3
11/17/97	3:12:21 PM	Service Control Mar	None	7024	N/A	D_S_TECH3
11/17/97	3:12:14 PM	Service Control Mar	None	7000	N/A	D_S_TECH3
11/17/97	3:12:13 PM	EventLog	None	6005	N/A	D_S_TECH3
11/17/97	3:12:14 PM	NetBT	None	4315	N/A	D_S_TECH3
11/5/97	8:57:02 AM	Service Control Mar	None	7024	N/A	D_S_TECH3
11/5/97	8:56:56 AM	Service Control Mar	None	7000	N/A	D_S_TECH3
11/5/97	8:56:54 AM	EventLog	None	6005	N/A	D_S_TECH3
11/5/97	8:56:56 AM	NetBT	None	4315	N/A	D_S_TECH3
11/4/97	12:47:39 PM	Service Control Mar	None	7024	N/A	D_S_TECH3
11/4/97	12:47:32 PM	Service Control Mar	None	7000	N/A	D_S_TECH3
11/4/97	12:47:31 PM	EventLog	None	6005	N/A	D_S_TECH3
11/4/97	12:47:32 PM	NetBT	None	4315	N/A	D_S_TECH3
10/29/97	12:19:54 PM	Service Control Mar	None	7024	N/A	D_S_TECH3
10/29/97	12:19:47 PM	Service Control Mar	None	7000	N/A	D_S_TECH3
10/29/97	12:19:45 PM	EventLog	None	6005	N/A	D_S_TECH3
10/29/97	12:19:47 PM	NetBT	None	4315	N/A	D_S_TECH3
10/24/97	11:41:50 AM	Service Control Mar	None	7024	N/A	D_S_TECH3
10/24/97	11:41:44 AM	Service Control Mar	None	7000	N/A	D_S_TECH3
10/24/97	11:41:42 AM	EventLog	None	6005	N/A	D_S_TECH3
10/24/97	11:41:44 AM	NetBT	None	4315	N/A	D_S_TECH3

Figure 14.11.

The details on an error message explain the cause.

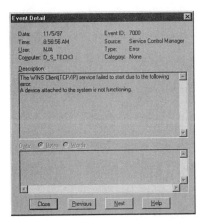

Event Detail

Date: 11/5/97
Time: 8:56:56 AM
User: N/A
Computer: D_S_TECH3

Event ID: 7000
Source: Service Control Manager
Type: Error
Category: None

Description:
The WINS Client(TCP/IP) service failed to start due to the following error:
A device attached to the system is not functioning.

Data: ⦿ Bytes ○ Words

| Close | Previous | Next | Help |

14.5. Choosing the Appropriate Action When a User Cannot Access a Resource

Windows NT's security system controls access to network resources through user and machine accounts. Your logon to a particular domain is validated by a domain controller and provides you with certain privileges and rights that are registered in the Security Accounts Manager (SAM) database.

When you log on to Windows NT, the system provides a Security Access Token (SAT) based on your user name and password. This SAT is a key that enables you to access objects that Windows NT manages by maintaining a Security Descriptor (SD) file. That SD file contains the access control list (ACL) for each resource.

Two types of accounts are created and managed in Windows NT: machine accounts and user accounts. Both of these accounts are stored in the Security Account Manager (SAM) database, which is located on the primary domain controller (PDC) and replicated to any backup domain controllers (BDCs) on the system. Accounts are then assigned an internally held system identification number (SID).

You create and manage accounts in the User Manager. Log on as an administrator so that you can fully access accounts for machines and different users. Other levels of users also have privileges, but what they can do is more limited.

An account is specified by the machine and user name, as in `computername\ username`. A *group* is an account that contains other accounts. Every computer contains a Users group to which all user accounts belong. There is also a Guest group that allows limited privileges to users who log in without a password (if you allow it).

The logon provides the definition of your group membership and other properties assigned to you. Groups are sets of users as well as other groups that are given the same access rights to resources. Access privileges (with the exception of No Access) are cumulative.

Local groups can be created to provide control over resource access. Windows NT also comes with some pre-built global groups that are available systemwide. You can also define additional global groups.

Users, groups, and domains offer a flexible system for managing resource access through security settings that you make either in the file system or on your desktop for various system objects.

14.5.1. Password Issues

Passwords enable you to log on to a particular user account. To log on successfully, you must know both the user name and the exact password. The important thing to know about passwords is that they are *case sensitive*. Therefore, one of the most common errors occurs when the Caps Lock key is pressed accidentally. A user can enter the correct password and still be denied entry to the system because the password is entered in the wrong case.

To protect passwords, Windows NT has an option that enables you to expire a password after a certain period. You can also set an option that requires Windows NT Workstation users to change the assigned password the first time they log on to the system. Users logging on after that time are also required to change their passwords.

Windows NT also provides a "no password" password for anonymous access that provides limited access to system resources. You might use this password, for example, for a Web server running an FTP service, which enables a user to access a PUB folder.

To change your system's password options, complete the following steps:

1. Open the Start menu and select Programs, Administrative Tools, User Manager to start the User Manager application.

2. In the Username panel, select an account name.

3. Choose Policies, Account; a dialog box resembling Figure 14.12 appears.

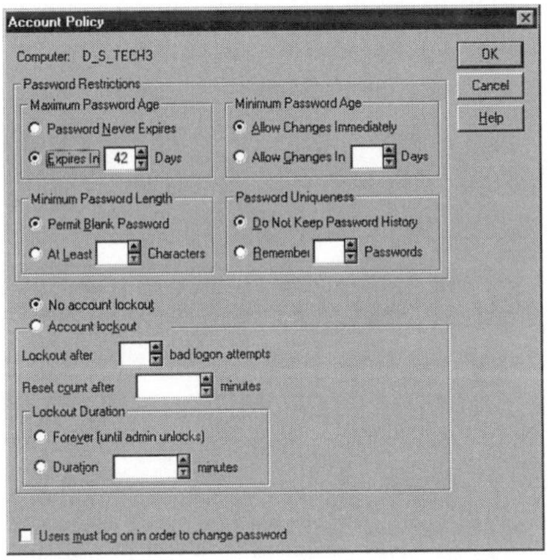

Figure 14.12.

The account policy for each user can be used to set his or her account options.

4. In the Account Policy dialog box, select the options you desire (which are described next), and then click OK.

The options of interest are as follows:

■ *Maximum Password Age and Minimum Password Age.* These settings control how long a user can use a particular password. The maximum age setting specifies whether the password expires and, if so, after how many days.

14

The minimum age setting needs a more detailed explanation. In the days of old, when a user had to change his password, he would often enter the existing value again (for example, change Bob to Bob) so it would be easy to remember. To prevent this, many network operating systems started requiring unique passwords, meaning that the user could not use the same password for a certain number of iterations (typically eight). Users then learned that when the change password prompt came up, they could change Bob to Bob1, then Bob2, then Bob3, all the way up to Bob7, and back to Bob—all on the same day. It took more work, but the end result was the same. Windows NT Workstation's minimum age setting makes this much more difficult. It forces the user to keep each password for the specified length of time before it can be changed to something else.

Used in conjunction, these settings require a user to change his password when it reaches the maximum age but then will not let him change the password again until it reaches the minimum age.

- *Minimum Password Length.* This setting enables you to require a password that's long enough to make it difficult to guess but not so long that the user must write it down. If the user has to write his password on a post-it note and stick it to the top of his terminal, he defeats the whole purpose of security. Somewhere between eight and ten characters is sufficient for most installations.

  You can also control whether blank (no character) passwords are permitted. Needless to say, allowing blank passwords does little for security. If security is of any concern at all, this option should definitely be disabled.

- *Password Uniqueness.* These options control whether a password list is maintained for an account and if so, how many used passwords are remembered. The password list ensures that each user must create unique passwords for a specified number of iterations. I highly recommend that the password history be used to prevent users from reusing expired passwords as their new passwords.

- *Account Lockout.* This option button enables you to control whether a certain number of failed attempts to log on with one user name locks up the account. If you enable Account Lockout, the subsequent settings control how many attempts are allowed within a specified time period. While a low number of logon attempts is good, it can add administrative overhead if the administrator must unlock every locked account. Every installation must use the perfect balance for that particular site.

If you use the Account Lockout feature, it is important to enter a lockout duration. If you choose Forever (Until Admin Unlocks), an administrator must unlock the account. If you choose the Duration option, after the account has been locked for that duration period, it becomes unlocked and can be used again. If you are greatly concerned about security, set this to require administrative action to unlock accounts, and you will be able to keep track of most break-in attempts.

In this author's opinion, the Lockout After...Bad Logon Attempts number should be relatively high. People using a guessing technique will have to guess many, many times to get the right password, and the system will lock out the account well before a person can guess it or use a password hacker program to get through.

It is important that you don't have a very large number of workstation passwords in one domain expiring at the same time. If 2,000 passwords were changed at the same time, the entire SAM would have to be resynchronized across the domain—a time-consuming procedure.

By the way, the common method used to change your own password is to press Ctrl+Alt+Delete and then click the Change Password button in the Windows NT Security dialog box. The Ctrl+Alt+Delete keystroke is one of the most difficult key sequences to trap and spoof. Therefore, it is used to initiate a logon or password change because it prevents someone from posting a spoofed Password Change dialog box and stealing a user account and associated password.

For the exam, know that the Change Password button can be used to change not only the Windows NT password, but other passwords (such as NetWare) as well. It will often trigger another utility for that system.

14.5.2. Troubleshooting Profiles and System Policies

A user profile is created whenever a user logs on to Windows NT Workstation the first time. User profiles can store a specific configuration of the desktop; programs, accessories, and printers; a Taskbar; a Start menu configuration; Help system bookmarks; and options in the Windows NT Explorer. This enables an administrator to provide a default profile that is used by a standard user in a domain.

14

Profiles also offer a method for creating an environment based on a particular user account. To set this option or to check to see whether a problem with the environment can be corrected, select the user account in the User Manager utility, and then click the Profile button. The User Environment Profile dialog box shown in Figure 14.13 appears.

Figure 14.13.

Login scripts can be specified from the Profile button of User Manager.

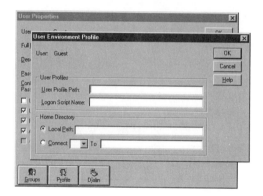

Check the User Environment Profile dialog box for the startup script that modifies the environment at logon. The script can be a BAT (batch), CMD (OS/2), or EXE (program or executable) file. You can also create a new script and specify its location.

A profile can be stored on the server and retrieved as a cached copy on a local machine when a user logs on. A stored local profile can be used when a problem occurs with a network connection or with a logon. If a user needs his profile and configuration to travel with him regardless of which workstation in the domain he logs on to, you can create a *roaming profile.*

User profile settings are located in the Windows NT Registry in the HKEY_CURRENT_USER key. To modify a user profile, complete the following steps:

1. Log on to the system with the user name whose profile you want to modify.

2. Open the Registry Editor (REGEDT32.EXE).

3. If you don't intend to make changes (optional), open the Options menu and choose the Read Only Mode command.

4. Click the HKEY_CURRENT_USER key to expand the settings (see Figure 14.14). Then alter the settings you desire.

Figure 14.14.

The Registry Editor (Regedt32) can be used to change current user settings.

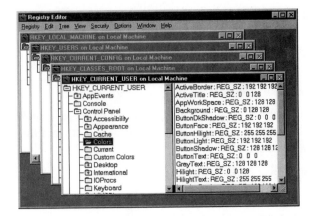

5. When you finish changing settings, close the Registry Editor; your new settings take effect.

The information that the Registry reads for a user profile is contained in the NTUSER.DAT file of the User Profile folder. This file is cached on a local computer when the user profile is read.

If you want to modify your user profiles, you can find them in the C:\WINNT\Profiles folder. The default profile is in the Default User folder, and other user accounts are located in folders with the same name as the user accounts. Each user profile folder contains a directory of shortcuts or LNK (link) files to desktop items and the NTUSER.DAT file. The following shortcuts are contained in these folders:

- *Application Data.* Application data and settings are stored in this folder.
- *Desktop.* Shortcuts to files or folders are stored in the Desktop folder.
- *Favorites.* Shortcuts to programs, folders, or favorite locations on the Web are stored in this folder.
- *NetHood.* This folder stores shortcuts to Network Neighborhood objects. (This is a hidden folder.)
- *Personal.* This folder contains program items.
- *PrintHood.* Network printer connections and settings are stored in this folder. (This is a hidden folder.)
- *Recent.* This folder contains the list of recently opened files that appears on the Documents menu. (This is a hidden folder.)

14

- *SendTo.* This contains shortcuts to document items.
- *Start Menu.* Items that appear on the Start menu are stored in this folder.
- *Templates.* This folder contains template items stored to disk by a user. (This is a hidden folder.)

The user profile is a binary file that cannot be opened and read with any text editor. The information contained in the USERNAME\NTUSER.DAT file is stored in the following subkeys of the Registry's HKEY_CURRENT_USER key:

- AppEvents (sounds)
- Console (command prompt and installed applications)
- Control Panel (which Control Panels are accessible and their settings)
- Environment (system configuration)
- Printers (printer connections)
- Software (which software programs are available and their settings)

14.5.3. Working with System Policies

To enforce a set of rules on a computer, a network administrator can create a system policy that applies to a single user, a group of users, or all users in a domain. You create a specific policy with custom options in the System Policy Editor. This utility enables you to edit portions of the Windows NT Registry or edit system policy. Policies that you see in the System Policy Editor are contained in the WINNT.ADM and COMMON.ADM system policy template files. *Template files* contain a set of standard stored Registry entries. You can modify a template file in the System Policy Editor, or you can create new template files.

 Note
The System Policy Editor is not installed by default on many installations of Windows NT Workstation. If it is not on your system, you can download it from the Microsoft Web site or get it from the Microsoft Windows NT Workstation Resource Kit.

System policy settings are stored in the Windows NT Registry in the HKEY_CURRENT_USER and HKEY_LOCAL_MACHINE keys. When you open the System Policy Editor in the Registry mode, you expose various keys in this area of the Registry.

System policy can restrict network logon or access, customize the desktop, or limit access to settings in the Control Panel. A system policy can be applied to a single user, a group of users, or all the users in a domain. Windows NT comes with two standard policies: Default Computer and Default User, both of which control options applied to all computers and users in a domain. You can create and enforce additional system policies.

To create a system policy, do the following:

1. Log on to the computer as an administrator.

2. Open the Start menu and select Programs, Administrative Tools, System Policy Editor. (You can also start it from the Run dialog box using the command `Poledit`.)

3. Choose File, New Policy. Two icons appear in the System Policy Editor window: Default Computer and Default User.

4. Select the Add User, Add Computer, or Add Group command to add a policy.

5. In the dialog box that appears, enter a name for the user, computer, or group. Then click the OK button.

6. Choose File, Exit to close the System Policy Editor.

With the System Policy Editor in Policy File mode, you can create or modify system policy (`.POL`) files for the domain. Any system policy modification you make for a user, group, or computer is written as an entry into the `NTCONFIG.POL` file. To enforce the policy with the modification, you must save this file in the `NETLOGON` share on the primary domain controller (PDC).

To have more than one system policy in a domain, you need to change the Remote Update setting from automatic to manual in the computer policy section of the system policy. Then the local policy is enforced instead of the default action when Windows NT searches the `NTCONFIG.POL` file on the domain controller to validate a user logon.

If a lot of users log on to the network at the same time, long delays occur if the `NETLOGON.POL` file contains a large number of different policies. To improve performance on Windows NT Workstation, enable manual updating and create system policy files on workstations other than the domain controllers to balance the load.

14

When a user presses Ctrl+Alt+Delete, the Logon Information dialog box appears, showing the name of the person who last logged on to the system in the User Name text box. To suppress this default action, you can change `DontDisplayLastUserName` in the `\Microsoft\Windows NT\Current Version\Winlogon` key of the `HKEY_LOCAL_MACHINE\SOFTWARE`. On most machines, you'll have to create this value by using the Edit, New command, as shown in Figure 14.15. The value should be set to 1, and the key is of the `REG_SZ` type.

Figure 14.15.

Suppressing the showing of the last user name to use the system can be done with Regedit.

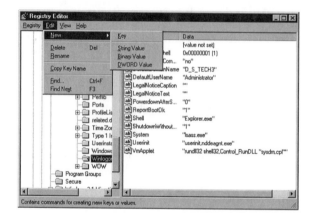

14.5.4. Accessing Shared Resources

Inability to access a share is one of the most common problems that requires resolution by an administrator. Files, shared folders (or simply shares), printer shares, and other shared resources require resource permissions. To create a share for an object, typically you right-click on the object and select the Sharing command. In many instances, the Sharing tab for the object appears, on which you can specify users, groups, and access privileges that are allowed.

The person who creates the resource "owns" the resource and has full privileges to it. The administrator doesn't have full access to a resource in many cases, but he or she can take ownership of it and thus receive the automatic full access. After an administrator takes ownership of a resource, the original owner is denied access to the resource. This is a safety mechanism to make it obvious that ownership has been removed and that the resource has been fully taken over.

If a user can't access a shared resource, he might not have the privileges required to do so. The administrator should try logging on under a different account and attempting to access that resource. If the resource has been accessed in the past under a particular user account, make sure that the resource's name is spelled correctly and that it has been located properly.

If there is a general problem accessing shared resources, you may want to open the Control Panel folder and check the Services Control Panel to see whether the various services responsible for validation are running properly. Those services include the following:

- NetLogon service
- Server service
- Workstation service

You should also check the Network Control Panel to ascertain whether the network bindings are configured correctly. These bindings are located on the Bindings tab. To check individual binding settings, select the binding and click the Properties button.

Inadvertent—or even intentional—changes to a user's group memberships in the User Manager or a change in System Policy can also cause a user to be denied access to a resource to which he was previously permitted access.

14.6. Modifying the Registry Using the Appropriate Tool

Windows NT 4.0 introduced the Registry database to this operating system, building on an early version in Windows NT 3.1 that stored OLE location information on object servers. The first complete Registry appeared in Windows 95, but the versions of the two are different.

The Registry is a database of settings and parameters. Among the features controlled by the Registry are the nature of the interface, operating system hardware and software settings, user preferences, and other settings. Prior to Windows NT, these settings appeared as sections and lines in various INI files.

The Registry is hierarchical, and each branch is referred to as a *hive*. Individual subbranches are also called *hives*. The top or first key of a hive is the primary key, and each primary key is composed of subkeys that take value entries.

Although most Registry entries are permanent, some are session dependent (transient) and are never written to disk. An example of a transient key is the

14

HKEY_LOCAL_MACHINE\Hardware key as generated by automatic hardware detection by the Hardware Recognizer (NTDETECT.COM for Intel computers). The Hardware key is a session value. Another transient value is the information, such as security tokens, that is written as part of a session logon.

When you install software, either a program or a part of the operating system, such as a device driver or service, writes new subkeys and value entries to the Registry. Uninstall these components to remove the information. Subkeys and value entries store information about hardware settings, driver files, environmental variables that need to be restored, or anything else the application developer requires reference to.

Only members of the Administrators or Power Users group can access the Registry by default. You can assign other users rights to modify all or part of the Registry by hives, but you should think long and hard before doing so. The potential to compromise security or corrupt an installation is high. By default, any user can see the Registry files but cannot edit, delete, or copy Registry files without specific permission to do so.

14.6.1. Modifying the Registry

You use the Registry Editor to view and modify the Windows NT Registry. Of the two versions of the Registry Editor, REGEDT32.EXE and REGEDIT.EXE, the former is more generally useful and offers more options. Figure 14.15 showed the menu and command you use to add an entry to the Registry using Regedit. Figure 14.16 shows the equivalent menu and command in Regedt32.

Figure 14.16.

You can suppress the display of the user name of the last user who used the system by using Regedt32.

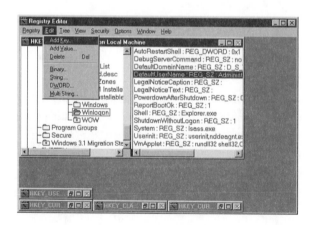

These programs are not listed on the Start menu and are not found in the Administrative Tools folder where you might expect to find them because Microsoft wanted to discourage their casual use. Instead, they're located in the WINNT folder, and you can add them to your Start menu or run them using the Run command on the Start menu.

Whenever you change a setting in a Control Panel or alter your desktop, you are writing changes to the Registry associated with the user account profile with which you logged on. If you want to view Registry information relating to services, resources, drivers, memory, display, or network components, you can use the Windows NT Diagnostic program (WINMSD). To access this utility, open the Start menu, choose Programs, select Administrative Tools, and look in the `%systemroot%\`
`system32` folder. WINMSD shows you the values that are currently there. For the most part, it is for viewing only, which prevents you from making destructive changes. Figure 14.17 shows the WINMSD interface. This utility is discussed in further detail in section 14.7.4.

Figure 14.17.

Viewing Registry settings with the Windows NT Diagnostics program.

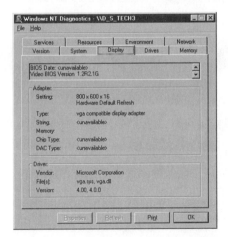

If you alter a value in the Registry using the Registry Editor, the changes you can make are unlimited and can be hazardous to your computer's health. If you delete or modify a required key, you could cause your computer to malfunction. In such a case, the only recovery methods that you can count on are reinstalling Windows NT and using the emergency repair disk. Therefore, you should proceed with caution when working in the Registry. You might even consider wandering around with the files opened as read-only to begin with (use the Read Only menu command in the Registry Editor).

14

These are the six root keys and their subtrees:

- HKEY_CLASSES_ROOT. This subtree stores OLE, file, class, and other associations that enable a program to launch when a data file is opened. Although the HKEY_CLASSES_ROOT is displayed as a root key, it is actually a subkey of HKEY_LOCAL_MACHINE\Software.

- HKEY_CURRENT_USER. All user settings, profiles, environment variables, interface settings, program groups, printer connections, application preferences, and network connections for the current user are stored in the subkeys of this root key.

- HKEY_LOCAL_MACHINE. This subkey contains information that identifies the computer on which the Registry is stored. Information in this key includes settings for hardware such as memory, disk drives, network adapters, and peripheral devices. Any software that supports hardware (device drivers, system services, system boot parameters, and other data) also is stored in this subkey.

- HKEY_USERS. All data on individual user profiles is located in this subkey. Windows NT stores local profiles in the Registry, and the values are maintained in this subkey.

- HKEY_CURRENT_CONFIG. The current configuration for software and any machine values are stored in this key. Among the settings stored in this root key are display device setup and control values required to restore the configuration when the program launches or your computer starts up.

- HKEY_DYN_DATA. Transient or dynamic data is stored in this last key in the Windows NT Registry. This root key cannot be modified by the user.

Most of the system data is stored in the HKEY_LOCAL_MACHINE and HKEY_USERS keys.

Individual settings that you make in the Control Panel applets are written to different keys in the Registry. You can modify those settings directly. Table 14.1 shows where the different Control Panel settings are located in the Registry. When you install a program using the Add/Remove Programs applet of Control Panel, for example, the data isn't written directly to the Registry, but the installer creates and deletes Registry entries in the Software hive.

Table 14.1. Control Panel relations to Registry keys.

Control Panel Option	Registry Data Location
Accessibility Options	`HKEY_CURRENT_USER\Control Panel\Accessibility`
Add/Remove Programs	`HKEY_CURRENT_USER\Console\Application` or `HKEY_LOCAL_MACHINE\Software\Microsoft\ Windows\CurrentVersion\Uninstall`
Console Date/Time	`HKEY_LOCAL_MACHINE\System\CurrentControlSet\ Control\TimeZoneInformation`
Devices	`HKEY_LOCAL_MACHINE\System\CurrentControlSet\ Services`
Display (machine settings)	`HKEY_LOCAL_MACHINE\Hardware\ResourceMap \Video`
Display (user settings)	`HKEY_CURRENT_USER\Control Panel\Desktop`
Fast Find	`HKEY_LOCAL_MACHINE\Software\Microsoft\Shared Tools\Fast Find`
Fonts	`HKEY_LOCAL_MACHINE\Software\Microsoft\Windows NT\CurrentVersion\Fonts`
Internet	`HKEY_LOCAL_MACHINE\Software\Microsoft\Windows \CurrentVersion\Internet Settings`
Keyboard	`HKEY_CURRENT_USER\Control Panel\Desktop` or `HKEY_CURRENT_USER\Control Panel\Keyboard`
Mail	Several places
Modems	`HKEY_LOCAL_MACHINE\Software\Microsoft\Windows\ CurrentVersion\Unimodem`
Mouse	`HKEY_CURRENT_USER\Control Panel\Mouse`
Multimedia	`HKEY_LOCAL_MACHINE\Software\Microsoft\Windows\ Multimedia` or `HKEY_LOCAL_MACHINE\Software\ Microsoft\Windows NT\CurrentVersion`
Network	Several locations
PC Card	`HKEY_LOCAL_MACHINE\Hardware\Description\System\ PCMCIA PCCARDs`
Ports	`HKEY_LOCAL_MACHINE\Hardware\ResourceMap`
Printers	`HKEY_CURRENT_USER\Printers`
Regional Settings	`HKEY_CURRENT_USER\Control Panel\International`

continues

14

Table 14.1. continued

Control Panel Option	Registry Data Location
SCSI Adapters	`HKEY_LOCAL_MACHINE\Hardware\ResourceMap\ScsiAdapter`
Server	Several locations
Services	`HKEY_LOCAL_MACHINE\System\CurrentControlSet\Services`
Sounds	`HKEY_CURRENT_USER\AppEvent\Schemes\Apps\Default` or `HKEY_CURRENT_USER\AppEvent\Schemes\Apps\.Default`
System	Several locations
Tape Devices	`HKEY_LOCAL_MACHINE\Hardware\ResourceMap\OtherDrivers\TapeDevices`
Telephony	`HKEY_LOCAL_MACHINE\Software\Microsoft\Windows\CurrentVersion\Telephony`
UPS	`HKEY_LOCAL_MACHINE\System\CurrentControlSet\Services\UPS`

If you make a mistake and delete a key or value from the Registry Editor, you cannot use an Undo command to recover from the error. The Confirm on Delete command on the Options menu offers only a limited safeguard. As everyone knows, it is easy to confirm a deletion and regret the mistake later.

To correct a critical deletion, complete the following steps:

1. Close the Registry Editor.
2. Immediately restart your computer.
3. Hold down the Spacebar while Windows NT loads, and then select the Last Known Good option.

When Windows NT boots your system, it uses the backup copy of the Windows NT Registry. Any changes you made to your system since your last startup are discarded. The Last Known Good configuration enables you to recover from a critical deletion that you've made in the Registry —provided that you recognize the error before successfully logging on to your computer again.

14.6.2. Backing Up the Registry

The most important thing you can do to protect your investment in your system's configuration is to back up the Registry files. When you create an ERD (as described earlier in this chapter), you back up specific hives of the Registry. You should keep a full backup of the Registry on hand.

You find the Registry file in the `%systemroot%\System32\Config` folder. For most installations, the `%systemroot%` is typically `C:\WINNT`. Individual user's Registry data is written to the `NTUSER.DAT` file in that user's folder at the location `C:\WINNT\Profiles\`*username*`\NTUSER.DAT`.

When a user logs on to his workstation, a Profile folder is created for him with an `NTUSER.DAT` file to hold his user profile. Roaming profiles for a domain are stored as the original copy of the `NTUSER.DAT` file on the domain controller.

The following `CONFIG` folder files store direct information on Registry hives:

- `DEFAULT`
- `NTUSER.DAT` (in Profiles subdirectory)
- `SAM`
- `SECURITY`
- `SOFTWARE`
- `SYSTEM`
- `USERDIFF`

Several files are associated with each Registry hive in the `CONFIG` folder. The first and primary file takes no extension. The `CONFIG` directory also contains auxiliary files for the Registry that are the backup, log, and event files. These files have the same names as those listed above, but they take the `.LOG`, `.EVT`, and `.SAV` extensions (respectively). The `SYSTEM` file also has a `SYSTEM.ALT` file associated with it. The EVT event files, viewable in the Event Viewer, contain audited events. Log files store changes that can be rolled back. The SAV backup files are part of the Last Known Good boot configuration that enables you to restore your Registry based on your last booted session. (The Last Known Good option was described earlier in this chapter.)

The LOG file is a backup file that enables changes to be rolled back. It is a fault-tolerance feature, as changes are written to the LOG file first. When the data is completely written in the LOG file, updating of the matching Registry hive begins.

14

First, the data section to be changed is marked, and the data is transferred. When the data transfer is complete, the update flag is reset to indicate successful transfer. Should there be a problem or should your computer malfunction during the transfer, the update starts again from scratch.

The SYSTEM file is updated in a somewhat different manner because your computer relies on that key to start up. The duplicate SYSTEM.ALT file is used and operates as the replacement for a LOG file. The entire file is mirrored and replicated. Then, in the event of a crash, the backup file is used, and the entire file is replaced.

It is unnecessary to back up the entire Registry. Much of the information is transitory and session dependent. Only specific portions of the Registry need be protected. The files of greatest importance are the SYSTEM and SOFTWARE files. They are generally small and can fit on a single floppy disk. You should also note that the SAM and SECURITY files can't be modified and cannot be copied or backed up.

To back up the Registry, use the RDISK program described earlier in this chapter and set that option. Do not try to copy the files directly to a disk. You can also back up individual hive files from within the Registry Editor by saving a branch using the Save Key command on the Registry menu. You can use the Restore Key command to load those backup files.

The hives of the Registry are locked and cannot be accessed to be copied directly. In a dual-boot system, or if you boot your system using MS-DOS or some other operating system, these files are not locked and can be copied directly. You could copy those files to another drive or volume, for example.

You can view Registry files on a FAT volume from any other operating system. If the file system is an NTFS volume, only a Windows NT or Linux system running a disk access utility can view the files, read them, and copy them. On Windows NT, one program that can do this is NTFSDOS.EXE.

 Note NTFSDOS poses a giant security risk because it allows you to bypass all NTFS security. Of course, you do have to boot the machine with a floppy containing the NTFSDOS driver, so it requires physical access to the machine.

14.6.3. Changing the Registry Size

Normally, the default size of the Windows NT Workstation Registry is sufficient for most configurations. If you have a large organization and store a lot of user profiles and application data configurations, the Registry might run out of room. In that case, you would need to alter the allotted size of the Registry.

To change the maximum Registry size, complete the following steps:

1. Double-click the System icon in the Control Panel folder.
2. Click on the Performance tab, and then click the Change button in the Virtual Memory section. The Virtual Memory dialog box appears.
3. Enter a size in the Maximum Registry Size (MB) text box, and then click OK.

The Registry can be somewhat larger than the value entered in the System Control Panel. It is related to the size of your paging file, which is related to the amount of RAM installed in your system. When the Registry exceeds the size you set, it brings your system to a halt with a STOP error. This problem is very rare unless you attempt to reduce the size of the Registry artificially. Keep the maximum Registry size set about 2MB larger than the current size in the Virtual Memory dialog box.

14.6.4. Troubleshooting the Registry

Several problems can be directly related to Registry errors. The most common problems include the following:

- Your computer won't boot properly or at all.
- Your computer looks or works differently than it once did.
- Your computer won't shut down correctly.
- The "Blue Screen of Death" occurs, resulting from a STOP error.
- A software or hardware component that once operated correctly stops working even though you haven't made any physical changes to the files or the device.
- Something stops working after you add new software or hardware, and the two are not known to be incompatible.

Most of these error conditions are at least correctable from backup. The one really frightening error is the STOP error because it prevents you from accessing your machine. To correct the Blue Screen of Death, try booting from your boot disk and running the Check Disk program to repair the type of errors associated with disk and file problems. The CHKDSK.EXE program is located in the %systemroot%\ SYS-TEM32 directory.

14

14.7. Implementing Advanced Techniques to Resolve Various Problems

Windows NT comes with several diagnostic tools to help you optimize and tune the system and to correct error conditions. In many ways, the operating system is meant to be *self-tuning* and to require that relatively few settings be altered to make the computer run well. To track errors, Windows records a system of events in log files. These events can be tracked and controlled, and they prove very useful in troubleshooting. This section delves into the Event logs in some detail.

To aid in solving network problems, Windows NT also offers you the Network Monitor. This utility enables you to examine and analyze network performance and utilization. Common network issues are also discussed in this section.

14.7.1. Working with the Event Logs and Event Viewer

Events are actions that occur on your system. The system itself generates events and records them in the System and Security log files. Applications record their events in the Application log. You see a standard set of events by default, but you can audit resources to add other events. Many application developers provide the event system to help administrators analyze their application. You view and analyze the Event logs in the Event Viewer.

The Event logs are normally accessible to everyone: Anyone who cares to can see the information. You can even view an Event log on another machine if you have the permission to do so.

An administrator might want to restrict access to these logs so that the information is secure and can't be erased. To restrict who can open the System or Application logs, you use the following Registry key:

```
HKEY_LOCAL_MACHINE\System\CurrentControlSet\Services\EventLog\log_name
```

Set the RestrictGuestAccess value of type REG_DWORD to 1. If this value is set to 0 or doesn't exist, the default condition enables anyone to access these two logs.

The log files use a first-in first-out (FIFO) system. When the ultimate limit of a log file is reached, the oldest events are deleted to make room for new events. The Event log holds events longer than the time limit as long as the size remains below the specified maximum size. The default size is 512KB, and the default time limit for storing an event is one week. You can modify these settings from within the Event Viewer.

To change the settings of the Event logs, complete the following steps:

1. Open the Event Viewer.

2. Open the Log menu and choose the Log Settings command. The Event Log Settings dialog box appears.

3. In the Change Settings for Log list box, select the log type.

4. Set the size of the log in the Maximum Log Size spinner.

5. Select one of the radio buttons in the Event Log Wrapping section to determine what happens to old events.

6. Close the Event Log Settings dialog box, and then close the Event Viewer.

A prudent administrator makes a habit of checking the Event logs on a regular basis. Many events occur so frequently that they can overwhelm the Event logs and make it difficult for the administrator to determine what other error conditions or trends exist. By analyzing the Event logs regularly, you can determine what event types are worth keeping and how often those should be noted.

Another useful feature of the Event Viewer is its capability to export Event logs to data files. Several output formats are available, so you can use whichever one makes it easiest for you to analyze the data in the logs. You can export your log data out to text files (TXT) or Event log files (EVT). Numerous third-party tools help analyze Windows NT Workstation log files.

The Event Viewer (like the Performance Monitor) is one of the Windows NT operating system's central diagnostic tools. Learning how to use this tool rewards the administrator with a better-running workstation, less time spent tracking down errors, and lowered stress.

If you want additional information about an event, double-click the event to open the Event Detail dialog box. That dialog box contains the following information for the selected event:

- Date of event
- Time of event
- User account that generated the event (when applicable, this information is recorded in the Security log)

14

- Computer on which the event occurred
- Event ID (the actual event code)
- Source or component that recorded the error
- Type of error: Error, Information, or Warning
- Category of event
- Description of event
- Data describing the event in hexadecimal form

You can find information on many of the possible error messages in the documentation and resource kits for Windows NT Workstation. Microsoft also maintains a technical database that contains many of the reasons a given error message might have been generated. You can search the Knowledge Base on the Microsoft Web site (as a premium service) or on the Microsoft network to obtain error information stored in the logs.

Another database on CD-ROM is delivered to programmers as part of their subscription to the Microsoft Developer Network program. This database contains information not only about error conditions, but also about internal error codes of interest to programmers. Participants at all levels of MSDN receive this database.

The Event log is very flexible. You can turn event logging on and off for a number of resources by specifying the auditing properties for that resource. Many developers use the Event logs to record information specific to their applications.

The Event log is almost an embarrassment of riches. To help you find the particular event you need, the Event Viewer has a find and search function. You can also filter the Event log derived from your own computer. The View menu commands enable you to filter the log by any of the following items:

- Computer
- Event date and time
- Event ID
- Event type
- User
- Source of the event

14.7.2. Network Diagnostics

Numerous network problems arise relating to both hardware and software configuration. Some of these problems require you to experiment with cabling and couplings; others can be solved with software that comes with Windows NT Workstation.

If you have a complex network installation, you may need diagnostic equipment to test your hardware. Often, you can test individual components by rearranging their positions in the network (swapping cables or boards) and isolating the offending piece of hardware.

Windows NT Server comes with a utility called the Network Monitor that can be very useful for diagnosing network activity. This Administrative Tools utility collects and filters network packets and analyzes network activity. This utility diagnoses only the computer that it is running on.

The Network Monitor service is a supplementary component of the Windows NT Workstation installation. To install this program, open the Control Panel's Network applet, choose the Service tab, and click the Add button. After Windows NT Workstation builds its list of services, you can select the Network Monitor Agent option from the list, as shown in Figure 14.18.

Figure 14.18.

Adding the Network Monitor Agent to the system.

Network Monitor is both statistical and graphical. The Network Monitor screen is divided into four panes: the Graph pane, the Session Stats pane, the Total Stats pane, and the Station Stats pane. In these four panes of the Network Monitor, the current activity appears in real time.

14

The Graph pane in the upper-left section shows the following bar graphs:

- % Network Utilization
- Broadcasts Per Second
- Bytes Per Second
- Frames Per Second
- Multicast Per Second

These parameters show you the level of activity your network is experiencing and how saturated your network bandwidth is.

The Session Stats pane shows you which nodes are communicating, and the number of frames (of the first 128 measured) sent and received from each.

The Total Stats pane (on the right side of the Network Monitor) shows complete network statistics in the following categories:

- Captured Statistics
- Network Card (Mac) Error Statistics
- Network Card (Mac) Statistics
- Network Statistics
- Per Second Statistics

You must scroll to see each of the panels in the pane for these categories.

The last pane at the bottom of the window is the Station Stats pane. Information here shows what your workstation is communicating to the network. Click on a column head to sort by that category. The following categories appear:

- Broadcasts Sent
- Bytes Rcvd
- Bytes Sent
- Directed Frames Sent
- Frames Rcvd
- Frames Sent
- Multicasts Sent
- Network Address

An amazing number of network problems are related to TCP/IP protocol addressing. Make sure that your workstation has a unique address or uses a DHCP (Dynamic Host Configuration Protocol) service for its TCP/IP assignments. Also, make sure that the subnet address you entered in the TCP/IP Properties dialog box is correct. To view such TCP/IP settings, complete the following steps:

1. Double-click the Network applet of the Control Panel.
2. Click on the Protocols tab of the Network dialog box.
3. Select the TCP/IP protocol, and then click the Properties button.
4. Examine the settings in the TCP/IP Properties dialog box to see whether they are correct.

 You can also use the IPCONFIG utility (particularly with the /ALL parameter) to view information about DHCP leases and other related IP information.

The PING utility is also included in Windows NT Workstation. You can ping other computers on the network to see whether they are active, and you can ping your own workstation with the specific address. You also can ping the Default Gateway or any computer on the Internet or your intranet. To learn more about this command, go to a command prompt and enter the PING command without any parameters. An informational screen appears, detailing the use of PING.

14.7.3. Resource Conflicts

Many configuration errors are resource conflicts. These can result from duplicate-interrupt or I/O assignments or from SCSI devices having duplicate or improper assignments. You might see these problems when you first boot your system, but they might not show up until later when a device doesn't work properly.

Check the Event log to see what error events are listed. Also run the Windows diagnostic program WINMSD (in the Administrative Tools folder) to examine your resource settings. You can roll back errors in software by using the Last Known Good configuration.

14

14.7.4. Using the Windows NT Diagnostics Program

The Windows NT Diagnostics program is the worthy successor to the MSD program in Windows 3.1. The Diagnostics dialog box shows you information on many of the Registry items in the HKEY_LOCAL_MACHINE subtree. Using WINMSD, you can obtain detailed information and reports on the state and configuration of your workstation. You cannot use this diagnostic tool to change any configuration settings, but you can use it to determine what conditions exist so that you can fix a problem.

This dialog box contains the following tabs:

- ■ *Display.* Provides information on your video adapter, its firmware, and any adapter settings.

- ■ *Drives.* Lists drives and volumes in a hierarchical display. Drives include floppy disk drives, hard disk drives, CD-ROM, optical drives, and mapped drives through any network connections. If you double-click a drive letter, the Drive Properties dialog box appears. The Drive Properties dialog box shows you sectors/clusters, bytes per sector, the current status of the use of the disk, and the file system in use.

- ■ *Environment.* Contains any environmental variables in use for a Command Prompt session.

- ■ *Memory.* Shows the installed memory and virtual memory, as well as usage of both.

- ■ *Network.* Displays any installed logons, transports (protocols and bindings), settings, and statistics.

- ■ *Resources.* Contains a list of device assignments. Specifically, this tab shows the IRQ assignments, port numbers, DMA channels, and UMB locations used by each device. If you suspect a device conflict, this is the place to go to attempt to locate the suspect.

- ■ *Services.* Displays the information stored in the HKEY_LOCAL_MACHINE\System\ CurrentControlSet\Services key. If you select a service and click the Devices button, the information stored in the HKEY_LOCAL_MACHINE\System\ CurrentControlSet\Control key appears, along with the status of that control.

- ■ *System.* Shows the information stored in the HKEY_LOCAL_MACHINE\Hardware key, including the CPU type and information on other installed devices.

■ *Version.* Contains the information stored in the HKEY_LOCAL_MACHINE\ Software\Microsoft\Windows\NT\CurrentVersion key. You will find the operating system version, build number, Service Pack update, and registered owner of the software.

Windows NT ships with several utilities for evaluating a workstation's configuration and performance.

Note

The exam tests you on the core product of Windows NT Workstation. In the real world, however, you should not limit your troubleshooting tools to only those. A great many other troubleshooting utilities can be found in the Microsoft Windows NT Workstation Resource Kit, on TechNet, and in the Service Packs that have been released since Windows NT Workstation 4.0 first came out (of which there are now three).

14

Lab

The following review questions will test your knowledge on the topics covered in this chapter.

Review Questions

1. Which of the following files are not on the emergency repair disk?

    A. `SETUP.LOG`

    B. `NTUSER.DA_`

    C. `CONFIG.NT`

    D. `NTSYSTEM.DA_`

2. Which of the following is a collection of configuration information Windows NT uses during the boot process?

    A. Last Known Good

    B. Control set

    C. `BOOT.INI`

    D. NTLDR

3. How do you boot with the Last Known Good configuration?

    A. Start WINNT with the `/L` switch.

    B. Select the option from the Boot Loader menu.

    C. Use the `/lastknowngood` switch in the `BOOT.INI` file.

    D. During the boot process, press the Spacebar when prompted.

4. Which utility is used to update the emergency repair information?

    A. `RDISK.EXE`

    B. `REPAIR.EXE`

    C. DISKPERF

    D. Server Manager

5. If you need to re-create the Setup boot disks, which command do you use?

   A. WINNT32

   B. WINNT

   C. WINNT/OX

   D. REPAIR

6. On an x86-based Windows NT Server, what is the default location of the NTOSKRNL.EXE file?

   A. *winnt_root*

   B. *winnt_root*\SYSTEM32

   C. *winnt_root*\SYSTEM32\CONFIG

   D. *winn_root*\SYSTEM

7. What section of the BOOT.INI file contains a reference for every OS on the Boot Loader menu?

   A. [initialize]

   B. [common]

   C. [boot loader]

   D. [operating systems]

8. What section of the BOOT.INI file defines the default operating system that will be loaded if a choice is not made on the Boot Loader menu?

   A. [initialize]

   B. [common]

   C. [boot loader]

   D. [operating systems]

9. Which of the following is an editable text file that controls the Boot Loader menu?

   A. NTBOOT.INI

   B. NTLDR

   C. BOOT.INI

   D. BOOTSECT.DOS

14

10. Evan calls and wants to know if you can reduce the amount of time his computer takes to boot. He also wants to change the default operating system from MS-DOS to Windows NT Workstation. Which utility do you use?

    A. Control Panel, Boot

    B. Control Panel, System

    C. Server Manager

    D. None of the above. You configure that on a user-by-user basis in the users profiles.

11. Spencer calls to say that he was playing around and accidentally changed the SCSI controller card driver, and now the computer won't boot Windows NT. It stops at the blue screen and gives him a system error. Given the following options, what should Spencer do?

    A. Boot into DOS and rerun the Windows NT Setup program.

    B. Purchase and install the SCSI device that he selected.

    C. Reinstall Windows NT.

    D. Select the Last Known Good configuration during Windows NT's boot process, and then remove the incorrect driver.

12. Annie works in the South building. She calls to say that the following message is showing up on her screen.

```
I/O Error accessing boot sector file multi(0)disk(0)rdisk(0)
partition(1):\bootsect.dos
```

    Which one of the critical boot files is *really* missing?

    A. NTLDR

    B. NTDETECT.COM

    C. BOOTSECT.DOS

    D. MSDOS.SYS

13. The BOOTSECT.DOS file contains:

    A. A copy of the information that was originally on the boot sector of the drive before Windows NT was installed. You use it to boot an operating system other than Windows NT.

    B. A copy of the information needed to boot a RISC-based computer.

C. The file that detects the hardware installed on a PC with a Plug and Play BIOS.

D. The file that contains the boot menu selections.

14. By default, in which of the following folders do spooled print jobs reside?

    A. `\winnt_root`

    B. `\winnt_root\SYSTEM32`

    C. `\winnt_root\SYSTEM32\SPOOL`

    D. `\winnt_root\SYSTEM32\SPOOL\PRINTERS`

15. A Windows NT-based computer is to function as a print server for the network. Which of the following is one of the most critical components?

    A. Free disk space

    B. Frequent backups

    C. A fast processor

    D. Accelerated PCI local bus video

16. What priority level is assigned to the print spooler service by Windows NT Workstation?

    A. 1

    B. 3

    C. 7

    D. 15

17. How do you change the location of the spool directory?

    A. In the Control Panel, choose the Printers option, and then change the entry on the Spool tab.

    B. In the Registry, add a value called `DefaultSpoolDirectory` to `HKEY_LOCAL_MACHINE\System\CurrentControlSet\Control\Print\Printers`.

    C. Map a drive to the new location.

    D. Change port settings at the printer.

14

18. Which two of the following extensions are used for files in the printer spool?

    A. .TXT

    B. .SHD

    C. .SHT

    D. .SPL

19. How long do files remain in the printer spool?

    A. Until there is a clean boot of the system

    B. Until the system is shut down

    C. Until the job finishes printing

    D. Until the administrator empties the spool

20. What becomes of spooled print jobs in the event of a computer crash?

    A. When the system restarts, the printer processes the files immediately.

    B. They remain inactive until the administrator restarts them.

    C. They do not restart.

    D. They perform a checksum operation to identify corruption that may have occurred.

21. To change the priority class of a print service, which component of the Registry do you edit?

    A. `HKEY_LOCAL_MACHINE\System\CurrentControlSet`

    B. `HKEY_LOCAL_MACHINE\System\CurrentControlSet\Control`

    C. `HKEY_LOCAL_MACHINE\System\CurrentControlSet\Control\Print`

    D. `HKEY_LOCAL_MACHINE\System\CurrentControlSet\Control\Printers`

22. Which of the following should be one of the first steps you take to resolve an error of insufficient disk space during a new Windows NT installation?

    A. Boot to a different operating system and run WINNT from there.

    B. Compress NTFS partitions.

    C. Open the Control Panel and verify that the local computer has a unique name.

    D. Call Microsoft Sales to replace the disks.

23. From which media can Windows NT 4.0 be installed?

  A. CD-ROM

  B. 5.25" floppies

  C. 3.5" disks

  D. A network share point

24. Which of the following is the correct method for installing Windows NT 4.0 over a previous version of NT and keeping all settings?

  A. Install in the same directory the old version was in.

  B. Install in a new directory.

  C. Do nothing. It will automatically find the old version and install over it.

  D. Run the MIGRATE utility.

25. How do you create a dual-boot machine with a previous version of Windows NT?

  A. Install in the same directory the old version was in.

  B. Install in a new directory.

  C. Do nothing. It will automatically find the old version and install over it.

  D. Run the MIGRATE utility.

26. Suppose you lose the startup disks you made during Windows NT installation. Which of the following commands do you use to remake them?

  A. WINNT32

  B. WINNT

  C. WINNT /OX

  D. WINNT /STARTUP

27. Which type of application is least likely to crash on Windows NT Workstation?

  A. MS-DOS–based

  B. Windows 16-bit

  C. Windows 32-bit

  D. Real-mode

14

28. How do you open the Task Manager?

    A. Click the Task Manager button in the Windows NT Security dialog box.

    B. Right-click the Taskbar.

    C. Select Task Manager from the Control Panel.

    D. Right-click on the desktop and choose Task Manager from the menu.

29. Which of the following services does Internet Information Server run?

    A. HTTP (WWW)

    B. FTP

    C. Gopher

    D. VRML

30. If you cannot log on to a workstation using any account, what is the next logical step toward solving the problem?

    A. Repair the accounts database by using the emergency repair disk.

    B. Verify that the SAM database contains the proper permissions.

    C. Look for CRC errors.

    D. Verify frame types.

31. Which of the following is one of the most common causes of logon problems?

    A. Programmable keyboard

    B. Hashing table error

    C. Duplicate SIDs

    D. The Caps Lock key

32. If a user can't access a file, a share, a printer, or some other resource, what should you check first?

    A. The resource permissions

    B. The global groups

    C. The local groups

    D. TechNet

33. You suspect a logon problem from a workstation. You should check the Control Panel's Services application to ensure that which of the following services is running properly?

    A. The NetLogon service

    B. The Server service

    C. The Workstation service

    D. The Bindings service

34. By checking the Bindings tab in the Control Panel's Network application, you can verify which of the following? (Choose two.)

    A. Services are bound to applications.

    B. Correct frame types have been selected.

    C. Dirty RAM is not causing a failure to update SAM.

    D. Services are bound to adapters.

35. Which tool should you use to find restrictions on a user's access to a computer?

    A. Network Monitor

    B. User Manager

    C. User Manager for Domains

    D. System Policy Editor

36. Karen calls to report that she cannot log on to the system. She is getting a message that says NT cannot log you on. Check your userid and password information and try again. As an administrator, what should you check first?

    A. Make sure that she types in the correct password and user ID combination. Also check to see whether she is entering the password in the correct case and specifying the correct domain name.

    B. Nothing. This is a normal message that the user will get when the server is down for maintenance.

    C. Log on as administrator and restart the domain controller to clear out any unused connections. When the server comes back up, the user should be able to log on.

    D. Check the System log in Event Viewer.

14

37. The System Tab in the Windows NT Diagnostics box displays information stored in the Registry under which hive?

    A. HKEY_LOCAL_MACHINE\SOFTWARE

    B. HKEY_LOCAL_MACHINE\HARDWARE

    C. HKEY_LOCAL_MACHINE\SOFTWARE\MICROSOFT\WINDOWS NT\CurrentVersion

    D. HKEY_LOCAL_MACHINE\SYSTEM

38. Version information is stored in which hive of the Windows NT Registry?

    A. HKEY_LOCAL_MACHINE\SOFTWARE

    B. HKEY_LOCAL_MACHINE\SOFTWARE\MICROSOFT\WINDOWS NT

    C. HKEY_LOCAL_MACHINE\SOFTWARE\MICROSOFT\WINDOWS NT\CurrentVersion

    D. HKEY_LOCAL_MACHINE\SYSTEM

39. Service information is stored in which hive of the Windows NT Registry?

    A. HKEY_LOCAL_MACHINE\SOFTWARE

    B. HKEY_LOCAL_MACHINE\SOFTWARE\MICROSOFT\WINDOWS NT

    C. HKEY_LOCAL_MACHINE\SOFTWARE\MICROSOFT\WINDOWS NT\CurrentVersion

    D. HKEY_LOCAL_MACHINE\SYSTEM

40. By default, who can view Event log information?

    A. Administrators

    B. Members of Domain Users

    C. Guests

    D. Anyone

41. To see information about DMA channels and UMB locations in the Windows NT Diagnostics tool, which tab do you select?

    A. Services

    B. Memory

    C. Resources

    D. Network

42. Which three log files can Event Viewer display?

    A. System

    B. Application

    C. Security

    D. NetLogon

43. When you view the Security log with Event Viewer, which of the following indicates a Failure Audit?

    A. A stop sign

    B. A key

    C. An exclamation mark

    D. A padlock

44. When you view the Security log with Event Viewer, which of the following indicates a Success Audit?

    A. A stop sign

    B. A key

    C. An exclamation mark

    D. A padlock

45. When you view the Security log with Event Viewer, which two symbols are displayed?

    A. A stop sign

    B. A key

    C. An exclamation mark

    D. A padlock

46. If you are not using any Win32 applications on a system, what are the contents of the Application log?

    A. It is empty.

    B. It contains only the Win16 application information.

    C. It mirrors the System log.

    D. It contains events for only those applications manually selected.

14

47. You configure recovery options by:

    A. Using Regedit to change parameters.

    B. Running the SYSTEM command-line utility.

    C. Changing values in the bottom frame of the Startup/Shutdown tab.

    D. Running Server Manager.

48. Which of the following logs is displayed in Event Viewer by default?

    A. System

    B. Application

    C. Security

    D. NetLogon

49. If you find a series of STOP errors in a System log, what is the most likely source of all the errors?

    A. The STOP error at the top of the list.

    B. The STOP error at the bottom of the list.

    C. Nothing. Each error stands alone.

    D. The error most replicated.

50. The System log, which you can view with Event Viewer, tracks what three kinds of events?

    A. Warnings

    B. Information

    C. Configuration

    D. Errors

Answers to Review Questions

1. D A compressed copy of the Registry's SYSTEM hive is stored as SYSTEM._ instead of NTSYSTEM.DA_.

2. B A control set is a collection of configuration information used during the boot process; Last Known Good is a special single control set used for troubleshooting.

3. D Press the Spacebar during the boot process, and the Hardware Profile/ Configuration Recovery menu appears. Then you can select a hardware profile and press L for Last Known Good configuration.

4. A RDISK will update the emergency repair directory.

5. C When used with the WINNT command, the /OX switch re-creates the Setup boot disks.

6. B The *winnt_root*\SYSTEM32 directory holds the NTOSKRNL.EXE file.

7. D The BOOT.INI file contains only two sections: [boot loader] and [operating systems]. The first defines the default operating system; the second contains a reference for each OS on the menu.

8. C The BOOT.INI file contains only two sections: [boot loader] and [operating systems]. The first defines the default operating system; the second contains a reference for each OS on the menu.

9. C The NTLDR calls the Boot Loader menu, but the BOOT.INI file controls the menu and its choices.

10. B In the System utility, you can choose a default operating system and reduce boot time.

11. D Booting with the Last Known Good configuration circumvents recent driver change problems.

12. C Never try to make a problem harder than it is. If the error message says BOOTSECT.DOS is missing, it is probably BOOTSECT.DOS that is missing.

13. A BOOTSECT.DOS is a copy of the information that was originally on the boot sector of the drive before Windows NT was installed. You use it to boot an operating system other than NT.

14. D By default, print jobs are stored in *winnt_root*\SYSTEM32\SPOOL\PRINTERS until they are completely printed.

15. A If a Windows NT-based computer is acting as a print server for the network, make sure plenty of free disk space is available on the partition that contains the default spool directory. Spooled print jobs can be quite large and can eat up disk space more quickly than you might think, especially during peak printing periods.

16. C Windows NT Workstation assigns a default priority level of 7 to the print spooler service.

14

17. B You can change the spool directory in the Registry by adding a value called `DefaultSpoolDirectory` of type `REG_SZ` to `HKEY_LOCAL_MACHINE\System\CurrentControlSet\Control\Print\Printers` and then entering the path to the new spool directory.

18. B, D When a document prints, two files are created for the print job in the spool directory (by default, *winnt_root*`\SYSTEM32\SPOOL\PRINTERS`). One of the files, which has an `.SPL` extension, is the actual print job spool file. The other file, which has an `.SHD` extension, is a shadow file that contains information about the job, including its owner and priority.

19. C When a document prints, two files are created for the print job in the spool directory (by default, *winnt_root*`\SYSTEM32\SPOOL\PRINTERS`). One of the files, which has an `.SPL` extension, is the actual print job spool file. The other file, which has an `.SHD` extension, is a shadow file that contains information about the job, including its owner and priority. These files remain in the spool directory until the job is printed, at which point they are deleted.

20. A In the event of a system crash, some spool and shadow files may be left over from jobs that were waiting to be printed. When the spooler service restarts (along with the rest of the system), the printer should process these files immediately.

21. C To change the priority class for the Spooler service, add a value called `PriorityClass` of type `REG_DWORD` to `HKEY_LOCAL_MACHINE\System\CurrentControlSet\Control\Print` and set it equal to the priority class desired.

22. B Compressing the partition can free up more disk space so the installation can execute successfully.

23. A, D Windows NT can be installed from a network share point or a CD-ROM. Although 3.5" floppies are needed to start the CD installation, Windows NT cannot be installed strictly from 5.25" or 3.5" floppy disks.

24. A To install 4.0 over a previous version of Windows NT and keep all settings, install it in the same directory the old version was in. If you install into any other directory, you do not upgrade; you create a dual-boot machine.

25. B To create a dual-boot machine, you install Windows NT 4.0 into any directory other that the one the previous version was in.

26. C Three startup disks are made at the time of installation. If you lose these disks, you can re-create them by running `WINNT/OX`.

27. C Windows 32-bit applications are least likely to crash on Windows NT Workstation.

28. A, B Task Manager can be opened from the status bar or the Windows NT Security dialog box.

29. A, B, C IIS runs HTTP, FTP, and Gopher applications as services.

30. A If you can't log on from any account, repair the accounts database by using the emergency repair process.

31. D One of the most common causes for logon problems is the Caps Lock key. Make certain that the user isn't typing the password in all caps.

32. A If a user can't access a file, a share, a printer, or some other resource, check the resource permissions.

33. A, B, C Check the Control Panel's Services application to ensure that the NetLogon service, the Server service, and the Workstation service are running properly.

34. A, D By checking the Bindings tab in the Control Panel's Network application, you can verify that the services are bound to applications and adapters.

35. D Check System Policy Editor for restrictions on the user's access to computers or other resources.

36. A If a user can't log on, he may be using an incorrect user name or password.

37. B HKEY_LOCAL_MACHINE\HARDWARE stores information about what is available on the machine.

38. C HKEY_LOCAL_MACHINE\SOFTWARE\MICROSOFT\WINDOWS NT\CurrentVersion stores information about the current version of Windows NT on the machine.

39. D HKEY_LOCAL_MACHINE\SYSTEM\CurrentControlSet\Services stores information about the current services available to Windows NT on the machine.

40. D By default, anyone can view Event log information. By editing the Registry, you can prevent guests from viewing the log information, but that is the only restriction available.

41. C DMA channel and VMB location information is located on the Resources tab.

42. A, B, C Event Viewer shows the contents of the System, Application, and Security log files.

43. D A padlock symbol indicates a failure audit.

44. B A key symbol indicates a success audit.

14

45. B, D A key symbol indicates a success audit, and a padlock symbol indicates a failure audit.

46. A The Application log stores information only on Win32 applications.

47. C The bottom frame of the Startup/Shutdown tab contains configuration information for the Recovery options.

48. A The System log is displayed by default when Event Viewer is started.

49. B The System log is written to in sequential order, with new entries at the top. The error most likely to be causing others would be the first one written to the file, which would appear at the bottom of the list.

50. A, B, D The System log tracks warnings, errors, and information events.

Exercises

The following exercises walk you through some of the steps discussed in this chapter.

Exercise 14.1: Creating a Boot Floppy Disk and Emergency Repair Disks

This exercise shows you how to create a disk with which you can start a workstation in case of boot failure and a set of disks with which you can repair a workstation that doesn't boot properly.

To create the boot floppy disk, follow these steps:

1. Insert a blank floppy disk in the disk drive and format that disk.

2. Open the Windows NT Explorer and select the BOOT.INI, NTLDR, NTBOOTDD.SYS, and NTDETECT.COM files.

3. Copy these four files to the floppy disk to create the Windows NT boot floppy disk.

4. Restart your computer without removing the floppy disk from the drive. If the disk is valid, it boots your computer.

5. Label the disk and store it in a secure location.

To create a set of emergency repair disks, follow these steps:

1. Open the Start menu, choose Programs, and choose Command Prompt.

2. Type RDISK /S and press the Enter key.

3. In the Repair Disk Utility dialog box, click the Create Repair Disk button.

4. Insert a formatted floppy disk, and then click OK.

5. After Windows NT Workstation creates the ERD, remove the floppy disk, write-protect the disk, and store it away.

6. Click the Exit button to close RDISK.

7. Click the Close box.

Exercise 14.2: Displaying Device Drivers at Startup

This exercise explores modifying the BOOT.INI file to enumerate your drivers when the kernel is loading. To display the device drivers, follow these steps:

1. Open the Start menu and choose Programs, Accessories, Notepad.

2. Select the File, Open command.

3. In the Files of Type list box, select All Files. Then select the BOOT.INI file from the root directory.

4. Find the line in the BOOT.INI file that reads Windows NT Server Version 4.00 [VGA] followed by /basevideo and /sos switches. If your system uses a VGA driver, skip to step 6.

5. Choose the File, Save As command and save the BOOT.INI file under a different name, such as BOOT.BAK.

6. Delete the /basevideo switch, but leave the /sos switch intact. Modify the text in brackets to read "Windows NT Server Version 4.00 [SOS]".

7. Select the File, Save As command and save the file as the BOOT.INI file in the root directory. (Note that the BOOT.INI file is read-only, system, and hidden. You will probably have to change the attributes to be able to save the file.)

8. Exit Notepad and reboot your system.

9. Select the SOS option from the boot menu when it appears. Your device drivers are now listed onscreen as they load in ARC format.

10. Log on to Windows NT Workstation.

11. Restore the original BOOT.INI file with the VGA configuration and /basevideo switch. Then reboot to test your system.

14

Exercise 14.3: Enabling Printer Auditing

In this exercise, you will turn on printer auditing for a share.

Before you can turn on auditing of a printer share, you must enable File and Object Access auditing in the User Manager. Then complete the following steps:

1. Click the printer icon in the Printers folder and press Alt+Enter to open the printer's Properties dialog box.
2. Select the Security tab of the printer Properties dialog box, and then click the Auditing button.
3. In the Printer Auditing dialog box that appears, click the Add button.
4. In the Add Users and Groups dialog box, select a group or user to be audited and click OK.
5. Back in the Printer Auditing dialog box, select a user or group. Then click the check boxes in the Events to Audit section to select events you want to log for that user and group.
6. Click OK to close the Printer Auditing dialog box, and click OK again to close the printer's Properties dialog box.

Exercise 14.4: Changing Password Options

In this exercise, you will change the password options for users. To change your users' password options, complete the following steps:

1. Open the Start menu and choose Programs, Administrative Tools, User Manager.
2. In the Username panel of the User Manager for Domains, select the account name.
3. Choose the Policies, Account command.
4. In the Account Policy dialog box, select the options you desire, and then click OK.

Exercise 14.5: Creating a System Policy

In this exercise, you will create a system policy. To create a system policy, do the following:

1. Log on to the computer as an administrator.
2. Open the Start menu and choose Programs, Administrative Tools, System Policy Editor.

3. Choose the File, New Policy command. Two icons appear in the System Policy Editor window: Default Computer and Default User.

4. Select the Add User, Add Computer, or Add Group command to add a policy.

5. In the dialog box that appears, enter a name for the user, computer, or group. Then click the OK button.

6. Select the File, Exit command to close the System Policy Editor.

Exercise 14.6: Changing Event Log Settings

In this exercise, you will change the settings governing the Event log. To change the settings of the Event logs, complete the following steps:

1. Open the Event Viewer.

2. Open the Log menu and choose the Log Settings command. The Event Log Settings dialog box appears.

3. In the Change Settings for Log list box, select the log type.

4. Set the size of the log with the Maximum Log Size spinner.

5. Select one of the radio buttons in the Event Log Wrapping section to determine what happens to old events.

6. Close the Event Log Settings dialog box, and then close the Event Viewer.

Appendix A

Last-Minute Study Tips

When you have finished reading this book and have studied as well as you can for the exam, read the information on each section of the exam presented here. This is a summary of the information already presented, highlighting the areas that will be stressed the most on the exam.

Planning

The command-line option to use an unattended installation script is /U:filename. The command-line option to use a uniqueness database file is /UDF:ID,filename. Not all options in the unattended installation file can be specified in the uniqueness database file. However, a single uniqueness database file (UDB) can contain multiple IDs, so a single uniqueness database file can contain unique settings for multiple systems.

The OEM structure gives you complete control of the installation process, but files in the OEM structure must conform to the 8.3 DOS file naming convention. The $$RENAME.TXT file, on the other hand, controls the renaming of files in the OEM directory. Said OEM directory contains a file called CMDLINES.TXT, which contains all the commands that are to be run after the setup is complete and which can include the SYSDIFF utility (used to automate the installation of applications as well as to configure Windows NT).

SYSDIFF must be run with the /snap mode to create a snapshot first. After the applications are installed and configuration is changed, the /diff mode is used to create a differences file from the snapshot. The differences file can then be applied to multiple computers (via the /apply mode).

SYSDIFF can create a completely different OEM directory from a differences file by using the /inf option. However, the differences files can be applied only to systems that have the same installation directory as did the system on which the differences file was created.

Installation and Configuration

Minimum hardware requirements for Workstation 4.0 include a 486DX/33 processor, 12MB of RAM, and at least 120MB of free disk space. The Setup programs are WINNT and WINNT32. WINNT is for DOS and Windows, and WINNT32 is for previous versions of Windows NT. Setup disks are created automatically at installation, but they also can be created at any later time by using the /ox switch with WINNT or WINNT32. Any number of different versions of Windows NT can be installed on the same system for dual booting as long as each version is installed in its own directory.

Windows NT Workstation supports FAT and NTFS file systems (OS/2's HPFS is no longer supported as of this release). FAT formatted file systems, while supporting no security at the file level, are required for dual booting to Windows 95 or DOS. NTFS, on the other hand, is a fault-tolerant file system with transaction tracking support that supports file-level security information and file-level compression.

Permissions and attributes between partitions can seem difficult to understand unless you remember what is going on behind the scenes. If you move a file between NTFS partitions, the file is copied to the destination folder first and then deleted from the first folder. Therefore, attributes of the target folder apply to the file. Just the opposite, when you move a file within the same NTFS partition, the file keeps its original attributes. When you copy a file, regardless of whether you're copying to the same partition or another, the new file always takes on the permissions of the target directory. If you copy or move a file from an NTFS partition to a FAT partition, the permissions are always lost, yet the long filename (if there was one) is maintained.

Windows NT Workstation supports membership in a workgroup or a domain. It allows you to control access to resources at a share level. File permissions are enforced through shares, and the *most* restrictive permissions between the share and file permissions are used.

If Windows NT Workstation is installed on an Intel-based machine, a hidden read-only file named BOOT.INI is created in the root directory. A sample of this file is shown here:

```
[boot loader]
timeout=30
default=multi(0)disk(0)rdisk(0)partition(1)\WINWKSTN
[operating systems]
```

continues

```
multi(0)disk(0)rdisk(0)partition(1)\WINWKSTN=
➥"Windows NT Workstation Version 4.00"
multi(0)disk(0)rdisk(0)partition(1)\WINWKSTN=
➥"Windows NT Workstation Version 4.00 [VGA mode]" /basevideo /sos
multi(0)disk(0)rdisk(0)partition(1)\WINNT=
➥"Windows NT Server Version 4.00"
multi(0)disk(0)rdisk(0)partition(1)\WINNT=
➥"Windows NT Server Version 4.00 [VGA mode]" /basevideo /sos
C:\="Microsoft Windows"
```

This file is important because it represents the choices relating to the boot menu. Note that there are only two sections: [boot loader] and [operating systems]. The first section defines the amount of time in seconds the system is to wait before defaulting to an operating system and what the default operating system is. Changing the timeout parameter to 0 prevents the display of the boot menu and forces the system to always boot the default. Making the timeout parameter –1 shuts off the menu countdown so the system will always wait for the user to make a choice. The second part of BOOT.INI, [operating systems], contains the valid choices installed on the workstation, which appear on the boot menu.

Managing Resources

Because Windows NT Workstation can exist in a workgroup or a domain, users can log on locally or they can log on and be authenticated by a server (Windows NT or NetWare). It is important to remember that when a user logs on locally, his least restrictive level of access (in other words, the level of permission for locally accessing an NTFS folder) determines his level of resource access. This is always the case unless there is a No Access permission anywhere in the mix, in which case No Access prevails over all other permissions, and the user has no access to the resource. If more than one user uses the workstation and you wish to customize environments, a user account must be created for each user.

When logging on to a domain, the domain controller's NetLogon folder is checked for a system policy (NTCONFIG.POL). If the file is found, HKEY_CURRENT_USER and HKEY_LOCAL_MACHINE hives in the local Registry are overwritten with entries from the system policy. For the entire domain, only one system policy needs to be created.

If logon scripts are used (their use is purely optional), they are replicated from \Winnt_Root\System32\Repl\Export\Scripts on the primary domain controller to \Winnt_Root\System32\Repl\Import\Scripts on all backup domain controllers.

A user can join a domain from her workstation (if an account has been set up for her in the other domain) by opening the Control Panel and choosing Network, then clicking the Change button. This displays the Identification Changes dialog box, which can be used to change the name of the domain with which the workstation is associated. When the user logs out and back in, she will be connected to the new domain, as an individual user can be connected to only one domain at a time.

Only members of the Administrators and Power Users groups can share folders in Windows NT Workstation. Other groups include Backup Operators, Guests, Replicator, and Users. Members are placed into groups and additional users are added from the User Manager utility (not to be confused with User Manager for Domains, which exists only in Windows NT Server).

When a printer is shared, a priority setting can be applied in the printer's Properties dialog box that will determine which jobs are serviced by the print spooler first. (Higher priority jobs are always serviced first.)

Connectivity

Installing and configuring Windows NT Workstation 4.0 networking components can be done in a very simple fashion. When you install Workstation, the installation process examines your system for a network card. If it finds one, services are installed at that time. If you add a card later or choose to change your services, follow the steps of the wizard to install services.

The *Network Device Interface Specification* (NDIS) is the specification that controls how network adapter card drivers are written. Windows NT 4.0 supports NDIS 3.0 and 4.0.

Although the names seem similar, don't make the common mistake of confusing the NetBEUI transport protocol with the NetBIOS API. NetBIOS and NetBEUI serve different functions in the networking components of Windows NT.

The default protocol for Windows NT Workstation 4.0 is TCP/IP. To configure it, you need an IP address, a subnet mask, and (optionally) a default gateway. An *IP address* is a unique, logical 32-bit address used to identify a TCP/IP host. The *subnet mask* is a value used to determine whether a host is on the same or a different network. A *default gateway* is an optional setting in TCP/IP configuration that identifies the router used to reach hosts not on the local network.

A DNS server is used for name resolution identifying TCP/IP hosts on the Internet. WINS is used for IP resolution from NetBIOS names. The IPCONFIG utility shows IP configuration information, and IPCONFIG /ALL shows all of this information. The DHCP service allows IP configuration information to be dynamically leased to client computers. Static host and NetBIOS name resolution can be done with the HOSTS and LMHOSTS files, respectively. They are located in \winnt_root\ SYSTEM32\DRIVERS\ETC.

Share names, computer names, and workgroup names are limited to 15 characters in length and are often referenced by a UNC name, which takes the form of http://www.microsoft.com/train_cert.

Microsoft Client Service for NetWare Networks (CSNW) must be installed with Windows NT Workstation to enable access to files or printers on a NetWare network. Similarly, Microsoft File and Print Services must be installed on a Windows NT 4.0 Server in order for NetWare clients to access files and printers on a Windows NT Server. (Microsoft File and Print Services is available from Microsoft but is not included in the Windows NT core product.) NCP is the standard Novell protocol for file and print sharing. Large Internetwork Protocol (LIP) is used to negotiate and determine the largest frame size that can be used to communicate with a NetWare server.

If a Windows NT Server is running Gateway Services for NetWare, a workstation client can access the NetWare network through the Windows NT server. CSNW detects the 802.2 and 802.3 frame types.

Windows NT Workstation 4.0 supports two different line protocols: SLIP and PPP. SLIP is an industry standard that supports TCP/IP (and only TCP/IP) connections made over serial lines. Within Windows NT Workstation, only the client functionality of SLIP is provided. PPP supports TCP/IP, NetBEUI, and IPX/SPX, as well as others. PPP also supports DHCP addressing, whereas SLIP does not. PPTP (the Point-to-Point Tunneling Protocol) is an extension of PPP that allows clients to connect to remote servers over the Internet and to create virtual private networks (VPNs).

A Windows NT Workstation is limited to one RAS session at a time. Its three settings are Dial Out Only, Receive Calls Only, and Dial Out and Receive Calls; Dial Out Only is the default. Dial-Up Networking supports most protocols, with the exception of XNS. Authentication and encryption settings are set individually for each phonebook entry.

Whereas Windows NT Server includes IIS (Internet Information Server), Windows NT Workstation includes PWS (Peer Web Services). The functionality of the two products is much the same except that IIS allows for an unlimited number of connections, while PWS is limited to 10.

Running Applications

Whether for DOS or for 16-bit Windows, all 16-bit applications are single threaded. DOS applications are executed in individual NT Virtual Device Managers (NTVDMs) and do not share memory with each other (they also do not support messaging).

16-bit Windows applications execute in a single Win16 NTVDM (although that can be changed to separate NTVDMs), share memory, and share a single message queue. They also employ cooperative multitasking, whereas 32-bit applications use preemptive multitasking. (Technically, applications in the Win16 NTVDM can be preemptively multitasked but they must always share a common message queue.)

The CONFIG.SYS and AUTOEXEC.BAT configuration files from the DOS world have been ported to Windows NT to configure 16-bit applications to properly run. They are now known as CONFIG.NT and AUTOEXEC.NT, but they serve the same purposes as they used to:

- CONFIG.NT loads system files.
- AUTOEXEC.NT primarily sets environment variables.

To run 16-bit Windows applications in their own NTVDMs, use the Run command from the Start menu, or execute the START command from the command line.

Monitoring and Optimization

A number of tools included with Windows NT Workstation simplify monitoring and optimization tasks. These include

- Performance Monitor, which shows statistics on just about everything, including memory usage. Physical disk counters are not visible in Performance Monitor, however, until you run DISKPERF. Likewise, network performance monitors are not visible until the Network Monitor Agent is installed (this still does not give TCP/IP statistics unless SNMP has been installed as well).

■ Task Manager, which can show running applications, CPU statistics, running processes, and memory usage. You open Task Manager by right-clicking the Taskbar or by pressing Ctrl+Alt+Del and choosing it from the menu.

The secret to preventing paging problems is to add more RAM. Short of that, you can move the paging file from the boot partition, or you can create multiple paging files (one for each physical disk except the boot partition). Another solution for increasing optimization is to convert all FAT partitions to NTFS. If you need to configure the paging file, choose System from the Control Panel. Then choose the Performance tab and click the Change button beside the Virtual Memory information. On the properties sheet that appears, you can adjust the size and location parameters of the paging file.

Troubleshooting

To hide a printer share, add a dollar sign to the end of the share name, as in sharename$. This prevents the printer from being displayed in the Connect To Printer dialog box (one of the steps in the Add a Printer wizard). A user must know that this printer share exists and be able to enter both the correct name and path to the printer share in order to connect to the printer.

A print job spooled to a printer is written as a temporary file to the %systemroot%\System32\Spool\Printers folder. The file is deleted after the printer indicates that the job has been printed. The most common print spool problem is a lack of available disk space. When you print to the spooler, you create two files for each print job: the SPL file, which is the actual print job spool file, and a shadow file, which is given the .SHD extension. The shadow file contains additional information about the print job that is not part of the print job itself, such as the owner and priority. If the computer crashes, SPL and SHD files remain in the default spool file until the service is restarted and they are processed and printed.

If you have a malfunctioning application, open the Task Manager and shut down the process. You can access the Task Manager by using the mouse or the keyboard. If you need to end a 16-bit Windows or an MS-DOS application, you must close the entire session. When you close a 32-bit Windows application, you only have to close that particular process or thread.

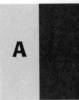

To restrict who can open the System or Application logs, you set this Registry key

`HKEY_LOCAL_MACHINE\System\CurrentControlSet\Services\EventLog\-<log_name>`

so that the `RestrictGuestAccess` value of type `REG_DWORD` is set to 1. When the `RestrictGuestAccess` is set to 0 or doesn't exist, the default condition is that anyone can access these two logs.

Appendix B

The Annotated Walkthrough Exam

The following practice test contains original questions culled from the material presented in this book, all designed to simulate in content as closely as possible the actual MCSE Implementing and Supporting Microsoft Windows NT Workstation 4.0 exam (#70–73).

At the time this book is going to print, there are 51 questions on the official exam, and candidates are given 90 minutes in which to complete it. The first time you use this practice exam, limit yourself to 90 minutes so you can pace yourself for the real thing. The current passing score is 70%, which means you need at least 36 correct answers to pass. When preparing for the exam, however, you should strive for complete mastery of the subject material and the highest score possible instead of simply attempting to gain the lowest possible passing score.

The answers are provided with annotations at the end of the exam. Take a deep breath, review, reread, and teach yourself how to master exam 70–73.

Good luck!

The Practice Exam

1. Kristin is running Windows NT Workstation on her machine at a small law firm that employs workgroups. After months of trying, she finally convinced her supervisors that she needed an HP 4000se laser printer. Now that it's properly installed and configured, she wants to share it, but only with select users. How can she hide the printer from most users so

they won't know it is there, yet make it available to those with whom she wants to share it?

    A. Select the Hidden option on the Properties tab.

    B. Do not install File Sharing.

    C. End the sharename with a $.

    D. Create a global group that includes only the selected users.

2. Evan is concerned because print jobs he sends to his printer are not coming out. He is not getting errors on his workstation to indicate that there is any problem with configuration, but he is not getting the printed document from his printer. He questions whether the documents are printing to another printer or staying in the spool. To troubleshoot the problem, you look to see if there are spool jobs in which of the following folders?

    A. `%systemroot%\System32\`

    B. `%systemroot%\System32\Spool\`

    C. `%systemroot%\System32\Spool\Printers`

    D. `%systemroot%\System32\Spool\Printers\Temp`

3. Spencer complains that he cannot share folders with other users in his workgroup. Spencer is running Windows NT 4 and suspects the problem might lie in his group memberships. What groups are allowed to share folders in NT Workstation?

    A. Administrators

    B. Backup Operators

    C. Replicators

    D. Power Users

4. Karen is attempting to troubleshoot a problem that's causing her applications to behave erratically. To that end, she has brought up the utility shown in Figure B.1. What utility is she using?

    A. Performance Monitor

    B. Task Manager

    C. Disk Administrator

    D. User Manager

Figure B.1.

The utility Karen is using to troubleshoot application problems.

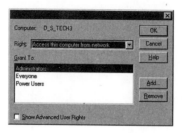

5. In reference to question number 4, what utility should Karen be using?

   A. Performance Monitor

   B. Task Manager

   C. Disk Administrator

   D. User Manager

6. Allan is installing Windows NT Workstation 4.0 on an Intel-based machine in an existing domain. What networking protocol(s) is/are installed by default?

   A. IPX/SPX

   B. NetBEUI

   C. TCP/IP

   D. NetBIOS

7. The head of the Finance department, Madonna, comes to you with news that the company has just purchased a small consulting company in a nearby town. The company has seven Windows NT Workstations that are currently functioning in a workgroup environment. What type of server can be added at the site to provide user authentication? (Choose all that apply.)

   A. NetWare

   B. Windows 95

   C. Windows NT Workstation

   D. Windows NT Server

8. Which of the following utilities is used to automate the installation of applications and to configure Windows NT?

A. Performance Monitor

B. Task Manager

C. SYSDIFF

D. Setupmgr

9. In the unattended setup automation utility, which parameter creates a snapshot?

   A. /snap

   B. /diff

   C. /apply

   D. /ox

10. Lorraine would like to know if her machine is capable of running Windows NT Workstation. To find the answer to that, she should look for the current:

    A. HAL

    B. HCL

    C. BOOT.INI

    D. LAH

11. Which of the protocols shown in Figure B.2 is considered nonroutable?

Figure B.2.

The currently installed protocols.

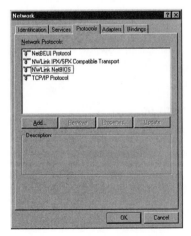

A. NetBEUI

B. NWLink IPX/SPX-Compatible Transport

C. NWLink NetBIOS

D. TCP/IP

12. Your company has an employee named Jerry who likes to tinker with the system until it no longer works. Therefore, you must implement a system policy. Which of the following names is typically given to the system policy?

A. CONFIG.POL

B. NTCONFIG.POL

C. USER.DAT

D. NTUSER.DAT

13. Suppose logon scripts must also be used on a domain network to curb rogue users like Jerry who like to tinker. Where should the logon scripts be placed?

A. On the PDC

B. On the BDC

C. On the local machine

D. In HKEY_CURRENT_USER

14. Jennifer, the system administrator for ABC Solutions, would like to restrict access on one particular file containing performance reviews. When she attempts to highlight the file and change the permissions, however, she sees only the rights and information shown in Figure B.3. Why is Jennifer unable to change the permissions on this file?

A. She does not have appropriate permissions.

B. The file is currently open.

C. The partition is FAT.

D. The owner has locked the account.

Figure B.3.

The properties on a selected file.

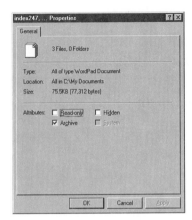

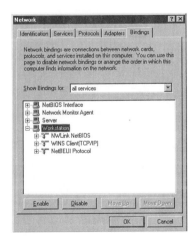

15. Tony Co. is running a small network that consists of only Windows 95 and Windows NT Workstation clients on a Windows NT Server network. The Workstation bindings match those shown in Figure B.4. Given this scenario, which protocol should be bound first?

    A. TCP/IP

    B. NetBEUI

    C. NWLink NetBIOS

    D. Order doesn't matter.

Figure B.4.

The binding order on Tony Co.'s Windows NT workstations.

B

16. The answer to most problems related with paging files is to:

    A. Increase the speed of the processor.

    B. Add more RAM.

    C. Decrease the load.

    D. Install more hard drives.

17. The paging file is configured from which Control Panel utility?

    A. Service

    B. Network

    C. Memory

    D. System

18. Windows NT Workstation can be installed into partitions currently formatted as which of the following?

    A. NTFS

    B. FAT

    C. HPFS

    D. CDFS

    E. Unformatted

19. Which of the following partitions contains the system files?

    A. boot

    B. system

    C. FAT

    D. NTFS

20. Which of the following partitions contains the boot files?

    A. boot

    B. system

    C. FAT

    D. NTFS

21. Which of these utilities is used to format a partition in Windows NT Workstation?

    A. User Manager

    B. User Manager for Domains

    C. Disk Administrator

    D. Format Manager

22. Edna calls and is as mad as you have ever seen her. She is attempting to gather statistical information about her physical disk usage by using Performance Monitor. However, the graph she is getting, shown in Figure B.5, shows a lack of activity. What is causing this lack of activity?

B

Figure B.5.

Edna's physical disk statistics in Performance Monitor.

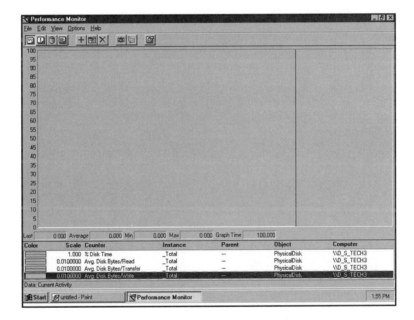

A. Her disk is experiencing no activity.

B. Performance Monitor is not the appropriate tool to use.

C. The physical disk counters are not turned on.

D. She has selected the wrong hard drive.

23. The Task Manager can be used to show running applications, memory usage, and so on. How do you bring it up?

    A. Right-click on the Taskbar.

    B. Press Ctrl+Alt+Del and choose it from the menu.

    C. Select it from the Programs, Administrative Tools menu.

    D. Right-click on the desktop and choose Task Manager.

24. Just when you are starting to enjoy work, Edna calls back again. This time she is furious that Performance Monitor is not showing her the TCP/IP statistics even though she knows she has selected the appropriate counters. What is the problem this time?

    A. She is probably not using TCP/IP; thus there is no activity.

    B. Performance Monitor is not the appropriate tool to use.

    C. The TCP/IP counters are not turned on by default.

    D. She has selected the wrong protocol.

25. Windows NT supports which two of the following line protocols?

    A. TCP/IP

    B. IPX/SPX

    C. PPP

    D. SLIP

26. How many concurrent RAS sessions is Windows NT Workstation limited to?

    A. 0

    B. 1

    C. 128

    D. 256

27. How many concurrent RAS sessions is Windows NT Server limited to?

    A. 0

    B. 1

    C. 128

    D. 256

28. Mitch loves to play computer games during his lunch hour. He is holding back on upgrading to Windows NT Workstation—although the rest of the department has already done so—because he is afraid he will lose this ability. Given that the true work Mitch does is very minimal and game playing is his biggest concern, which operating system should he be using?

    A. Windows for Workgroups

    B. Windows 95

    C. Windows NT Workstation

    D. Windows NT Server

29. Which of the following statements are true of 16-bit Windows applications?

    A. They employ preemptive multitasking.

    B. They run in their own message queues.

    C. They share a single message queue.

    D. They employ cooperative multitasking.

30. What is the effect of the command line command shown in Figure B.6?

Figure B.6.

A command line command.

    A. Task Manager is started.

    B. Physical disk statistics are no longer available in Performance Monitor.

    C. FAT partitions are converted to NTFS.

    D. Disk compression is activated.

31. Two configuration files from the DOS world have been ported to Windows NT to configure 16-bit applications to run properly. They are now known as:

    A. CONFIG.SYS and AUTOEXEC.BAT

    B. USER.DAT and SYSTEM.DAT

    C. CONFIG.NT and AUTOEXEC.NT

    D. CONFIG.NT and AUTOEXEC.BAT

32. Which system file is shown in Figure B.7?

Figure B.7.

One of the system files.

    A. CONFIG.NT

    B. AUTOEXEC.NT

    C. USER.DAT

    D. BOOT.INI

33. In the startup file, the TIMEOUT= number should be changed to what to prevent the menu from appearing?

    A. -1

    B. 0

    C. 1

    D. ;

34. The startup file can be safely edited without using a command-prompt editor through which System utility tab?

A. BOOT

B. STARTUP/SHUTDOWN

C. ENVIRONMENT

D. GENERAL

E. PERFORMANCE

35. Landon is a temporary employee on a long-term assignment. Although he will be working for the company for quite some time, he must work at a different machine each day, depending upon whose regularly scheduled day off it is. To best accommodate these circumstances, Landon should be set up with a:

A. User profile

B. Mandatory profile

C. Roaming profile

D. System profile

36. To create a mandatory profile for a user, you use which of the following file extensions?

A. .DAT

B. .PRO

C. .NT

D. .MAN

37. Which of the following utilities is used to examine the System log?

A. Performance Monitor

B. Event Viewer

C. System Manager

D. Task Manager

38. McKenzie is trying to determine what type of machine she should purchase to run Windows NT Workstation at home. She has already decided to purchase a Pentium with a 5GB IDE drive. How much RAM is considered the minimum?

A. 4MB

B. 8MB

C. 12MB

D. 16MB

39. The share name is traditionally limited to how many characters?

    A. 8.3

    B. 10

    C. 15

    D. 256

40. The UNC path takes the form of:

    A. `\\computername\sharename [\optional path]`

    B. `\\sharename\computername [\optional path]`

    C. `\\sharename [\optional path]`

    D. `\\computername [\optional path]`

41. What would be the UNC path for a file named `SPENCER.DAT` in a directory named `EVAN` in a share named `KRISTIN` on a server named `KAREN`?

    A. `\\KRISTIN\KAREN\EVAN\SPENCER`

    B. `\\SPENCER\EVAN\KRISTIN\KAREN`

    C. `\\KAREN\KRISTIN\EVAN\SPENCER`

    D. `//SPENCER/EVAN/KRISTIN/KAREN`

42. In order for Jeff's workstation to join a domain, he must have network connectivity to which of the following?

    A. A member server

    B. The backup domain controller

    C. The primary domain controller

    D. Another workstation

43. A Windows NT Workstation can access NetWare servers via a Windows NT Server if the server is running which of the following?

    A. Gateway (and Client) Services for NetWare

    B. Microsoft Client Services for NetWare Networks

    C. Microsoft File and Print Services for NetWare

    D. IPX/SPX

44. CSNW is installed from which Control Panel applet?

    A. Network

    B. System

    C. Services

    D. User Manager for Domains

45. Which of the following is the command line option for using an unattended installation script?

    A. /ox

    B. /U:*filename*

    C. /UDB:*filename*

    D. /S:*filename*

46. Figure B.8 shows which of the following utilities?

Figure B.8.

One of the system utilities.

    A. Windows NT Diagnostics

    B. User Manager

    C. Disk Manager

    D. Event Viewer

47. Tracy calls with a question about some errors that are appearing in the System log. Figure B.9 shows the errors in the Event Viewer. Of the four events shown, which one most likely caused the other three?

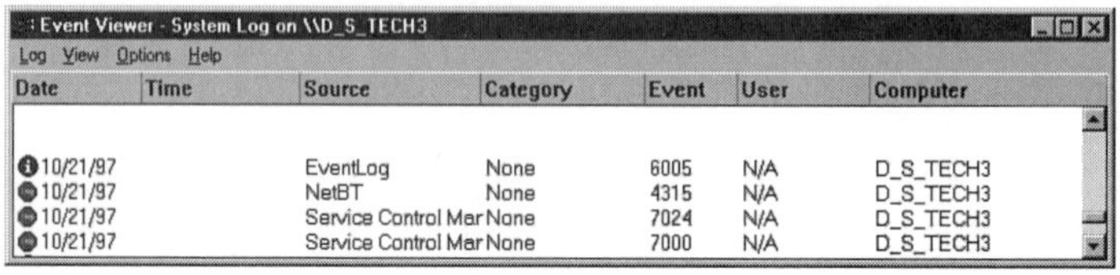

Figure B.9.

The System log in Event Viewer.

    A. Event 6005

    B. Event 4315

    C. Event 7024

    D. Event 7000

48. Which parameter in the SYSDIFF utility is used to create a differences file from a snapshot?

    A. /snap

    B. /diff

    C. /apply

    D. inf

49. Lori has lost her Windows NT Startup disks, and now she needs them to correct a problem. What command can she issue to re-create the disks on a Windows 95 machine?

    A. WINNT

    B. WINNT32

    C. WINNT /OX

    D. WINNT /START

50. Which of the following is the TCP/IP optional setting that identifies the router?

    A. Default Gateway

    B. Subnet mask

    C. IP address

    D. DNS server address

51. Big Bill's Real Estate Consortium has a Windows NT Workstation 4.0 with two modems and two ordinary phone lines. You want to help them establish the fastest possible connection to a remote network. Which protocol do you recommend they use?

    A. Serial Line Internet Protocol (SLIP)

    B. Point-to-Point Tunneling Protocol (PPTP)

    C. Point-to-Point Multilink Protocol

    D. Remote Access Service (RAS)

Answers

1. C Ending the sharename with a $ makes it hidden.

2. C A print job spooled to a printer is written as a temporary file to the `%systemroot%\System32\Spool\Printers` folder.

3. A, D Administrators and Power Users can share folders in Windows NT Workstation 4.0.

4. D Figure B.1 shows a dialog box in User Manager.

5. B Task Manager should be used for diagnosing application problems.

6. C TCP/IP is installed by default. In previous versions, NetBEUI and IPX/SPX were installed by default, but that is no longer the case. NetBIOS is not a networking protocol.

7. A, D Both NetWare and Windows NT Server can be used to provide user authentication. User authentication cannot be established in the absence of a server, and neither Windows 95 nor Windows NT Workstation qualifies as a server.

8. C SYSDIFF is used to automate the installation of applications and to configure Windows NT.

9. A The /snap mode is used to create a snapshot first.

10. B The Hardware Compatibility List (HCL) documents what hardware is currently compatible with Windows NT.

11. A NetBEUI is a nonroutable protocol ideal for small networks.

12. B The system policy is usually named NTCONFIG.POL.

13. A If they're used, optional logon scripts should be placed on the PDC. Replication will then be required to replicate the logon scripts to the associated BDCs.

14. C Permissions exist only on NTFS partitions, not on FAT.

15. A In the described environment, TCP/IP should be bound first.

16. B Adding more RAM to a system is a universal answer to most paging file related problems.

17. D The paging file is configured from the System utility in Control Panel.

18. A, B, E Windows NT Workstation can be installed into FAT, NTFS, or unformatted partitions.

19. A The system files are in the boot partition.

20. B The boot files are in the system partition.

21. C Disk Administrator is the utility used to format partitions.

22. C By default, the physical disk counters are not turned on. To turn on the disk counters, run the command DISKPERF -Y.

23. A, B You can bring up the Task Manager by right-clicking on the taskbar or by pressing Ctrl+Alt+Del and choosing it from the menu.

24. C By default, the TCP/IP counters are not available until SNMP has been installed as well.

25. C, D Windows NT supports both the PPP and SLIP line protocols. The other two choices are networking protocols, not line protocols.

26. B Windows NT Workstation is limited to only one inbound RAS connection.

27. D Windows NT Server is limited to 256 concurrent RAS sessions.

28. B Computer games are very graphics-intensive. Windows 95 can handle and maximize this; Windows NT Workstation is more concerned with security and work-related robustness.

29. C, D Windows 16-bit applications share a single message queue and employ cooperative multitasking.

30. B Physical disk statistics are not available in Performance Monitor after DISKPERF -N has been executed.

31. C The configuration files from the DOS world that have been ported to Windows NT to configure 16-bit applications to run properly are now known as CONFIG.NT and AUTOEXEC.NT.

32. D Figure B.7 shows a BOOT.INI file.

33. B Setting TIMEOUT=0 effectively prevents the boot load menu from appearing.

34. B The STARTUP/SHUTDOWN menu is used to safely edit the BOOT.INI file.

35. C A roaming profile enables a user to carry configuration settings from one workstation to another when he must work on different machines.

36. D A mandatory profile has the extension .MAN.

37. B Event Viewer is used to view the System log.

38. C 12MB RAM should be considered the bare minimum Windows NT Workstation can run in.

39. C A share name is traditionally limited to 15 characters.

40. A The UNC path takes the form of \\computername\sharename [\optional path].

41. C \\KAREN\KRISTIN\EVAN\SPENCER is the correct UNC path.

42. C To join a domain, Jeff must be able to get to the Primary Domain Controller.

43. A A Windows NT workstation can access NetWare servers via a Windows NT Server if the server is running Gateway (and Client) Services for NetWare.

44. A CSNW is installed from the Network applet in the Control Panel.

45. B The command line option for using an unattended installation script is /U:filename.

46. A Figure B.8 shows Windows NT Diagnostics.

47. D The file is written to with the newest entries at the top. The oldest STOP error will be at the bottom of the list and is likely to have caused the other errors.

48. B The /diff parameter is used with the SYSDIFF utility to create the differences file.

49. C WINNT /OX creates the Windows NT Startup disks.

B

50. A The Default Gateway is an optional TCP/IP parameter used to define the router.

51. C The Point-to-Point Multilink Protocol enables you to combine multiple physical links into one logical connection.

Index

B

C

I

M

R

V

W-X-Y-Z

NT Utilities

Because you've purchased this book, you qualify for a special discount on two utilities designed to allow you to deploy Windows NT Workstation in your environment:

ChangeINI

This utility allows you to change entries in INI-type files from a command line. This can be used to change entries in BOOT.INI, WIN.INI, and SYSTEM.INI, as well as in any other file that uses the INI file structure of headings surrounded by brackets.

ChangeREG

This utility allows you to change Registry entries from a command line. This can be used in login scripts to change the legal message that appears when a user logs in or to add a missing setting for a custom application.

Each of these programs is normally licensed at $10 per program per server, or $15 per server for both. An enterprise license for each of these programs is normally $50 per program, or $75 for both. But because you've purchased this book, you can get an enterprise license for both programs for just $50. All you need to do is write the code TNW9712 on the order form that accompanies either of the programs. You'll also receive a 10% discount on other programs from Thor Projects, including

RegReplace

This utility searches the Registry and replaces all values. This is useful when a server name has been changed and you don't want to reinstall all the applications.

Runner

This utility enables you to run programs on a remote system, even at administrative authority. It's great for when you need users to be able to run a particular fix command but when you don't want to allow them physical access to the server or give them administrative privileges.

ChangeINI and ChangeREG can be downloaded from http://www.ThorProjects.com/programs, where you can also find descriptions and current pricing of RegReplace, Runner, and others. For additional information, contact

Thor Projects
P.O. Box 1624
Carmel, Indiana 46032
http://www.ThorProjects.com
sales@ThorProjects.com

In a fast-paced, ever-changing environment, who has the *TIME*?

You do. . .with Media Consulting's Web University!

Check us out at *http://www.media-consulting.com* and experience for yourself:

Over 240 engaging, interactive computer-based courses

= a fun learning *TIME*

Authentic simulations that provide the next best thing to the actual application

= a productive, stimulating learning *TIME*

Many courses tracked to Microsoft, Novell, Oracle, and SAP certification

= a profitable, career-boosting *TIME*

College credit available for many courses through *American Council on Education*

= a rewarding, worthwhile *TIME*

Pretesting to determine what you already know

= a means to save you *TIME*

For 20% off our list price, use the following promotional code when registering: 260-NTTEACH

REGISTRATION CARD

Sams Teach Yourself MCSE Windows NT Workstation 4 in 14 Days

Name _____ Title _____

Company_____ Type of
business _____

Address _____

City/State/ZIP _____

Have you used these types of books before? ☐ yes   ☐ no

If yes, which ones? _____

_____

How many computer books do you purchase each year? ☐ 1–5   ☐ 6 or more

How did you learn about this book? _____

Where did you purchase this book? _____

Which applications do you currently use? _____

_____

Which computer magazines do you subscribe to? _____

_____

What trade shows do you attend? _____

_____

Comments: _____

_____

_____

Would you like to be placed on our preferred mailing list? ☐ yes   ☐ no

> ☐ **I would like to see my name in print!** You may use my name and quote me in future Sams products and promotions. My daytime phone number is: _____

Sams Publishing   201 West 103rd Street ◆ Indianapolis, Indiana 46290 USA

Fax to **317-581-4663**

Fold Here

NO POSTAGE
NECESSARY
IF MAILED
IN THE
UNITED STATES

BUSINESS REPLY MAIL
FIRST-CLASS MAIL PERMIT NO. 9918 INDIANAPOLIS IN

POSTAGE WILL BE PAID BY THE ADDRESSEE

SAMS PUBLISHING
201 W 103RD ST
INDIANAPOLIS IN 46290-9058

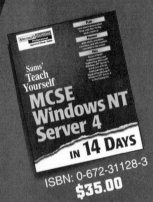